A Bunch of Stories in Which I Am Killed

Mick Malone

A Bunch of Stories in Which I Am Killed
copyright © Mick Malone, 2018
all rights reserved

No part of this book may be used or performed without written consent from the author, except for critical articles or reviews.

Cover art by Mick Malone

to contact the author,
send an email to mpmmick [at] gmail [dot] com

For Airheads...

A very good film

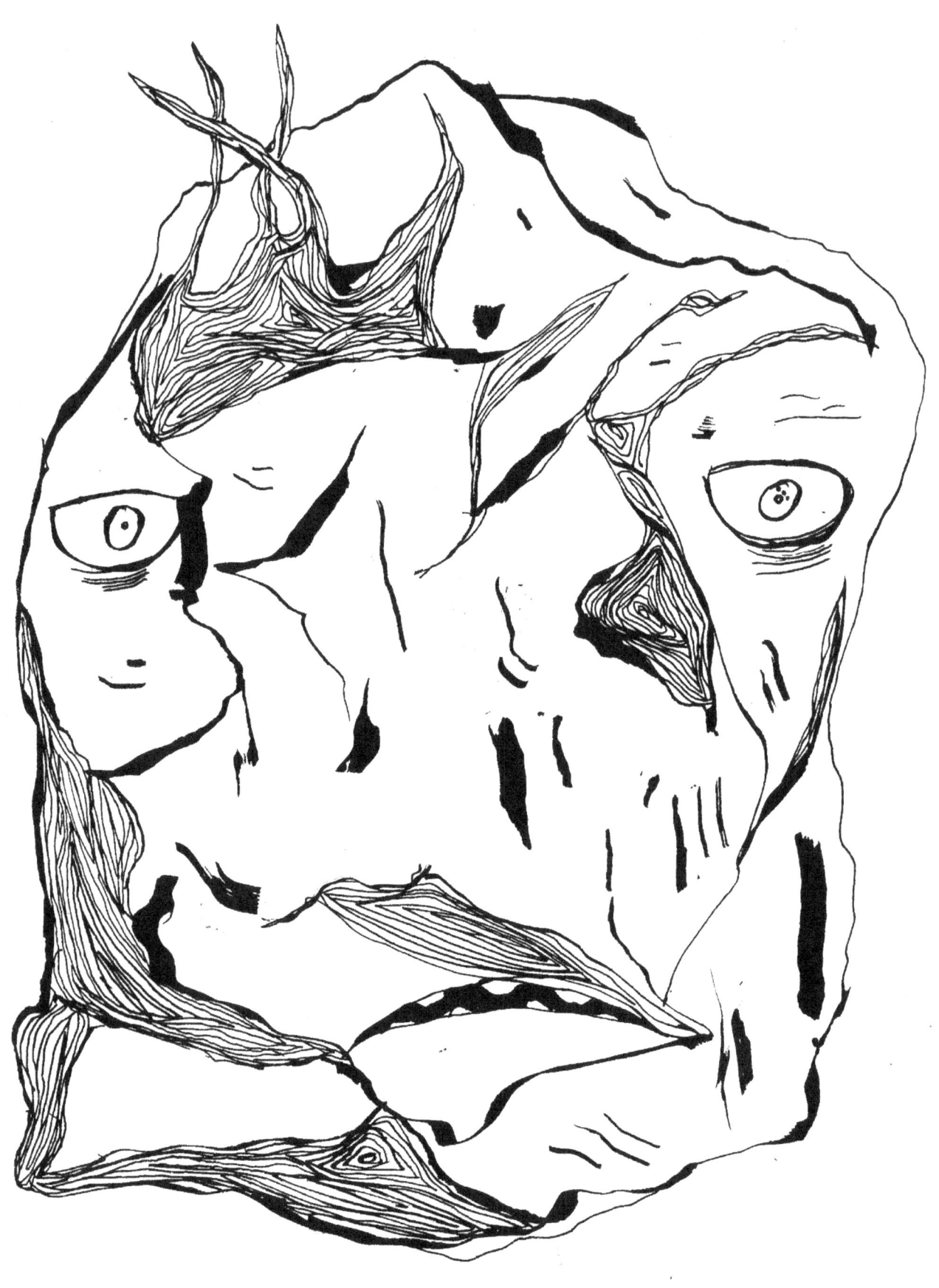

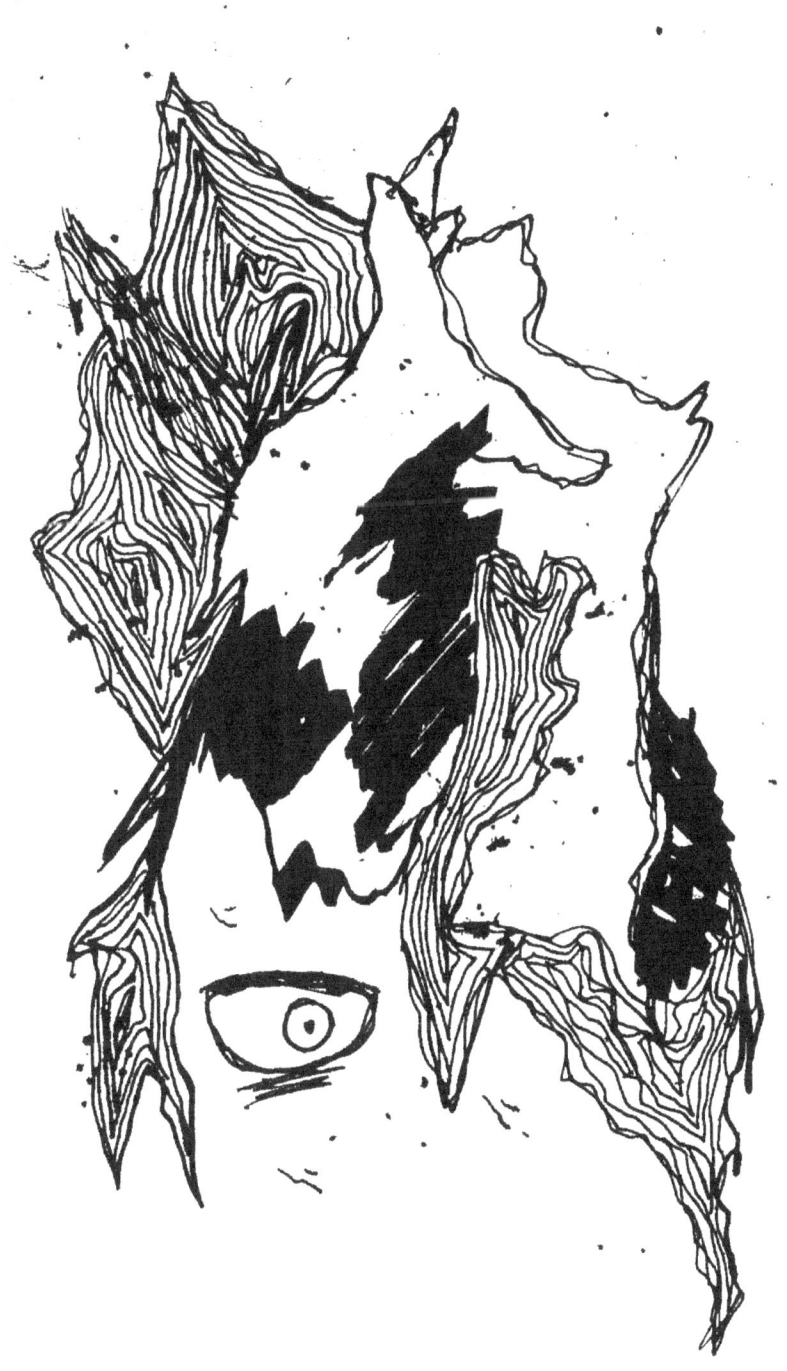

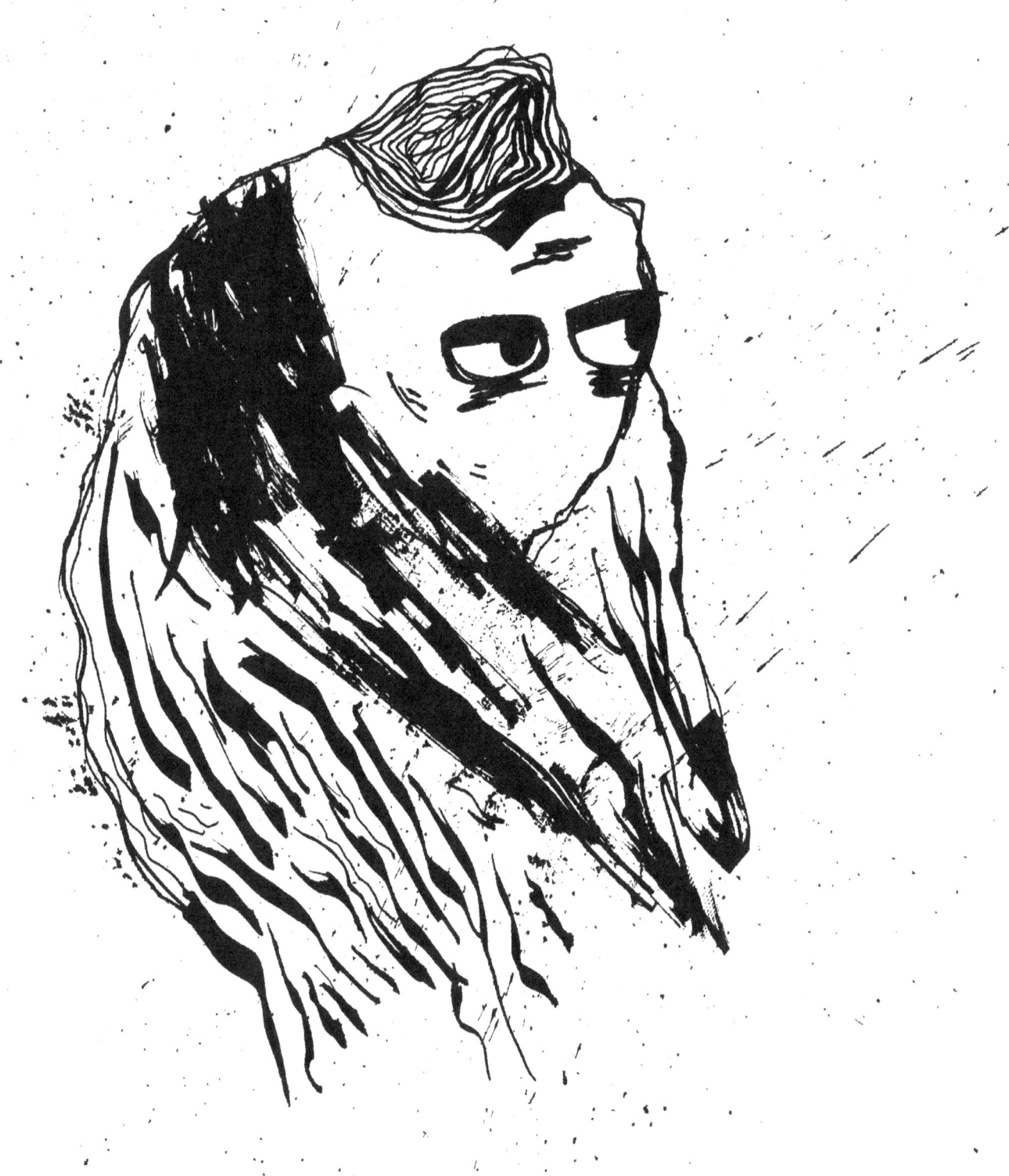

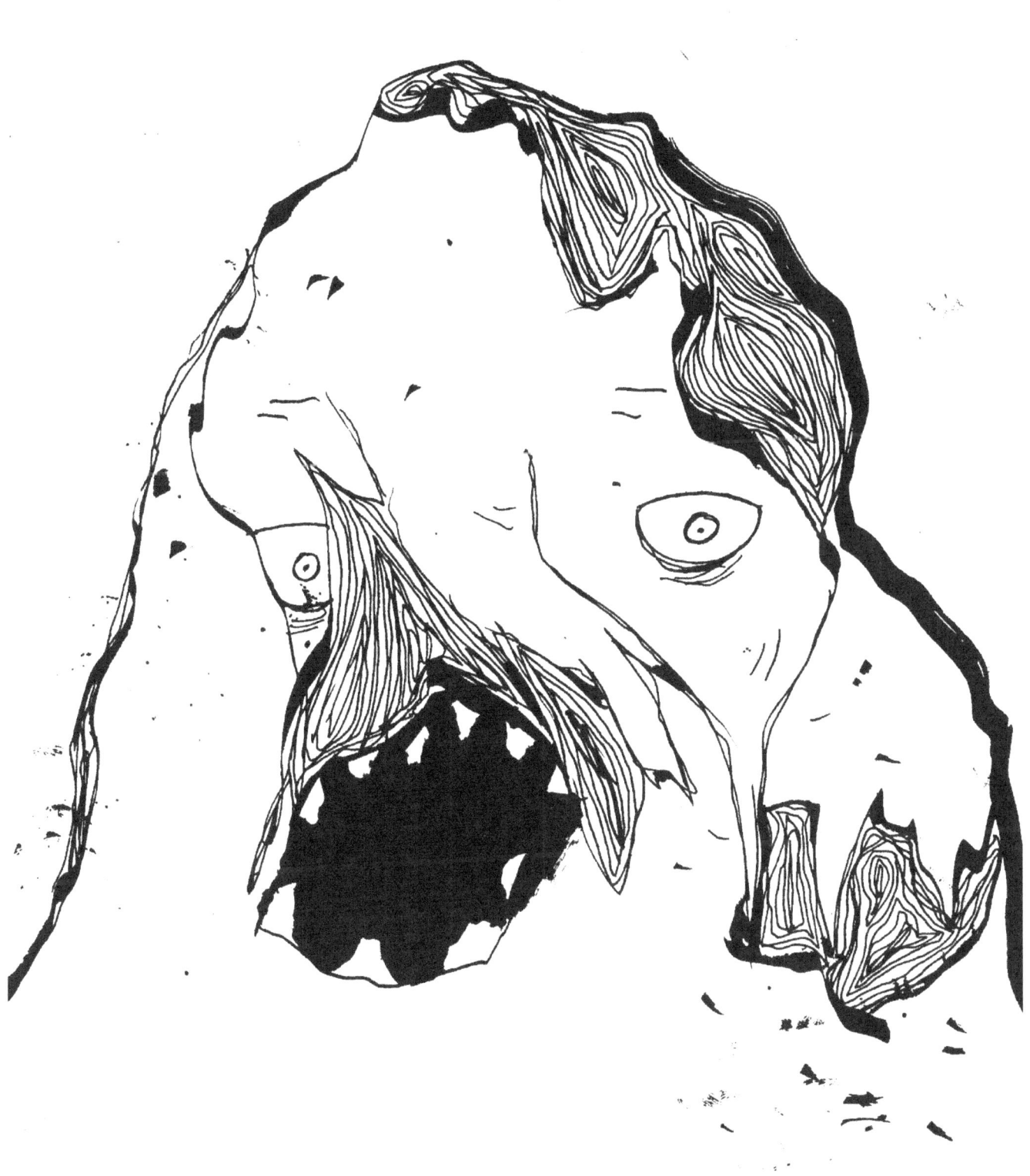

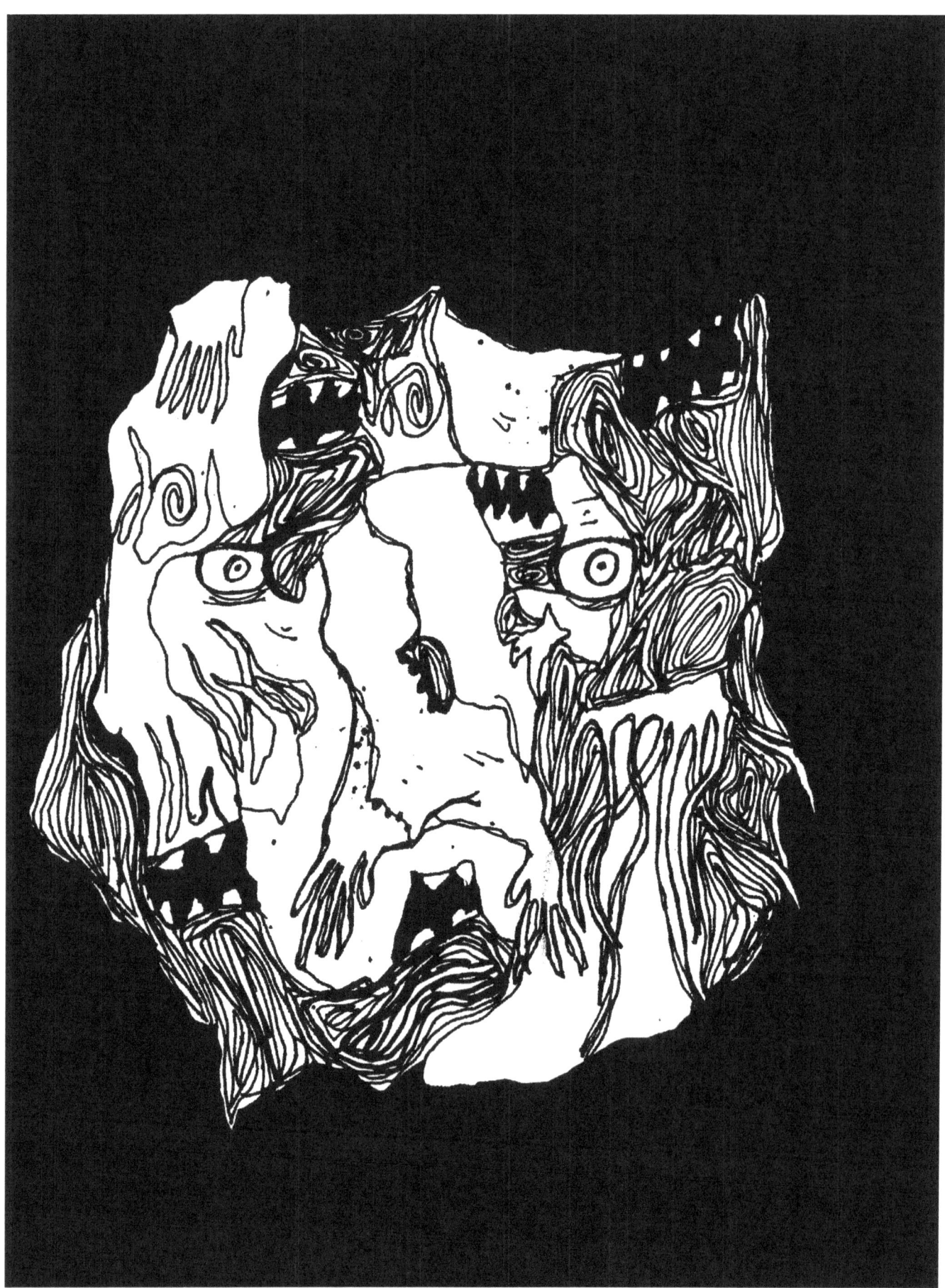

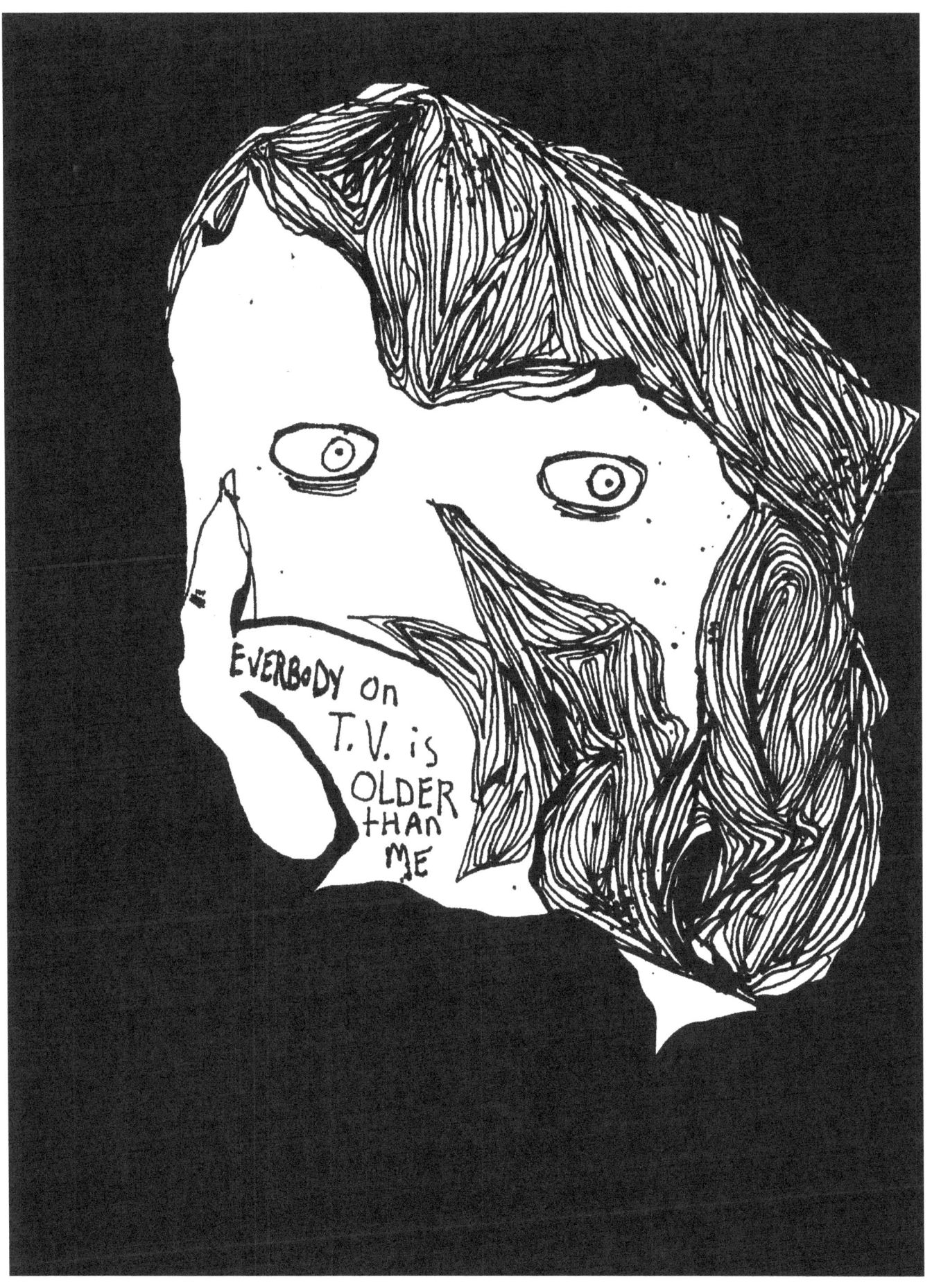

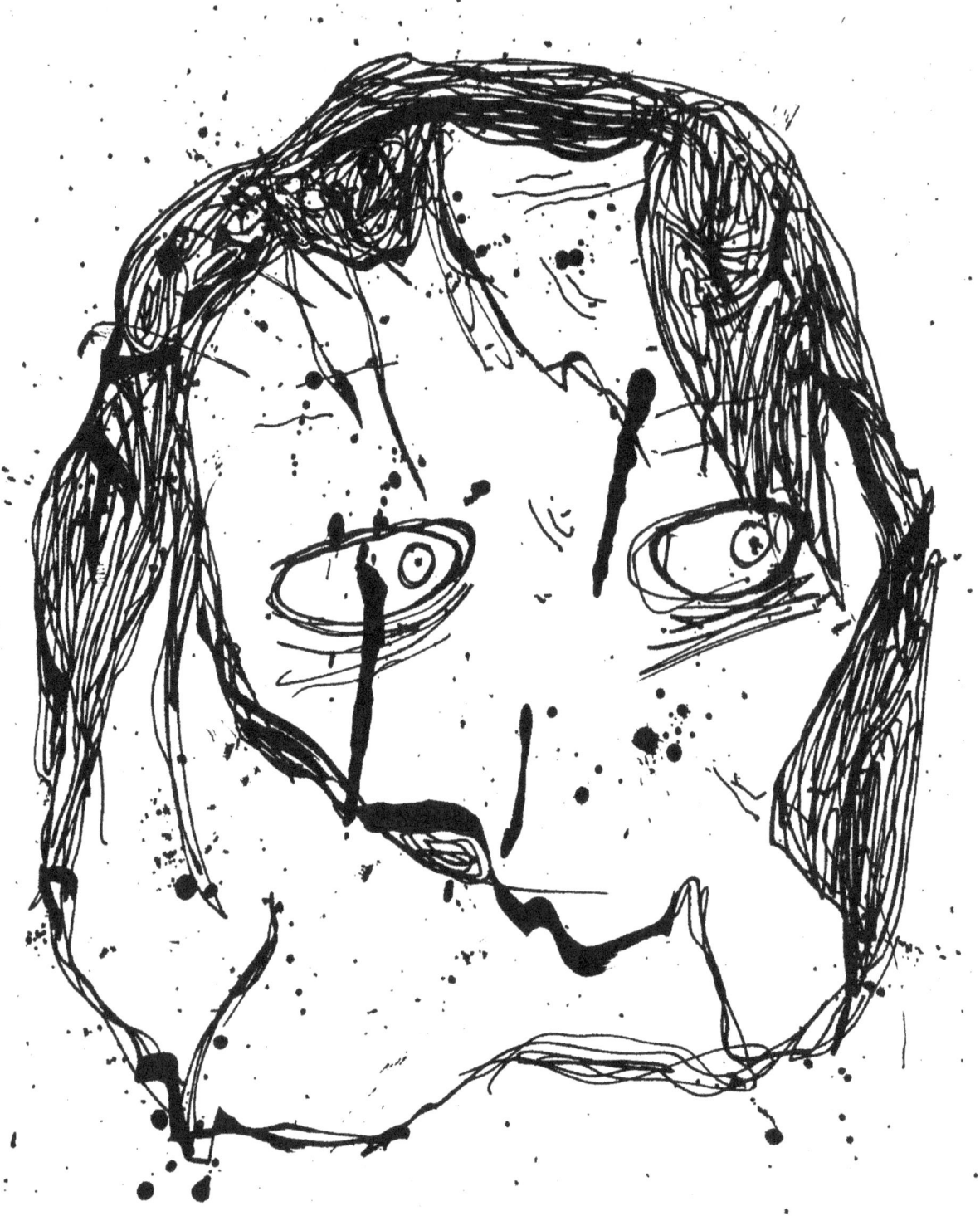

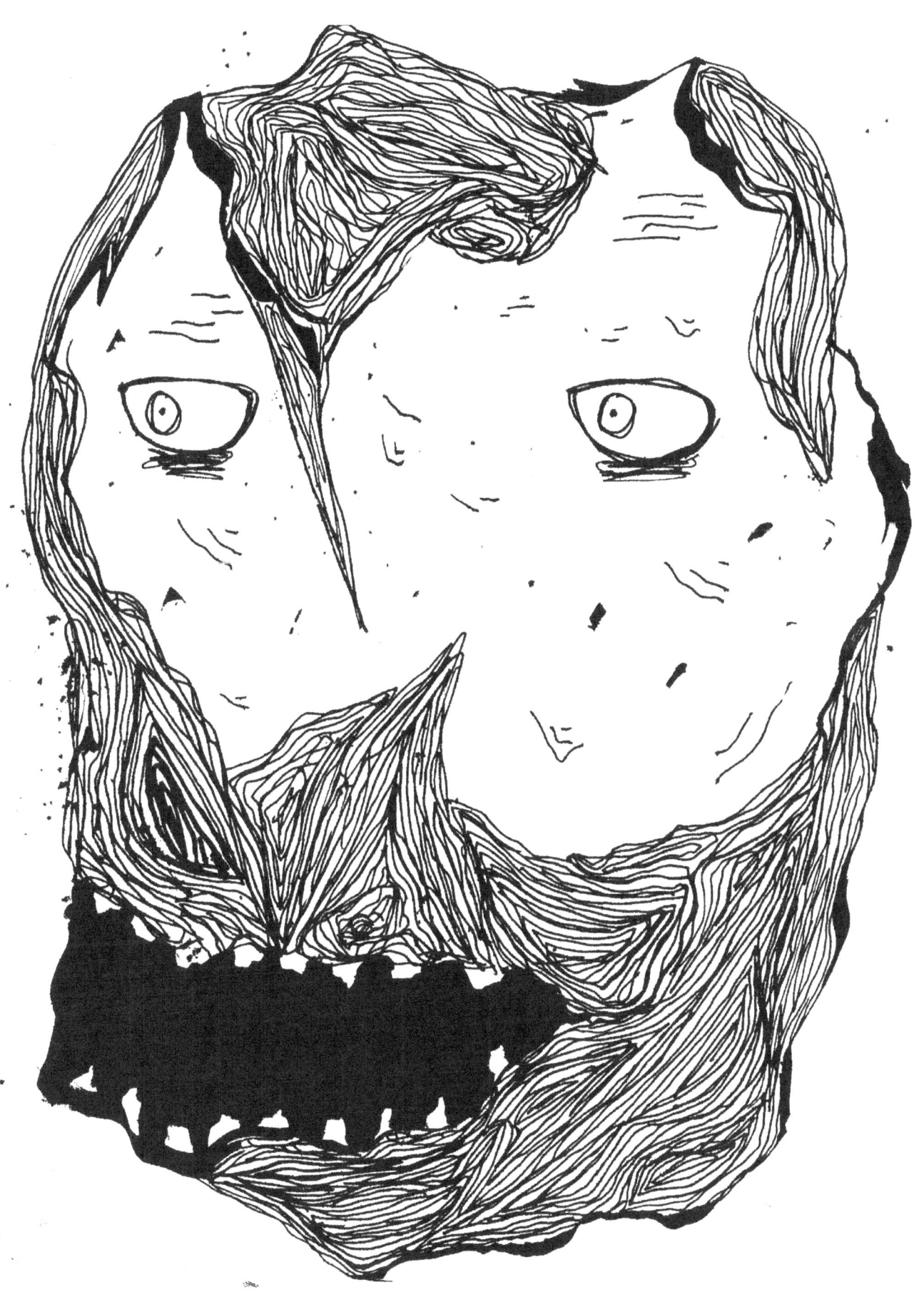

THE FIRST SKY BIRTH

I am awakened by the tearing of the sky
and deafened by the roar of ripping flesh.
Streaming open, a deluge of fat
gristle, guts and blood rains down on us.
The sky gives birth.

I thought I was wearing my new hat, fashioned after a supremely
long piano, but it was just a shadow.
It offered me no protection.

The afterbirth got into my mouth and eyes.
I am deaf, blind and cannot speak.
My ears never cease their bleeding.
My eyes have scabbed shut.
My teeth have grown and fused together
forming an impenetrable wall of braided bone guarding my
throat.
While the afterbirth made us virtually immortal
I worry where my vomit will escape from
I wonder if I'll drown in my own sick.
I cannot wait to die.

Centuries later, as a decrepit old man
I will stumble down the stairs
My bones will shatter and splinter into my pulverized flesh
My teeth will break; my jaws will separate once again
My tongue will spill out my chapped lips
It's gotten so big, a pregnant organ

THE FIRST TONGUE BIRTH

I stagger out of my own swollen tongue as a tiny being. I am covered in blood, sweat and taste buds.
I can taste with my entire body.
I will be gifted a pair of hideous shoes
and when I refuse I am rolled about in salt, lemon juice
and my least favorite foods.
I am miserable.
There is no sympathy for a tongue being
There is no satisfaction in the taste without a swallow
I am executed in front of a cheering crowd
Diced into cubes
And fed to sea

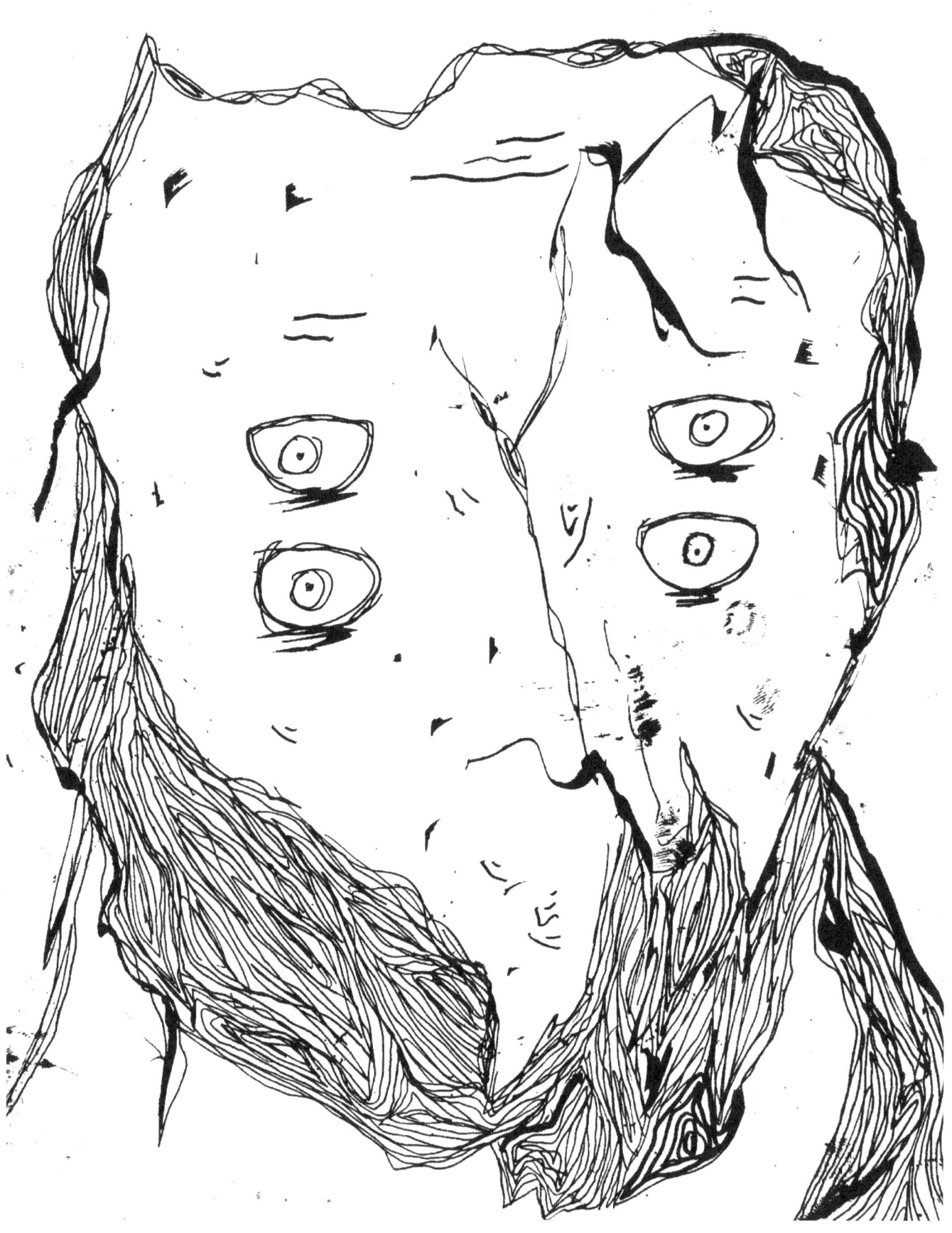

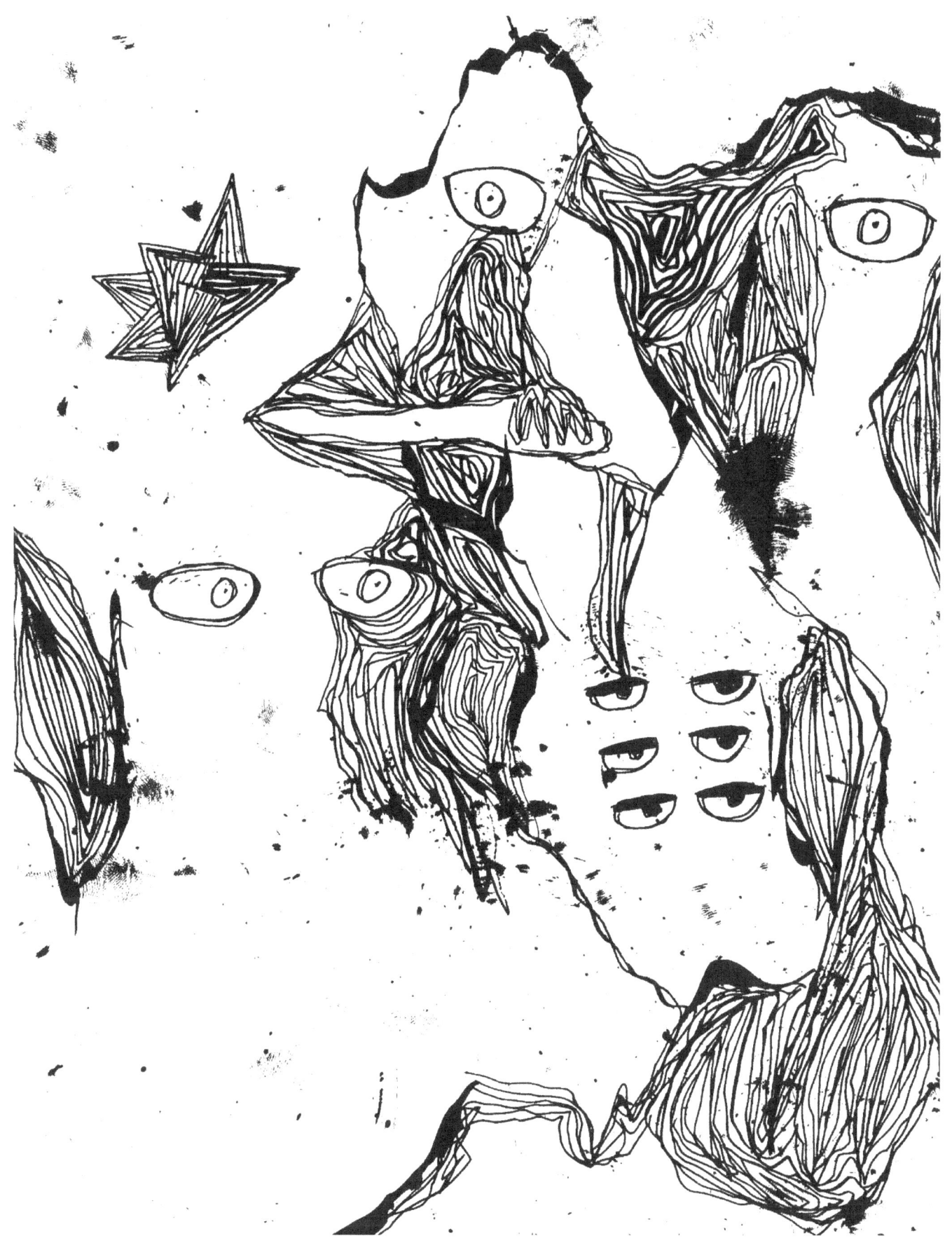

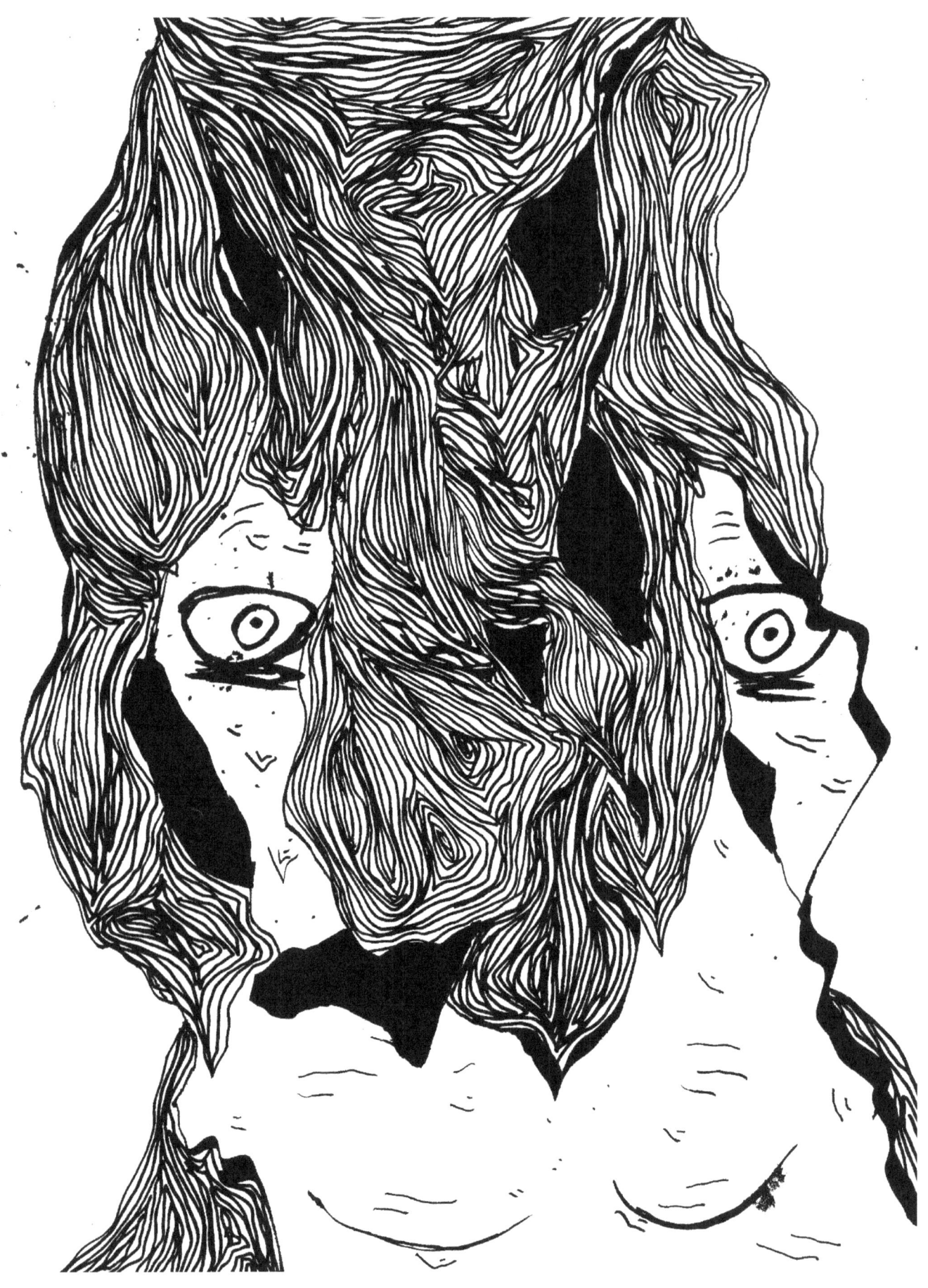

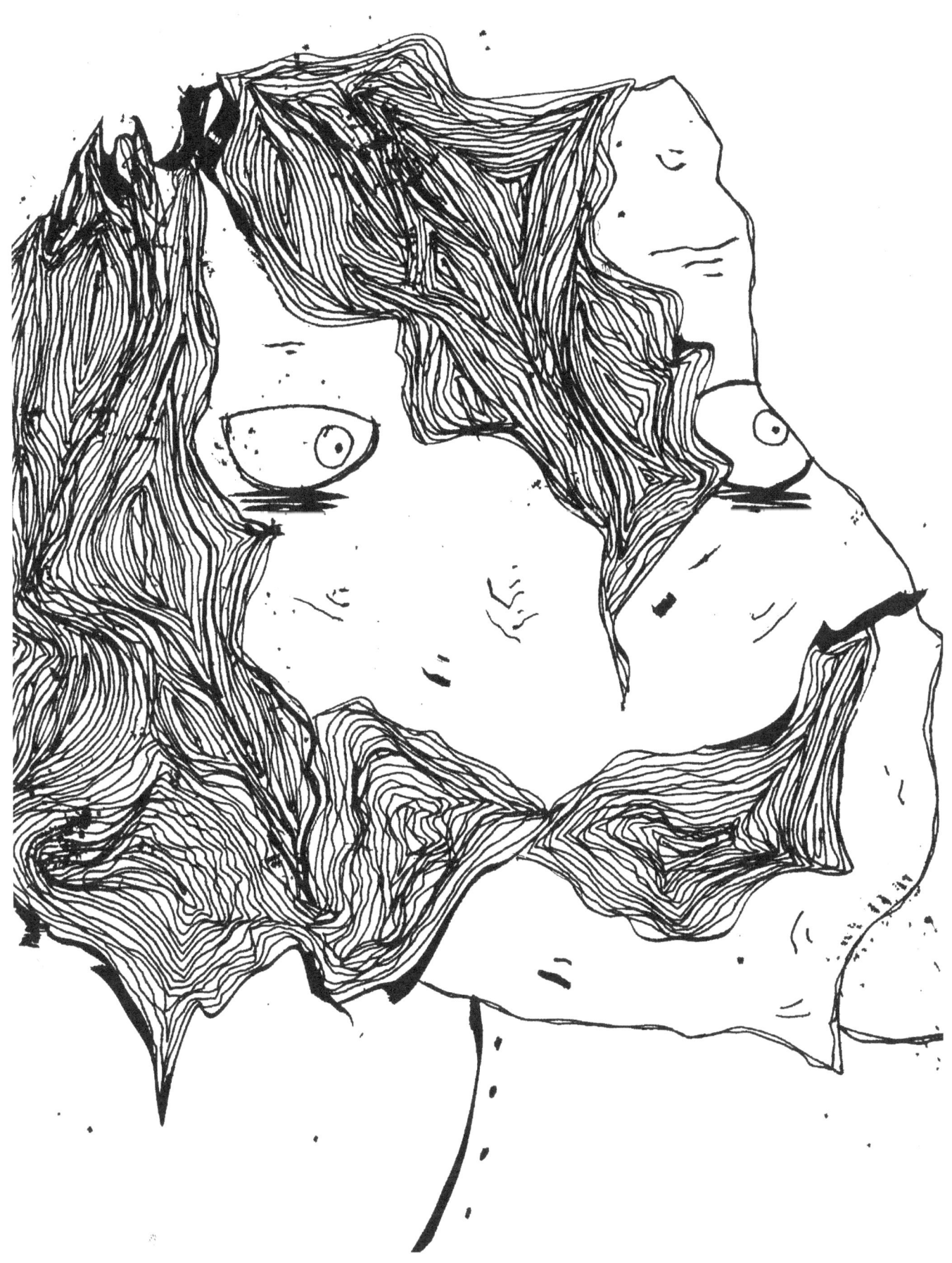

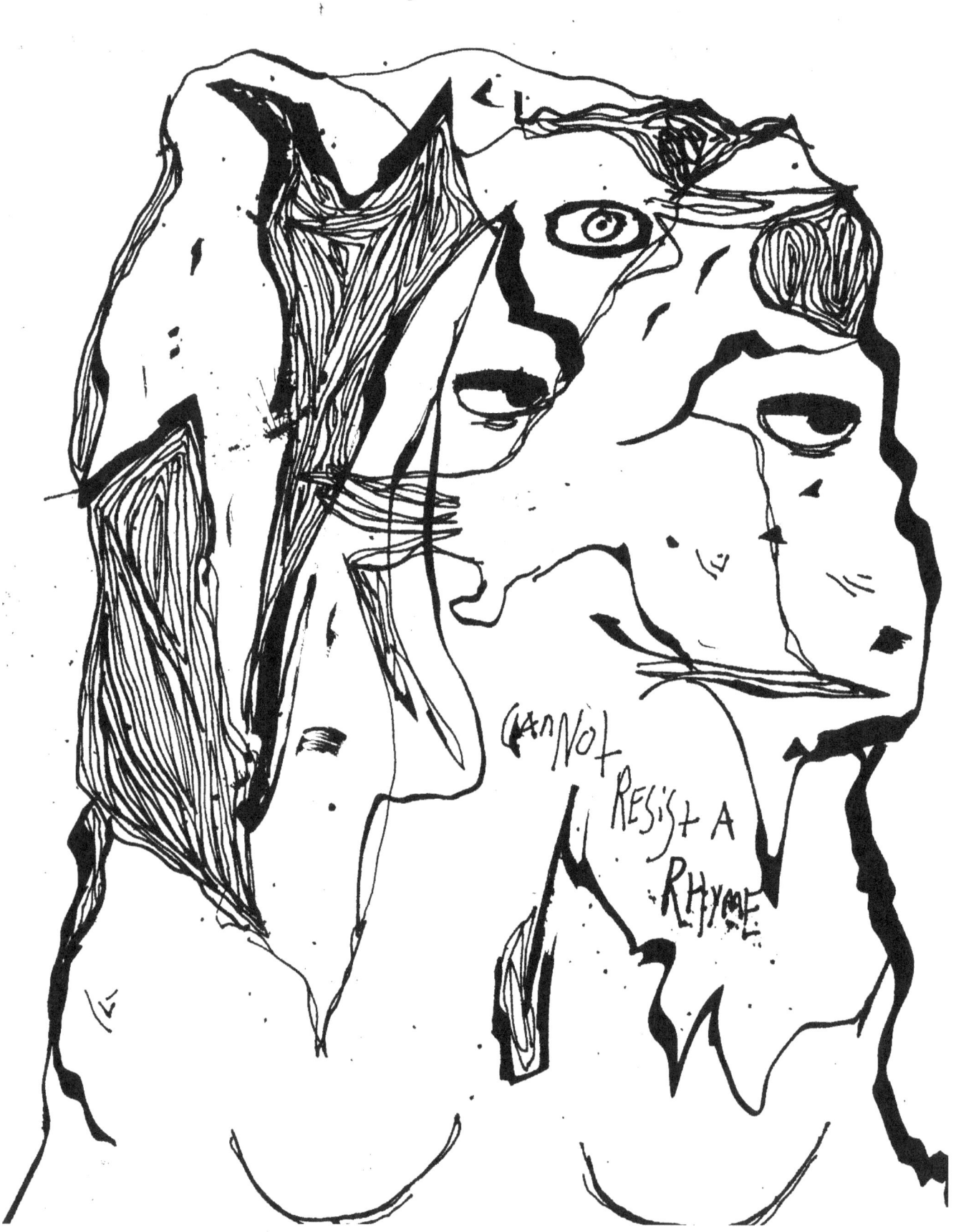

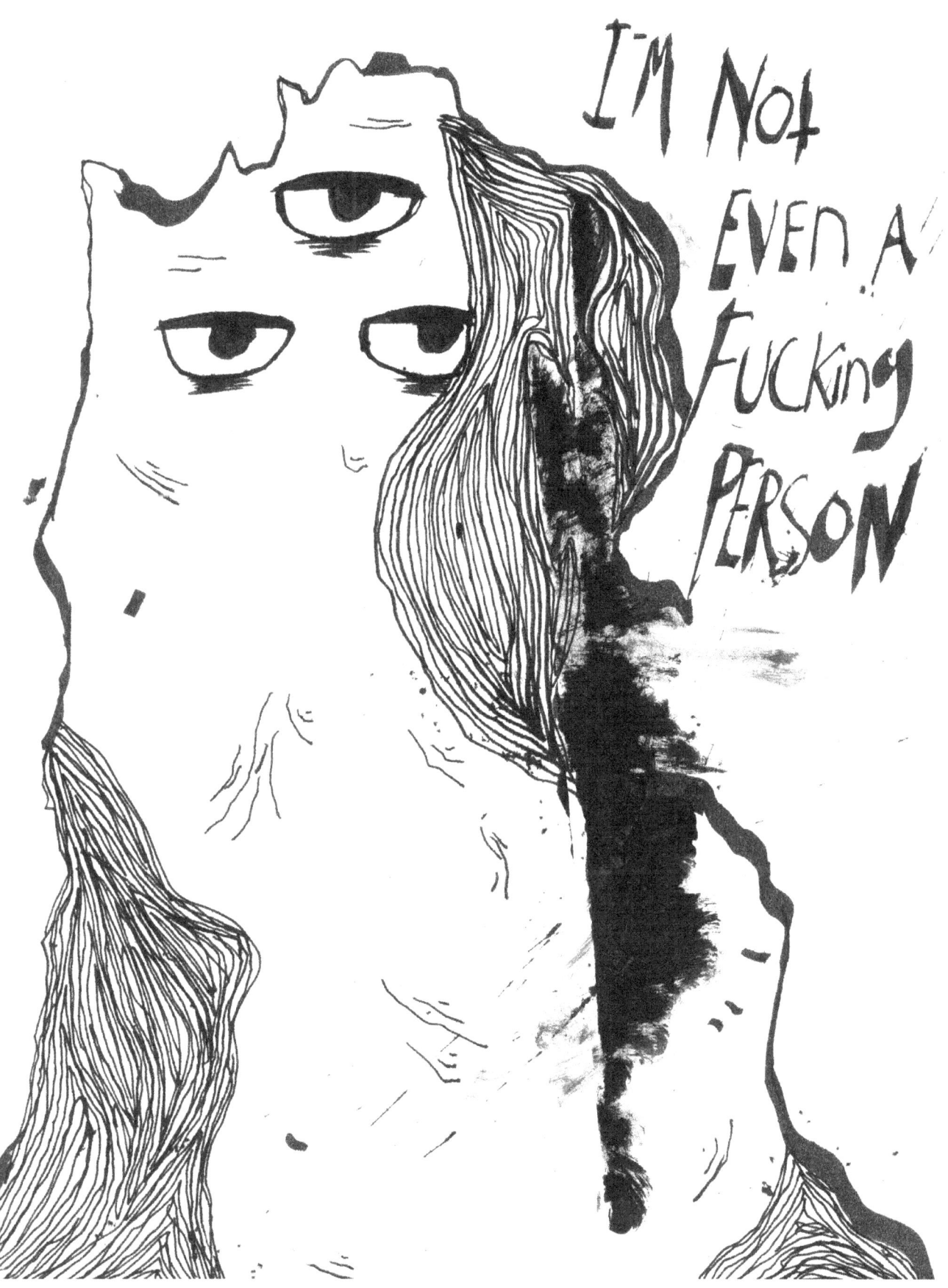

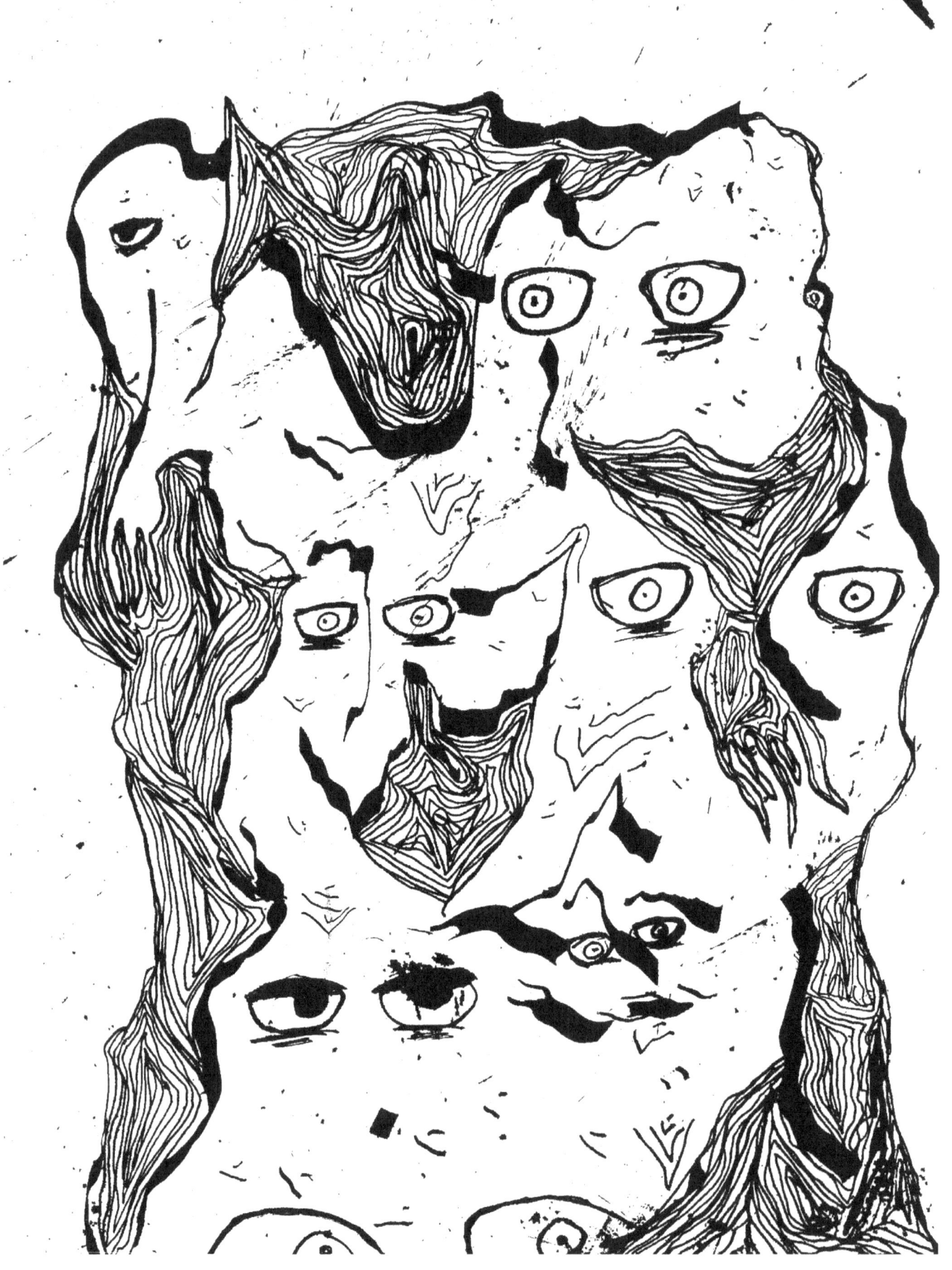

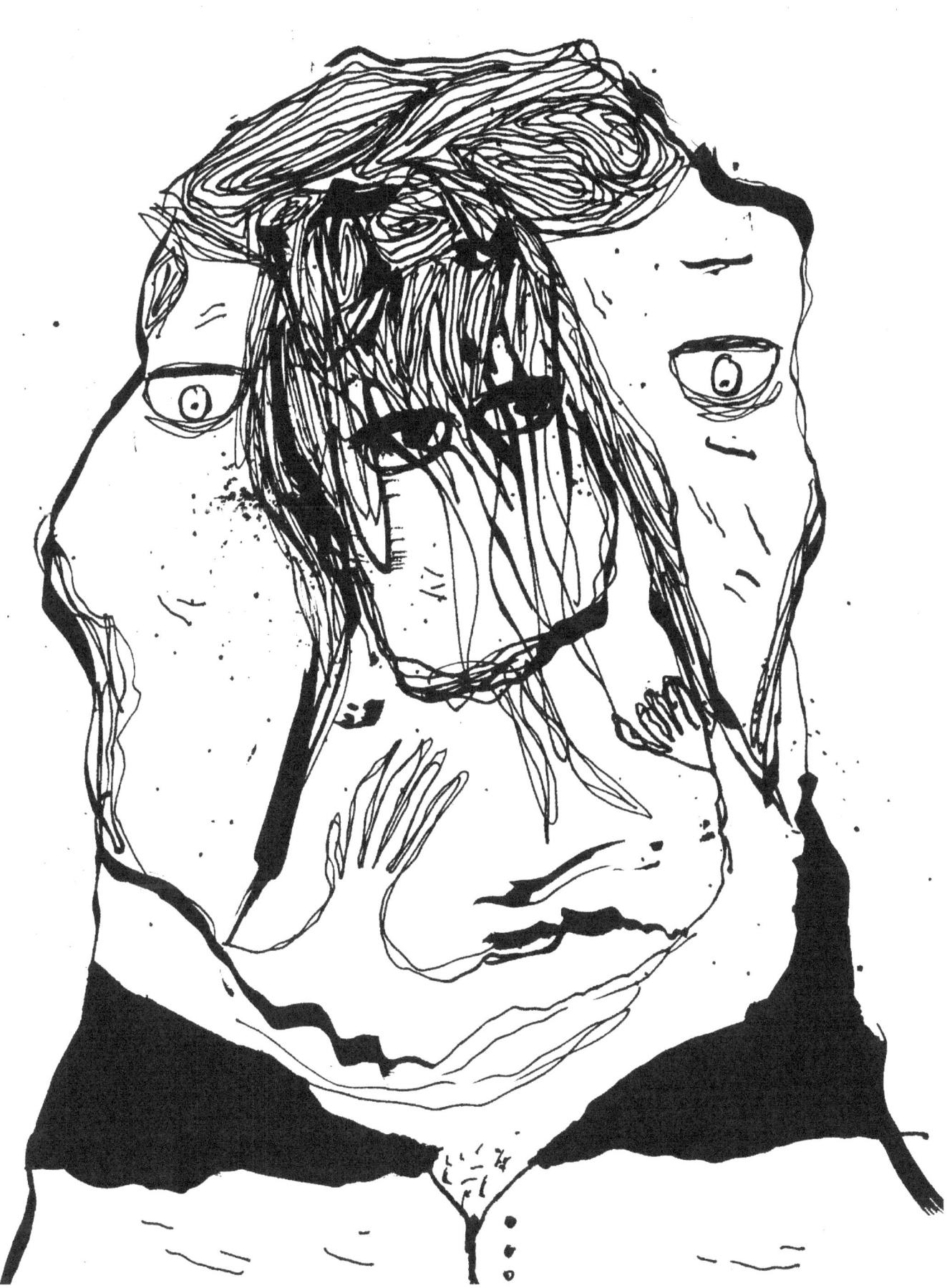

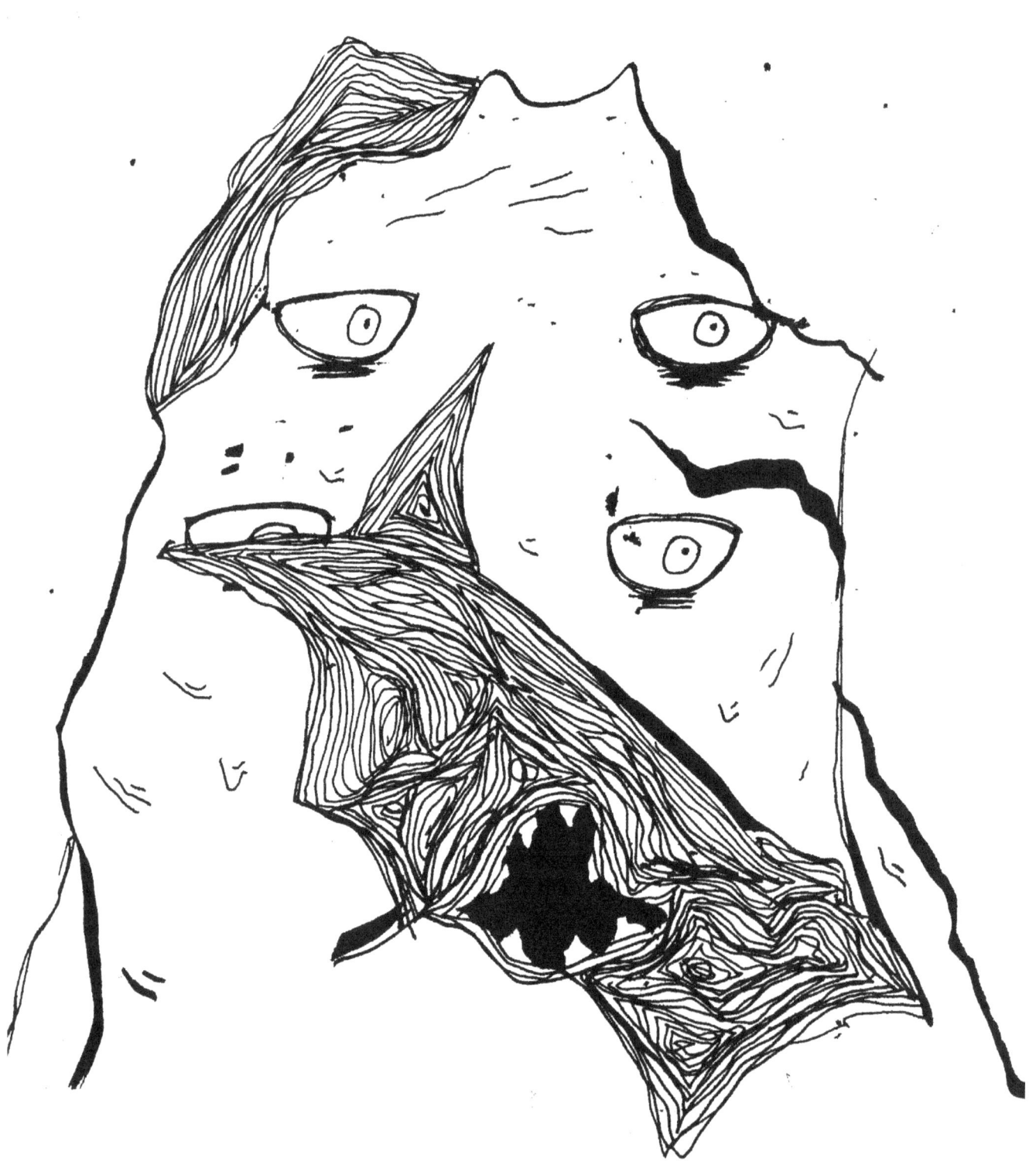

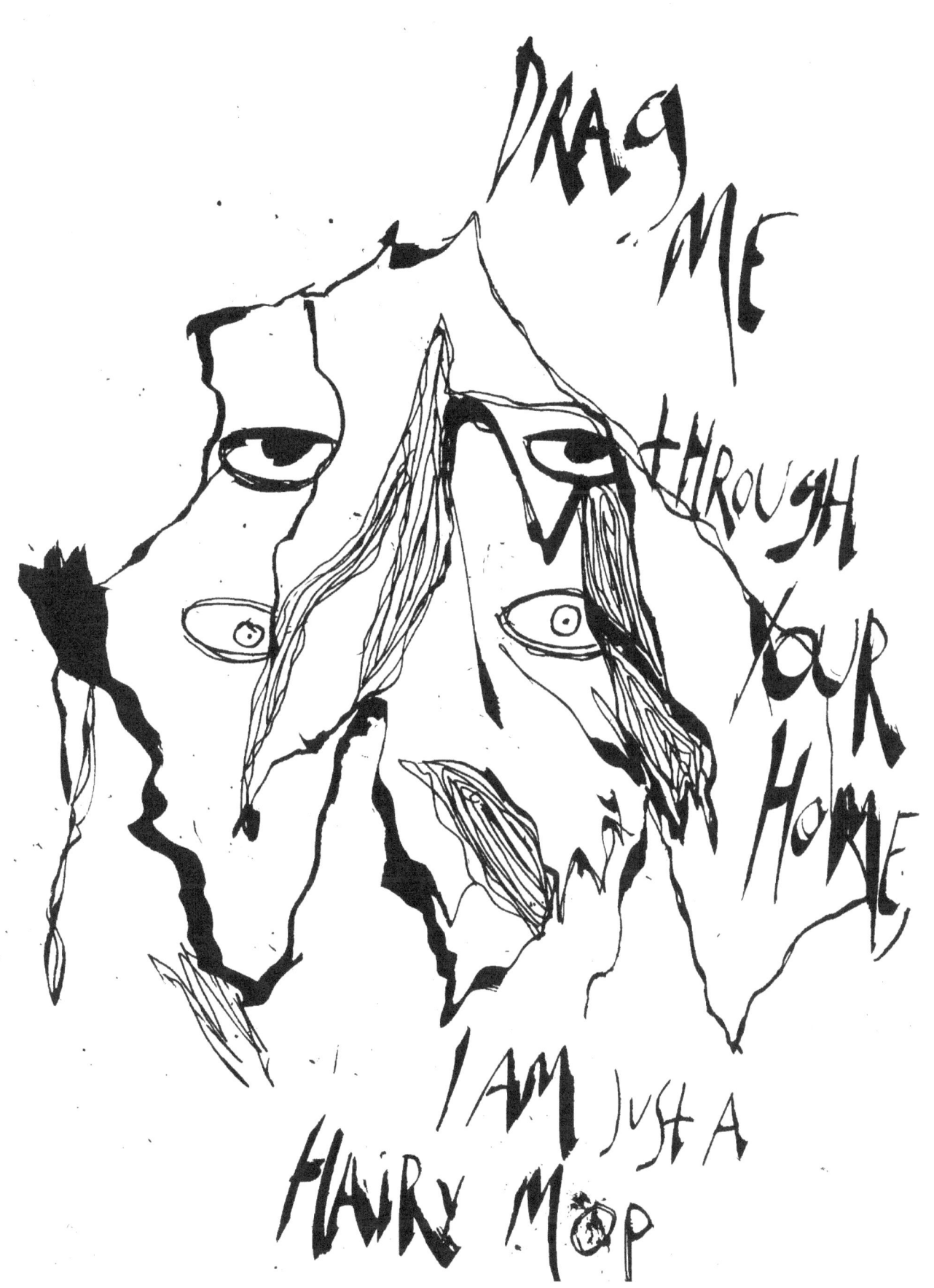

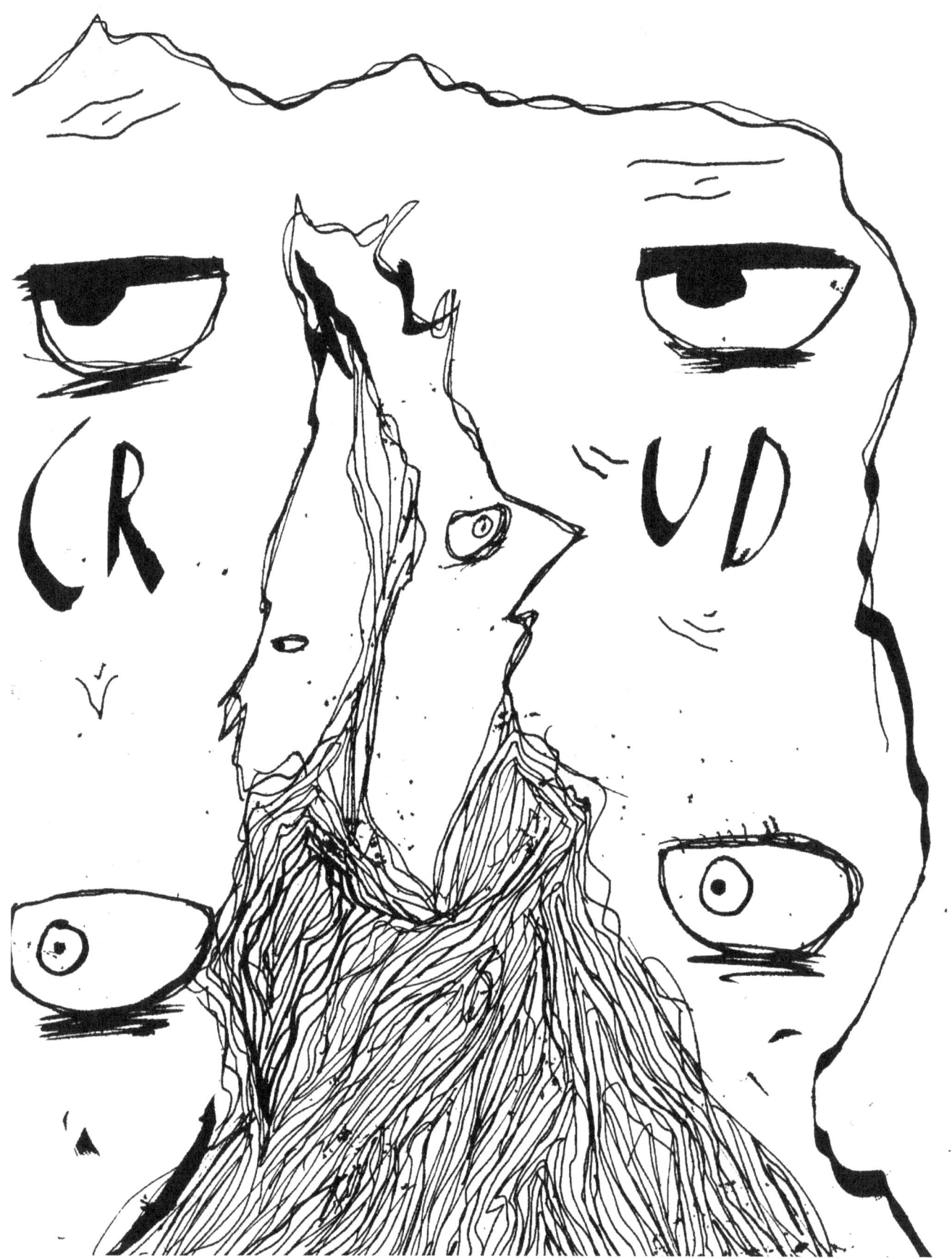

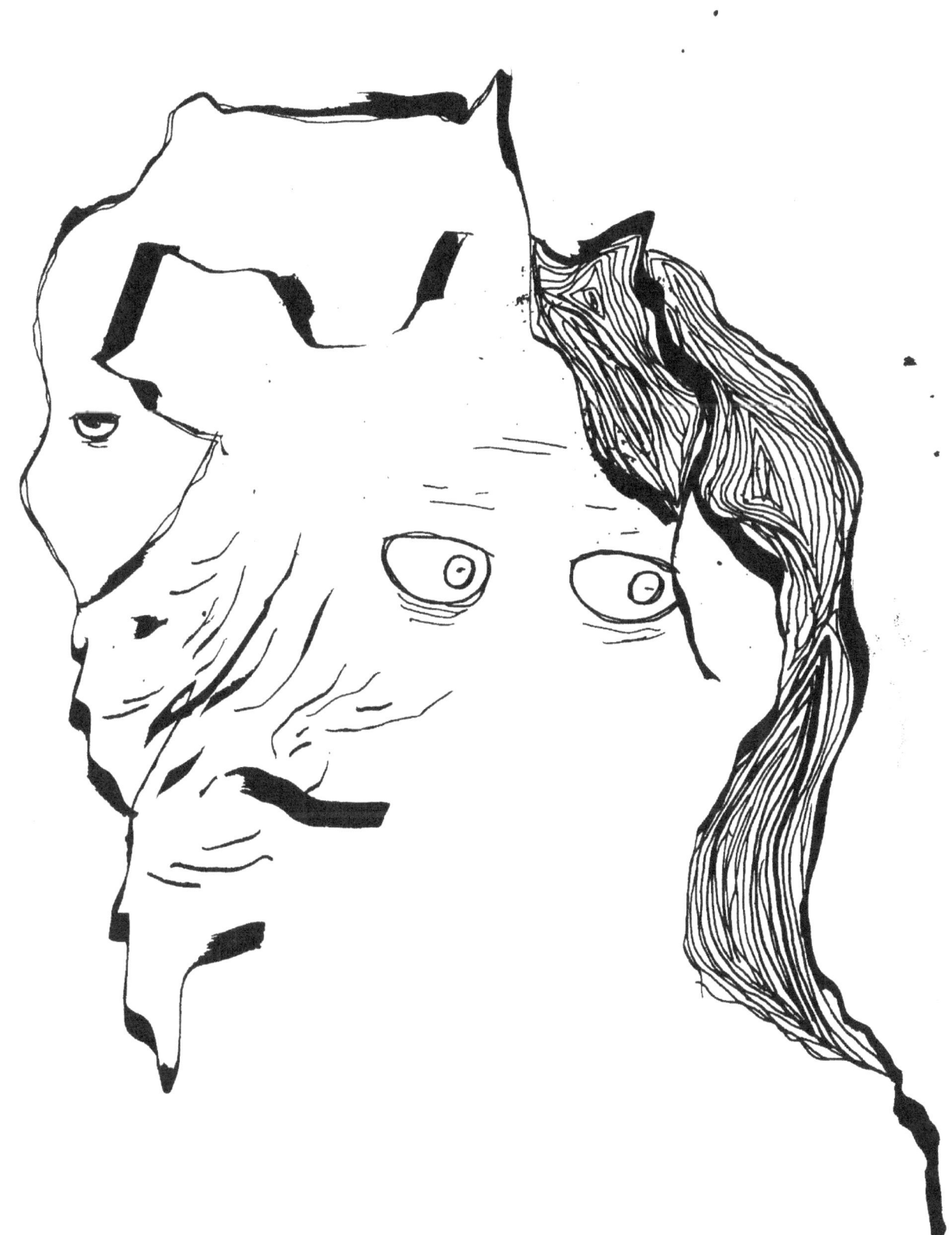

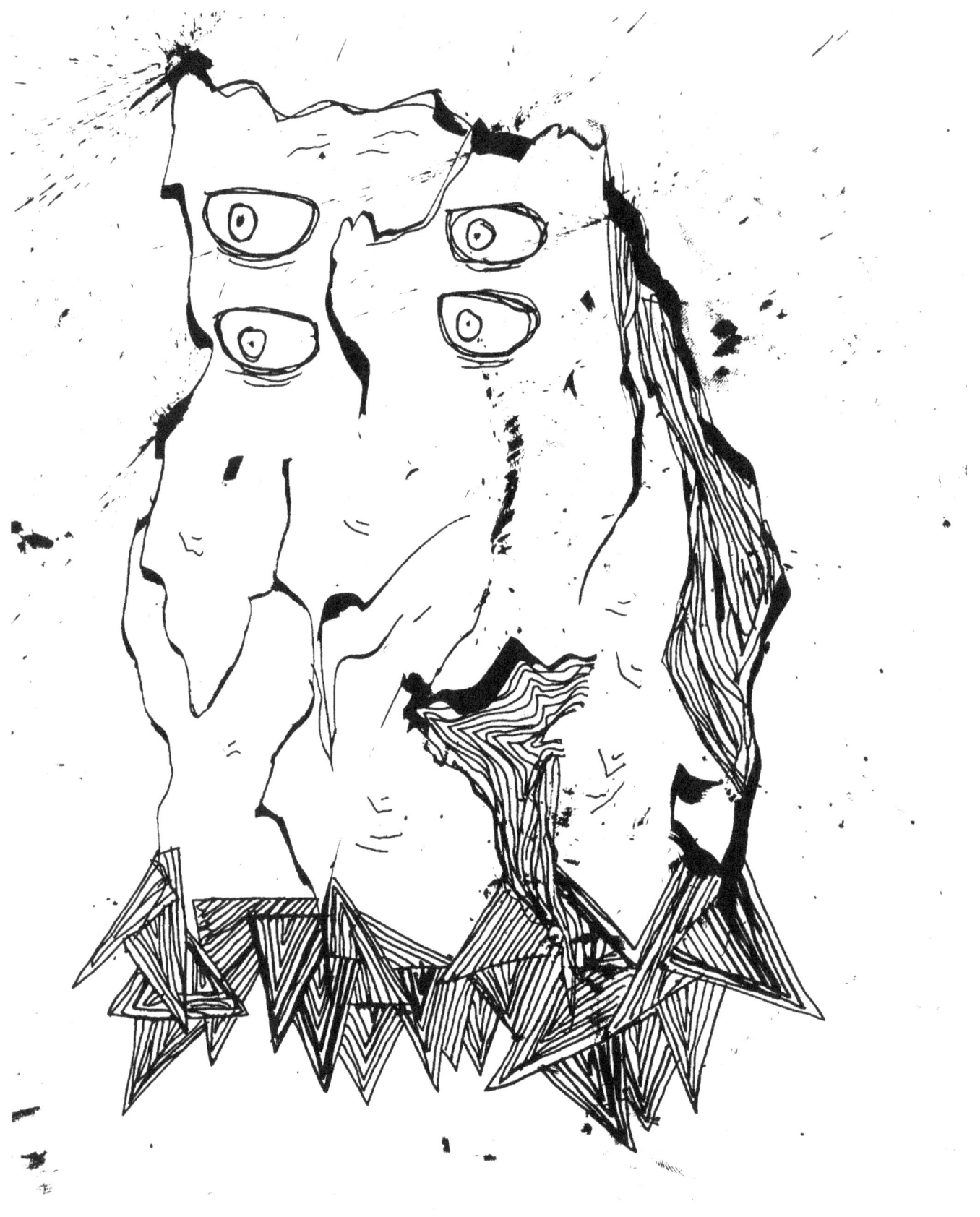

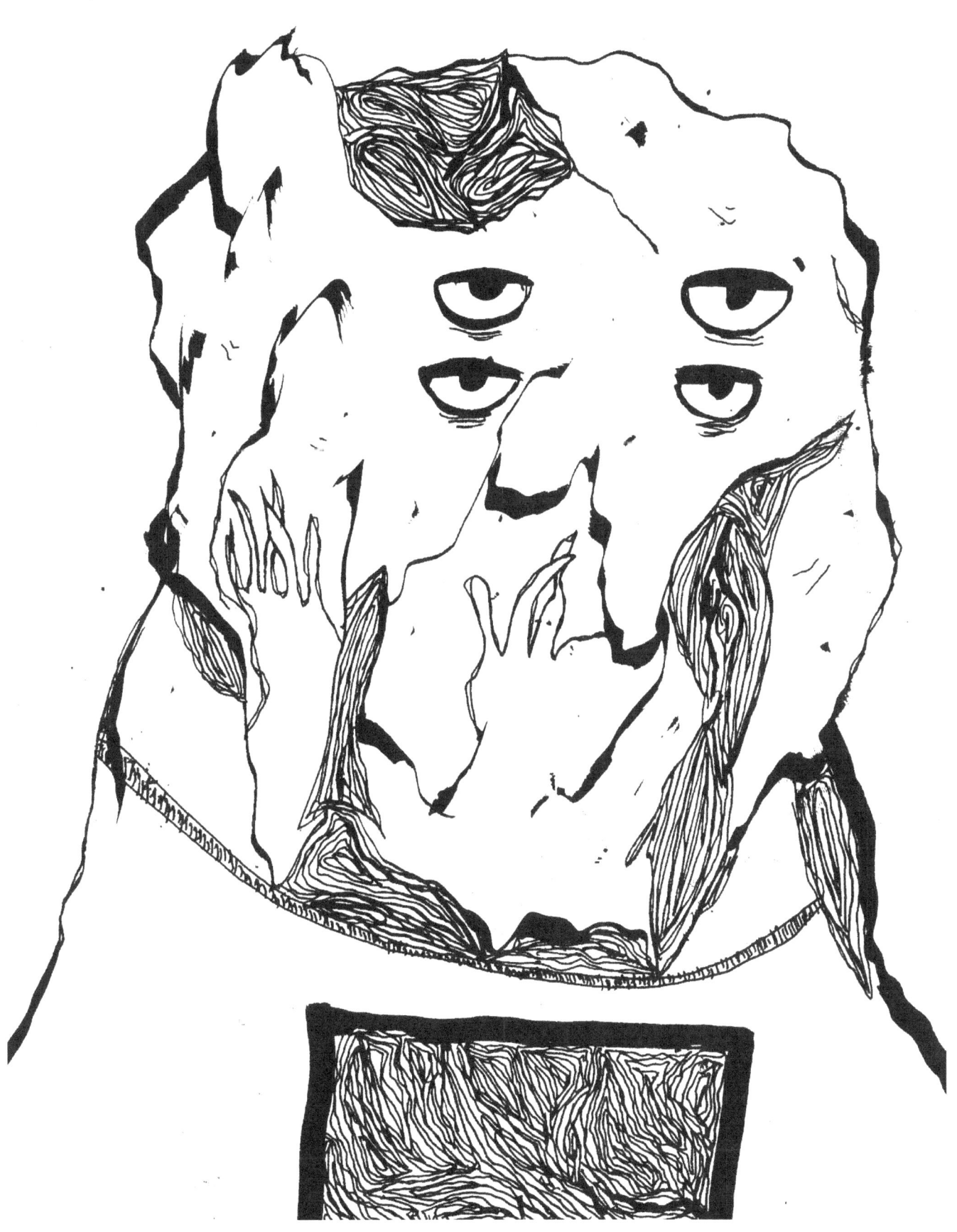

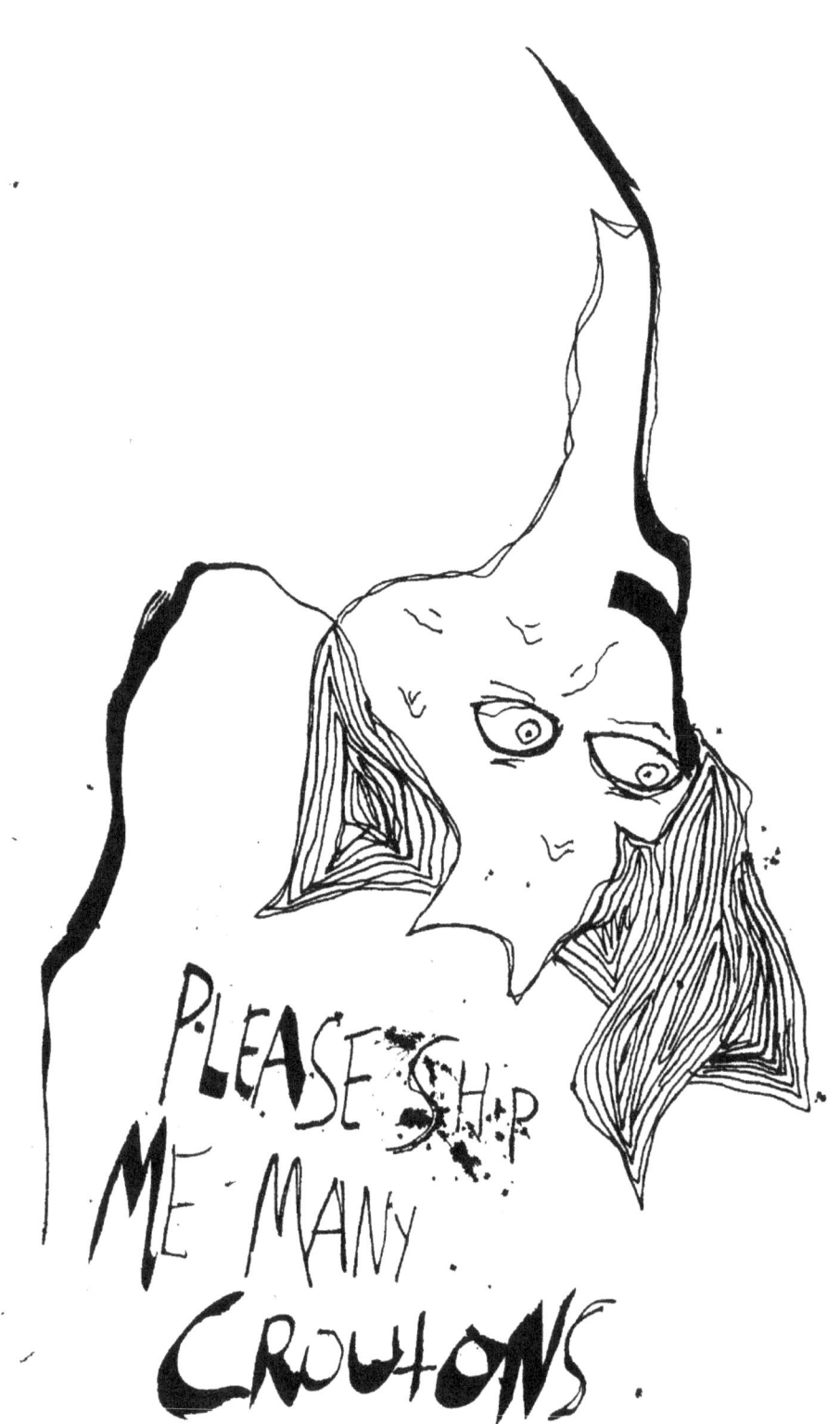

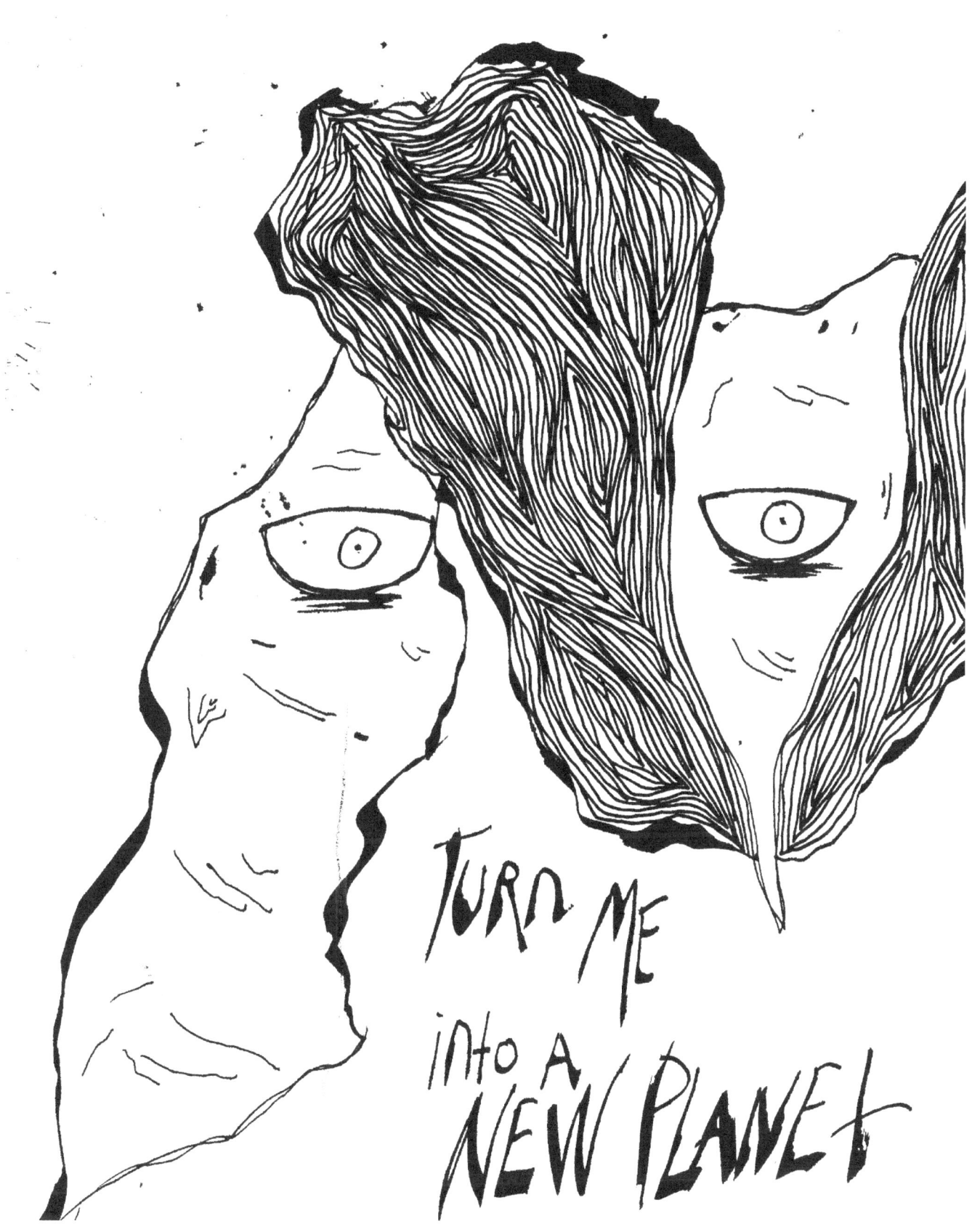

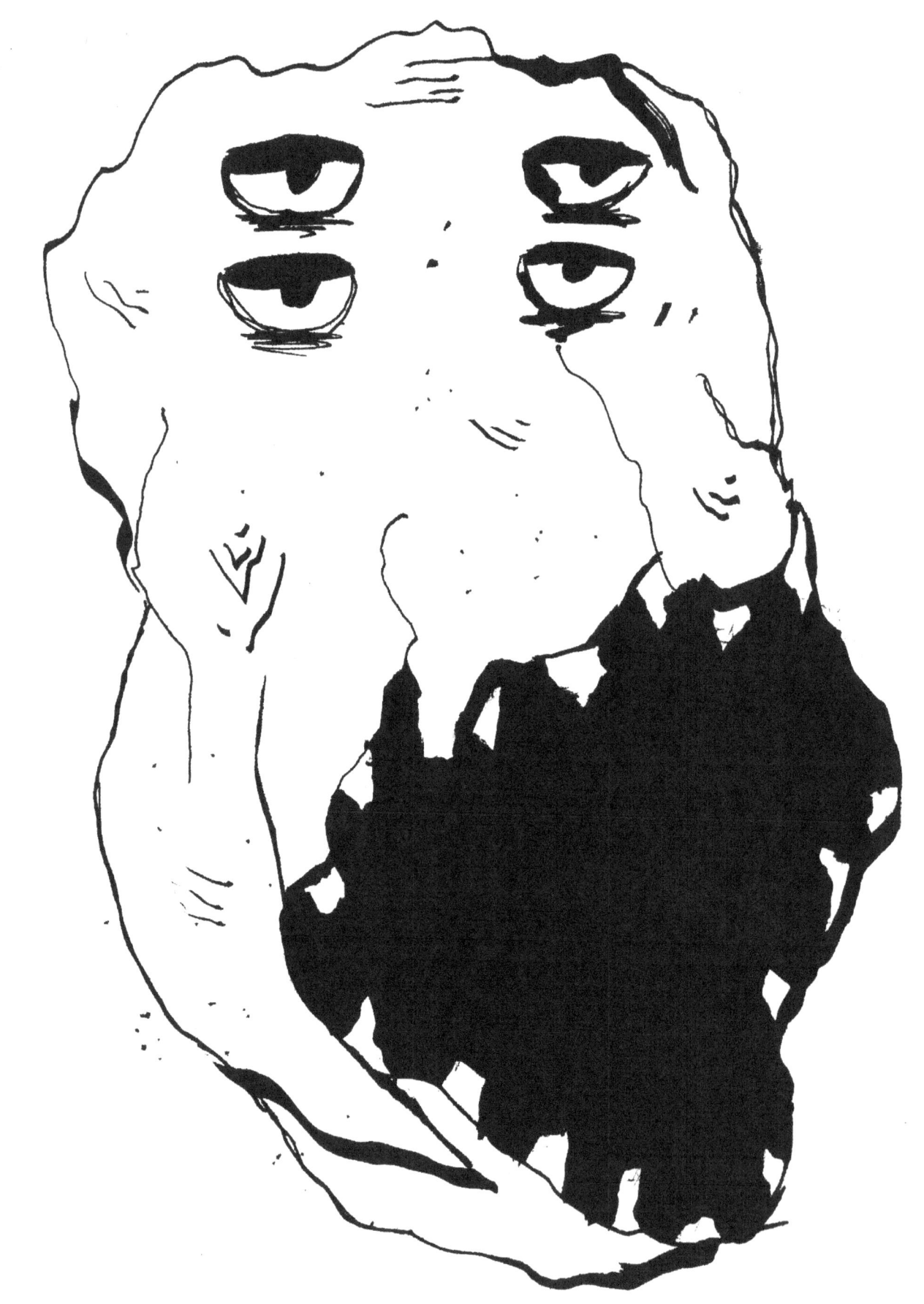

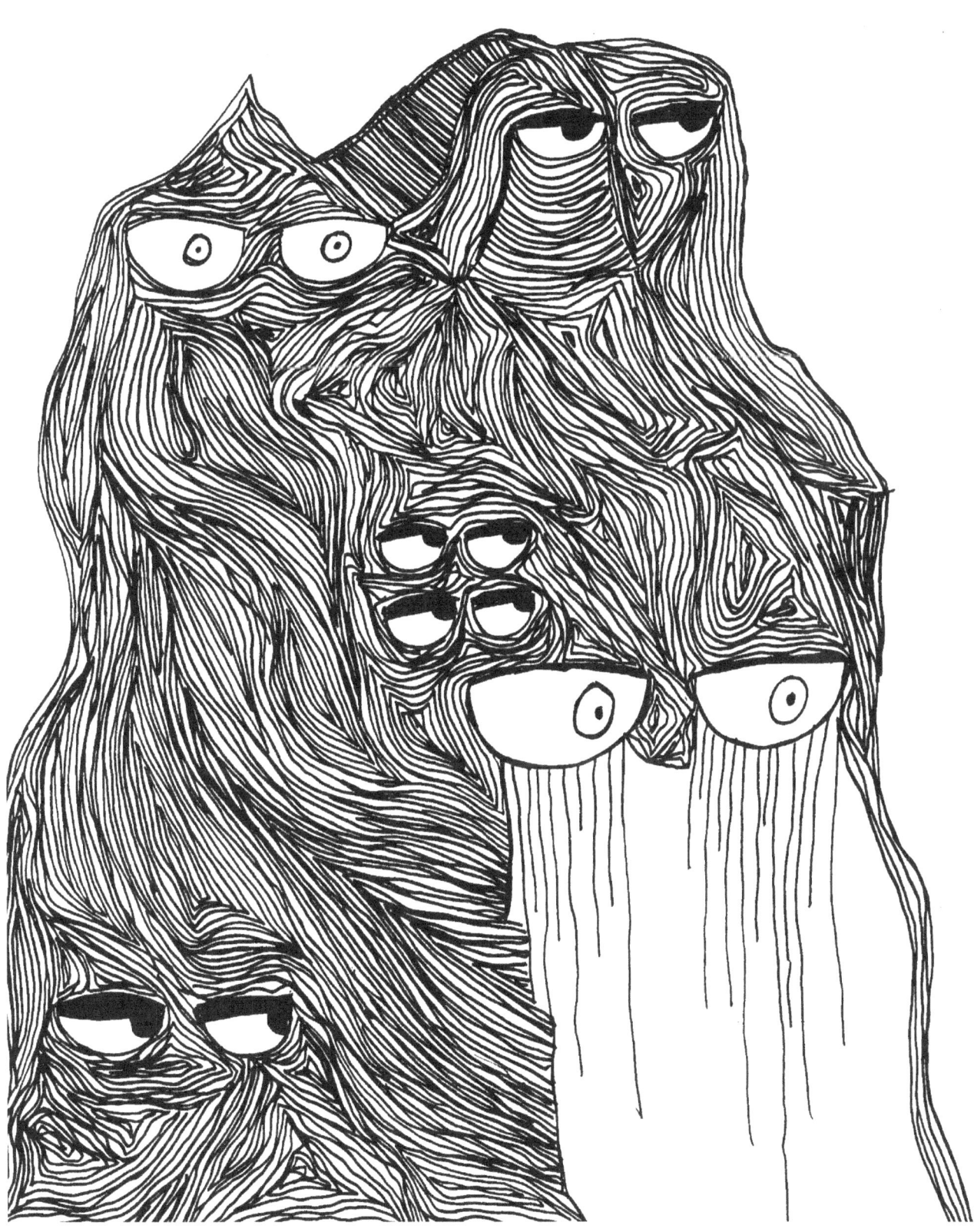

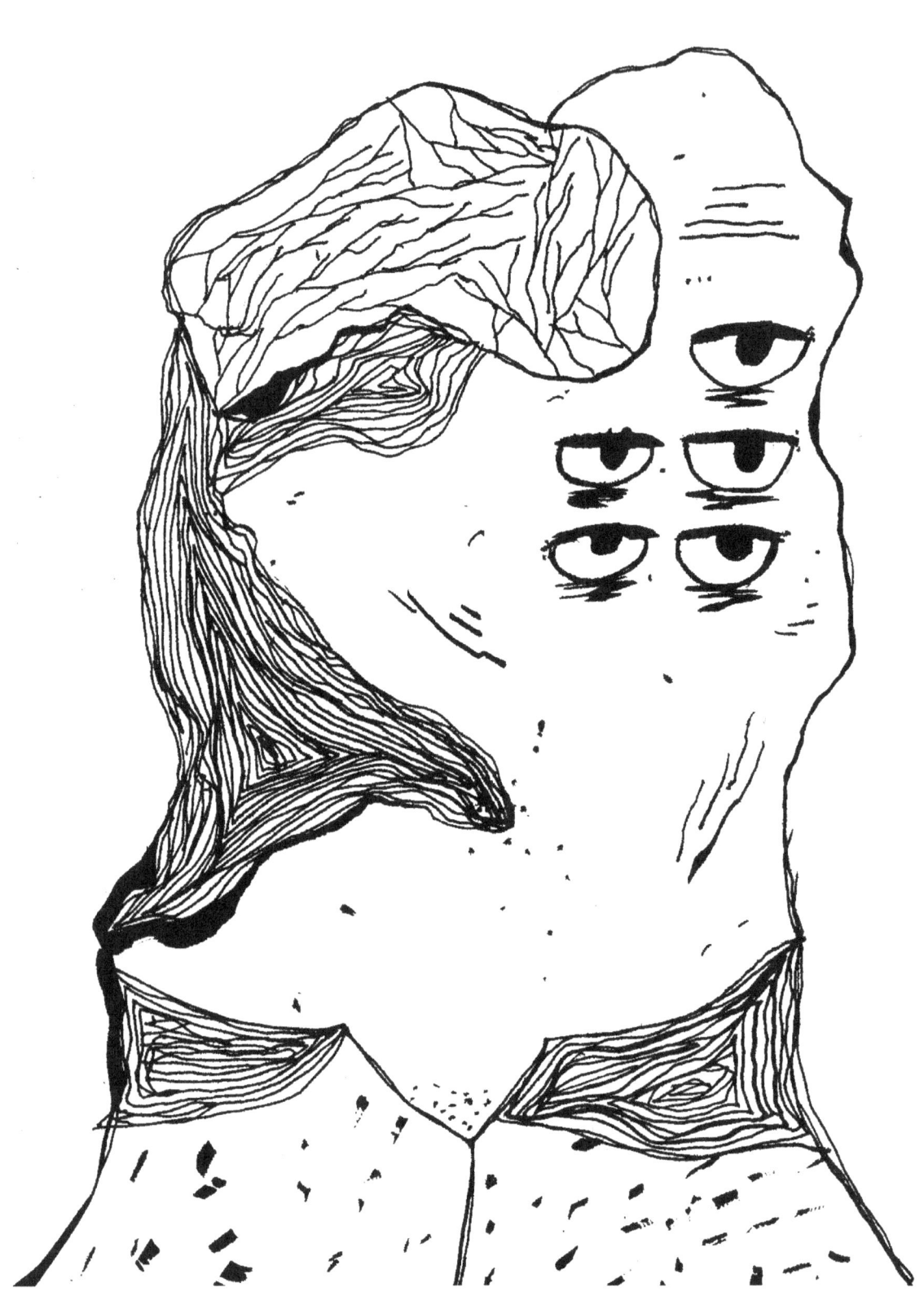

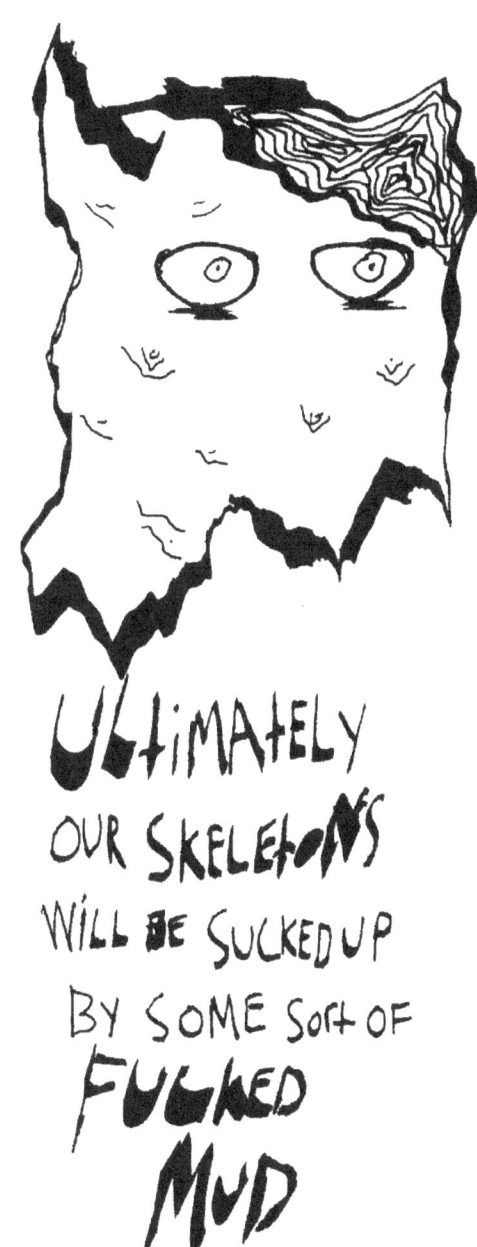

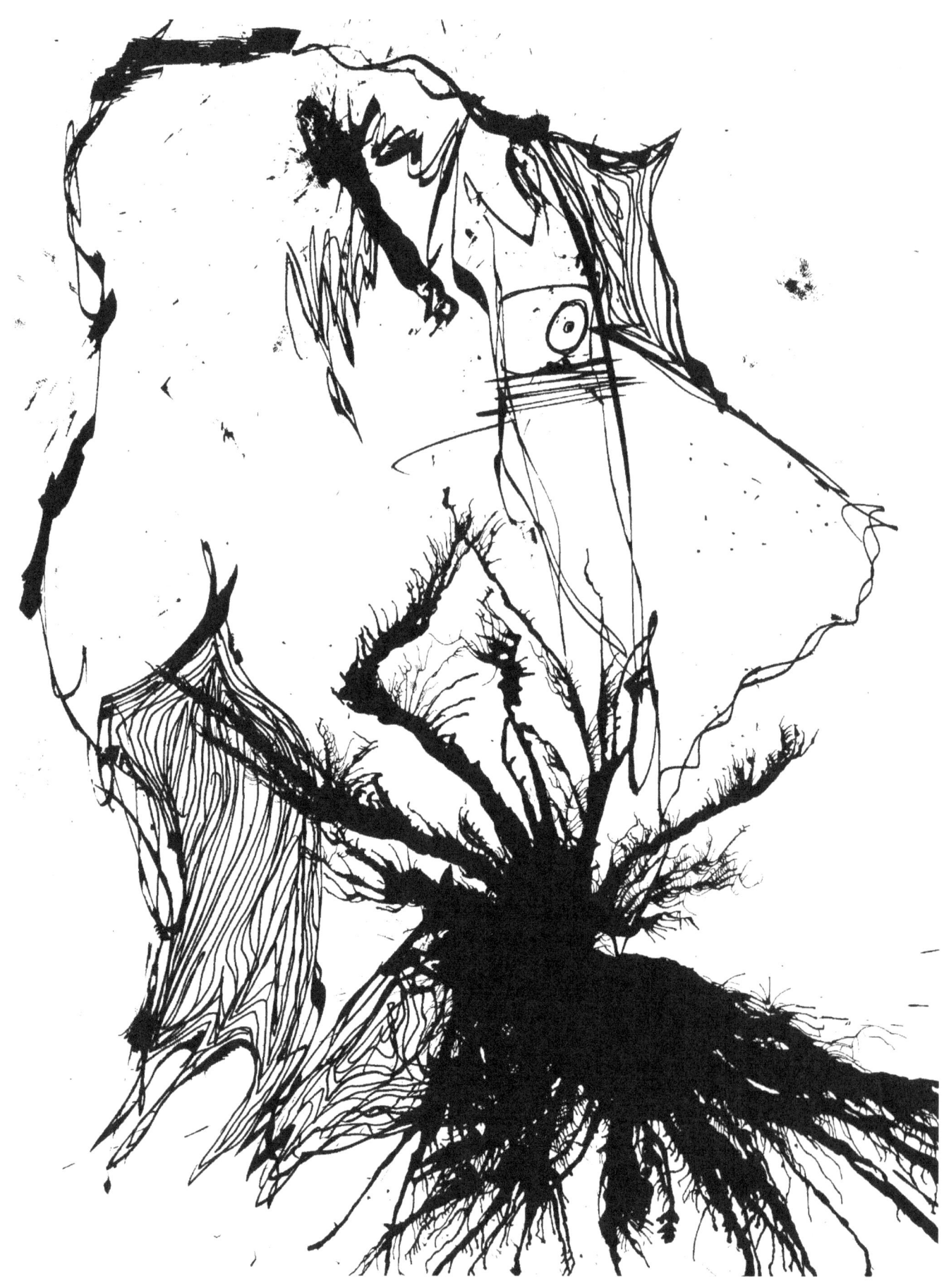

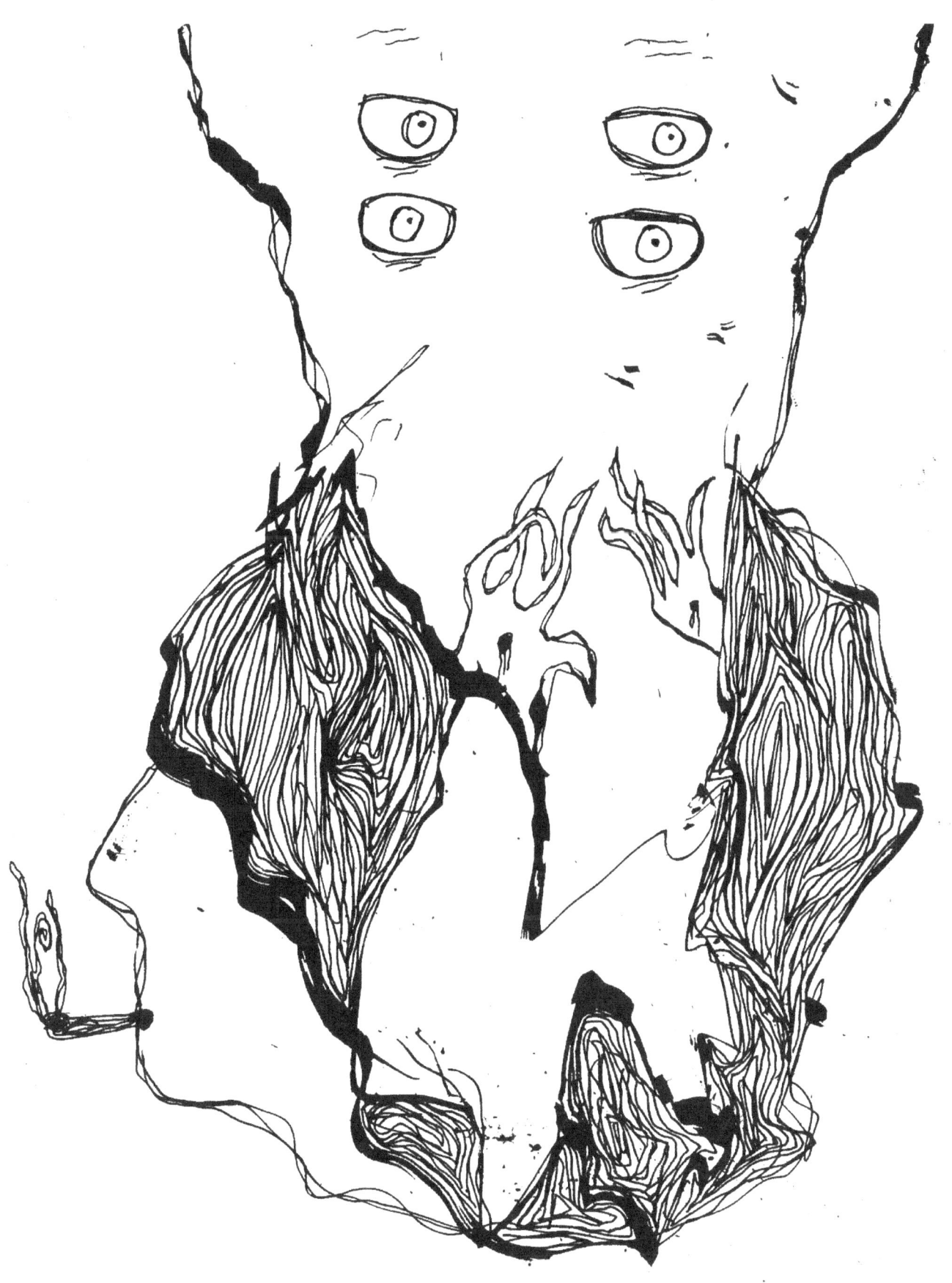

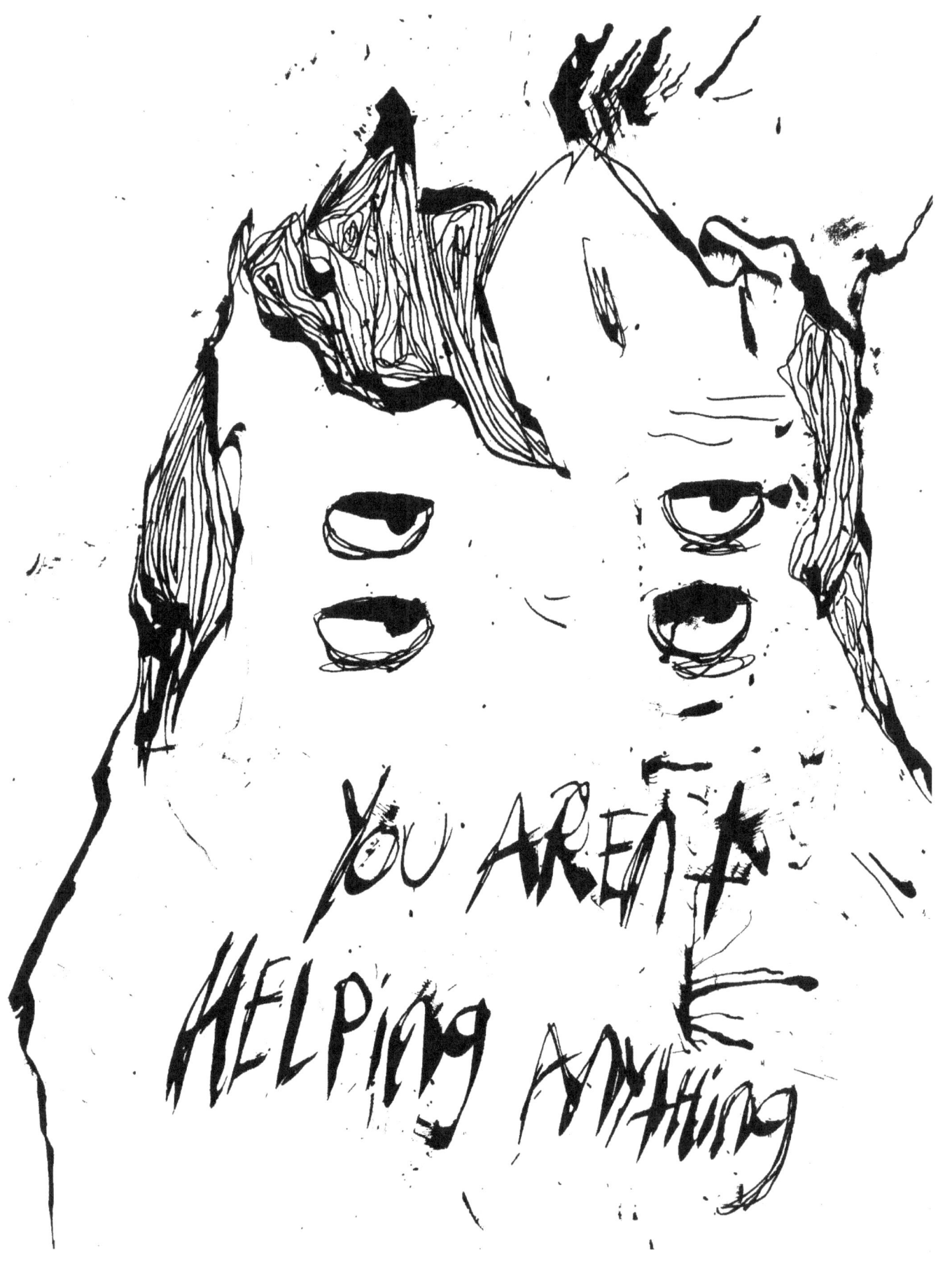

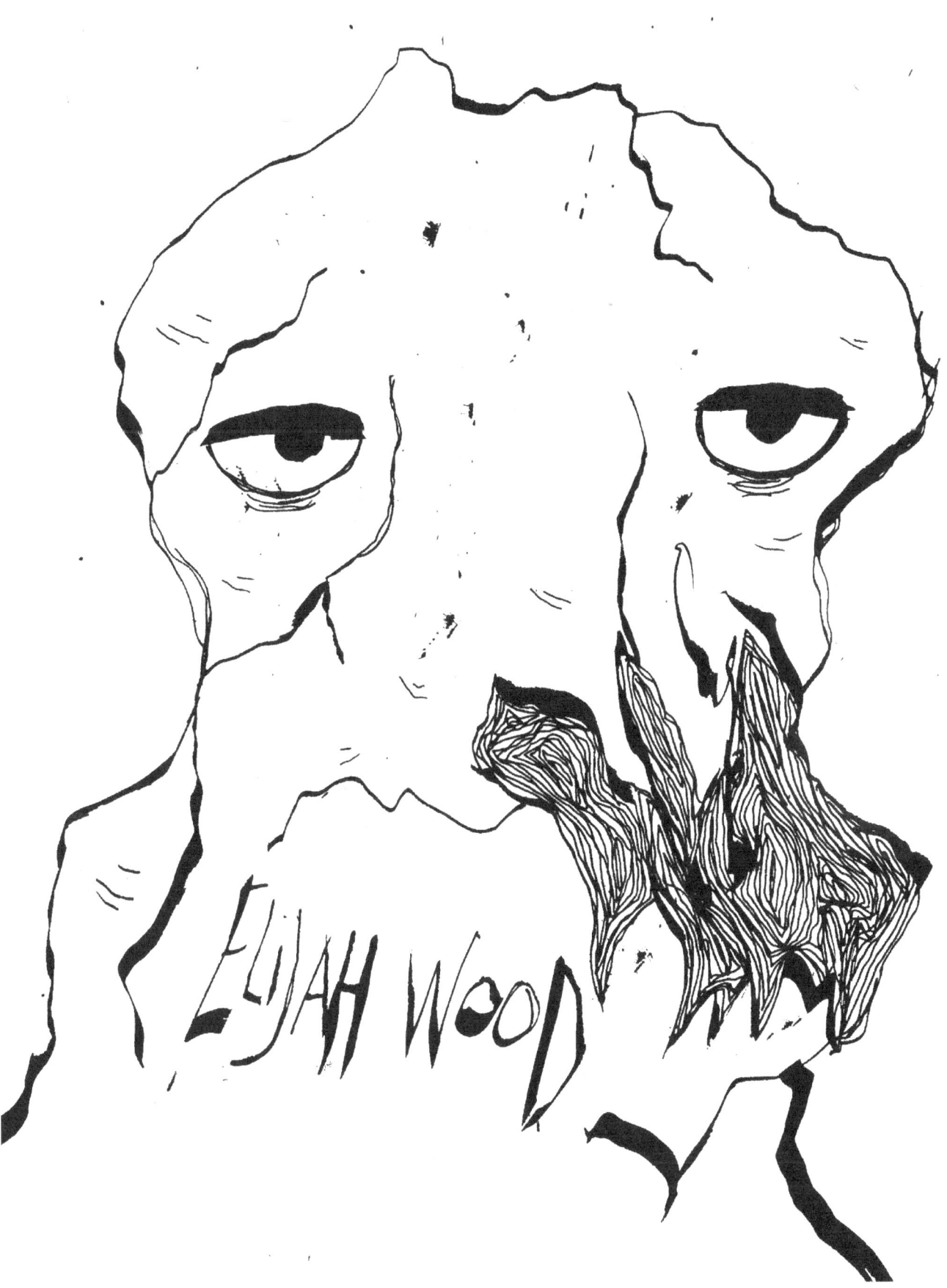

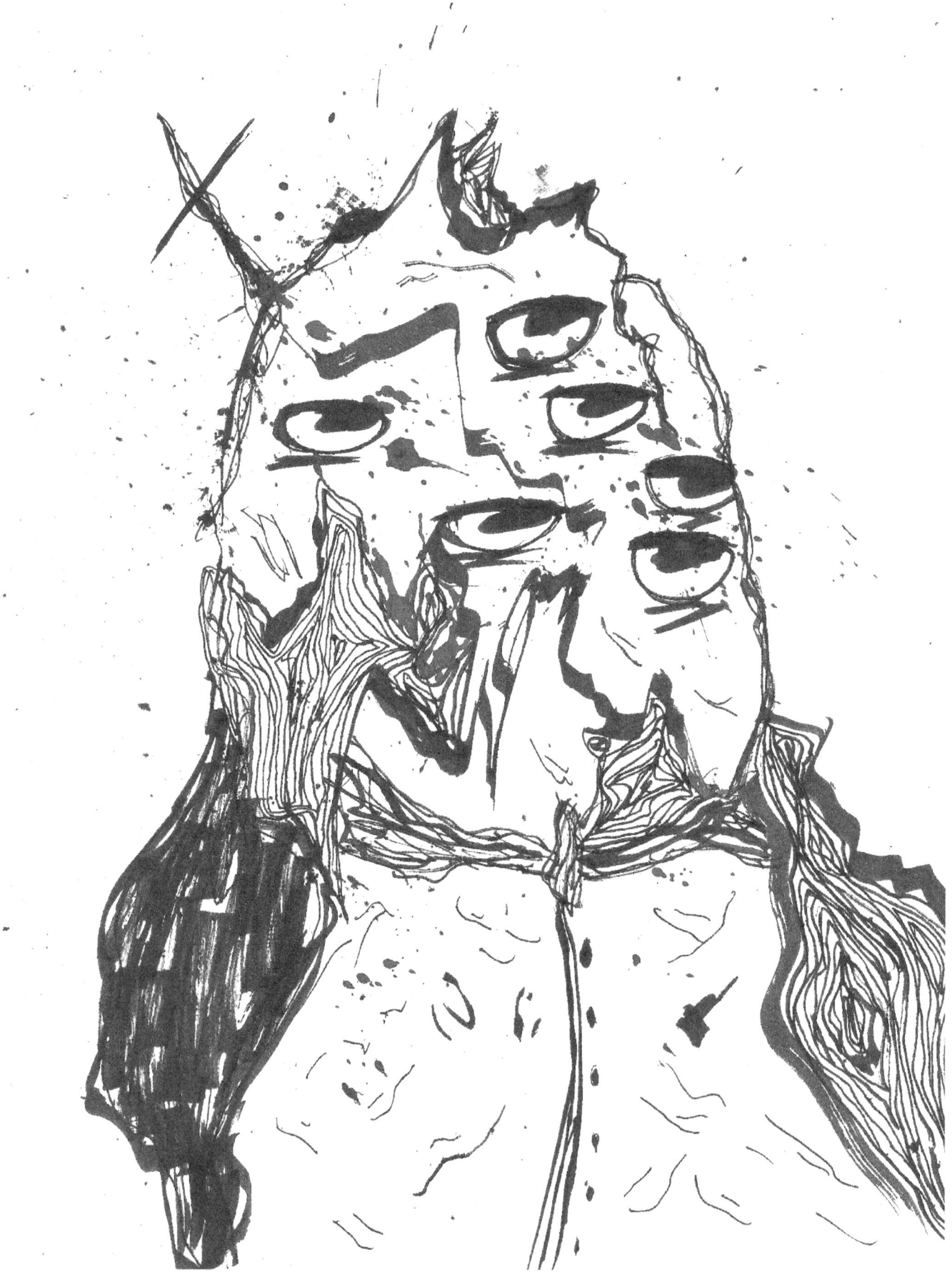

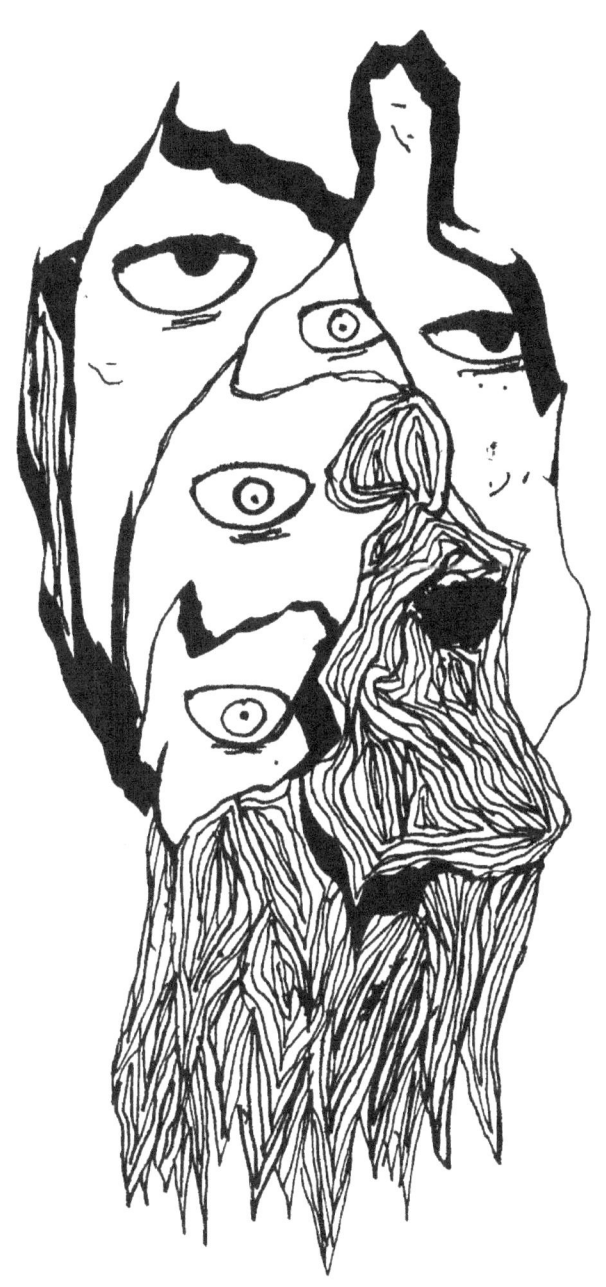

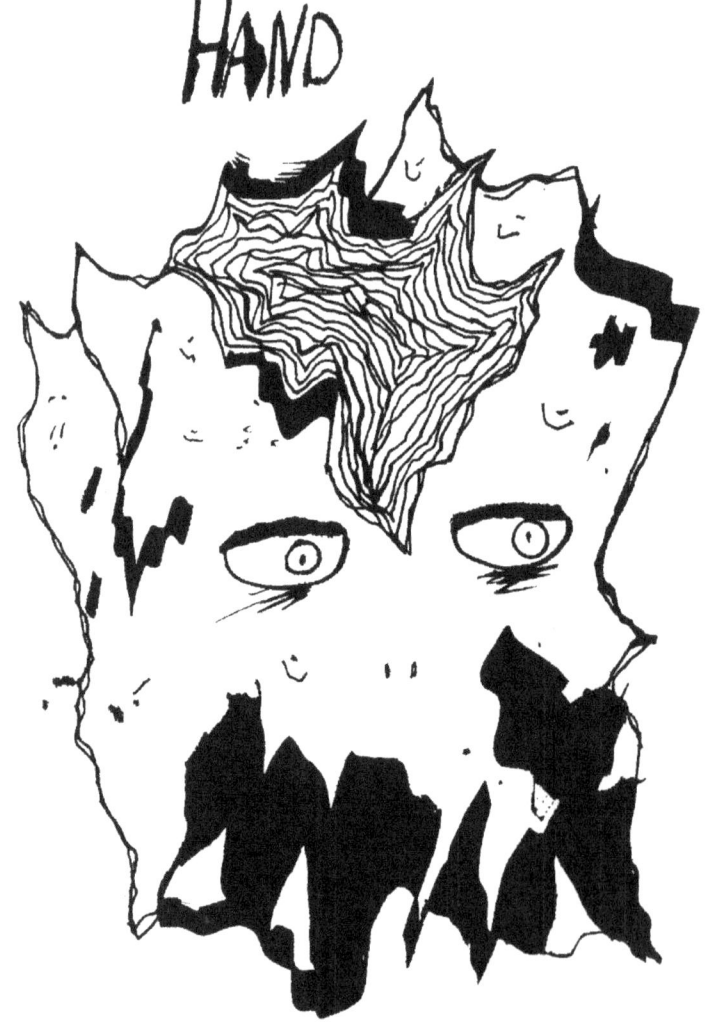

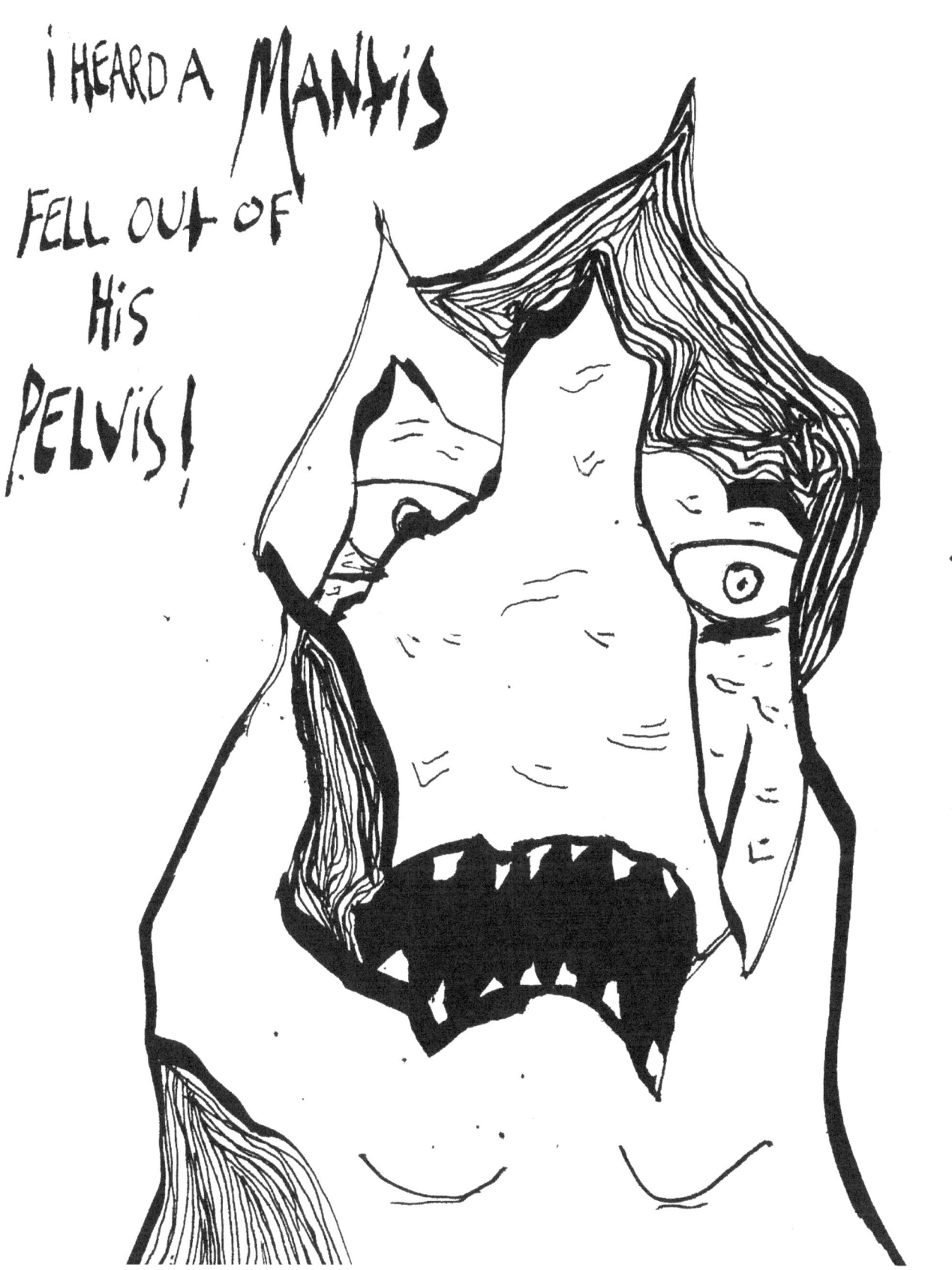

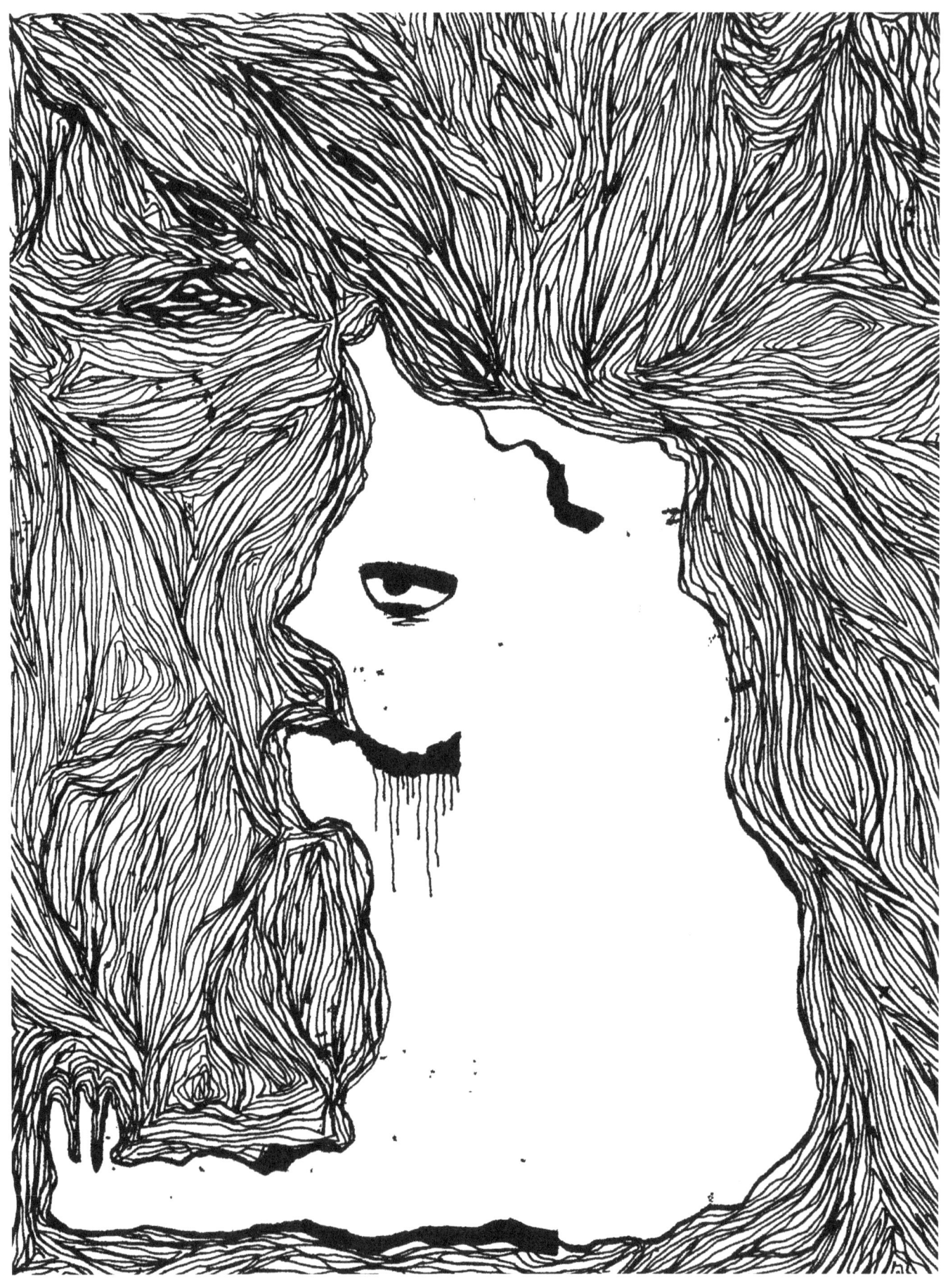

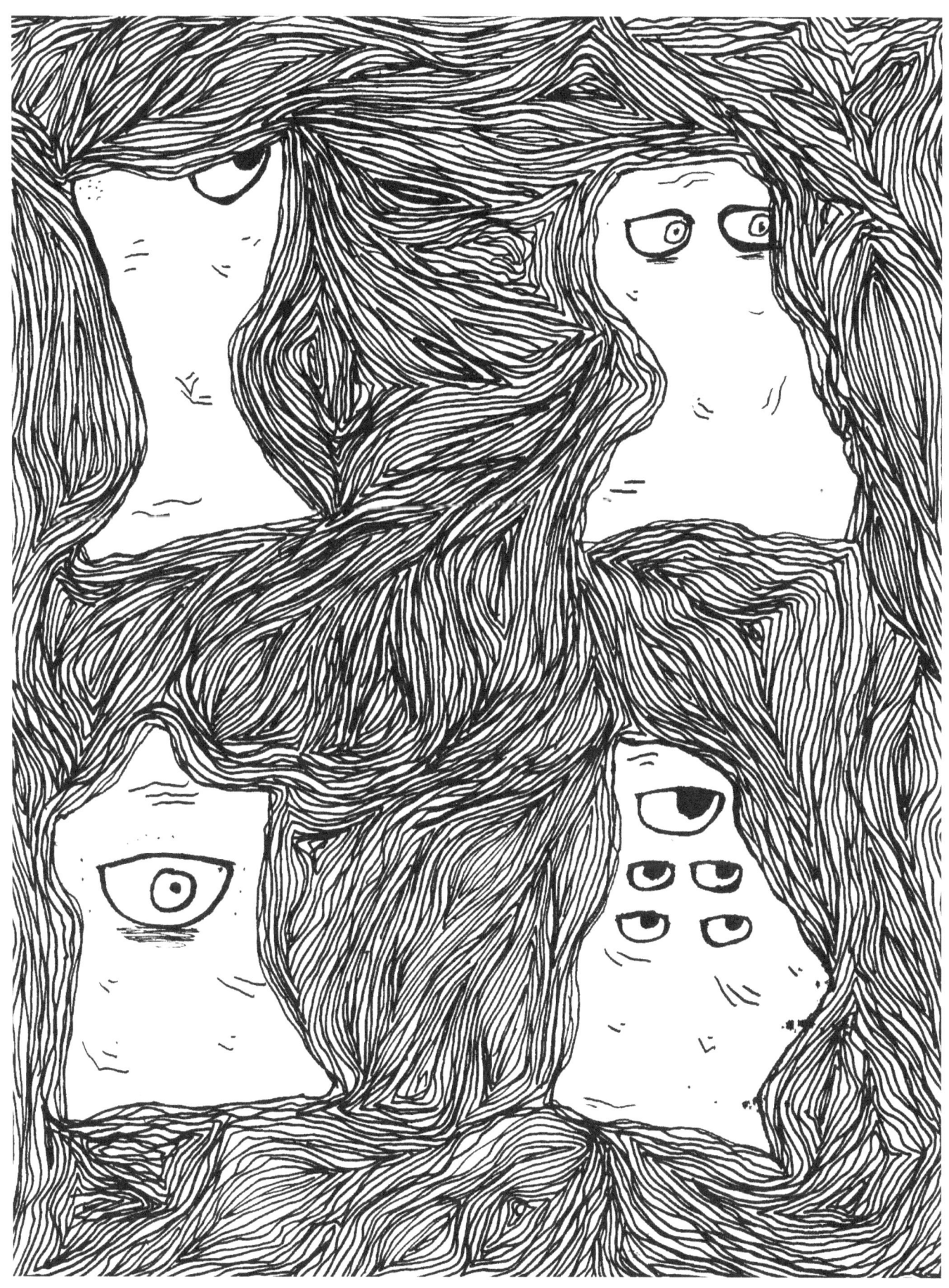

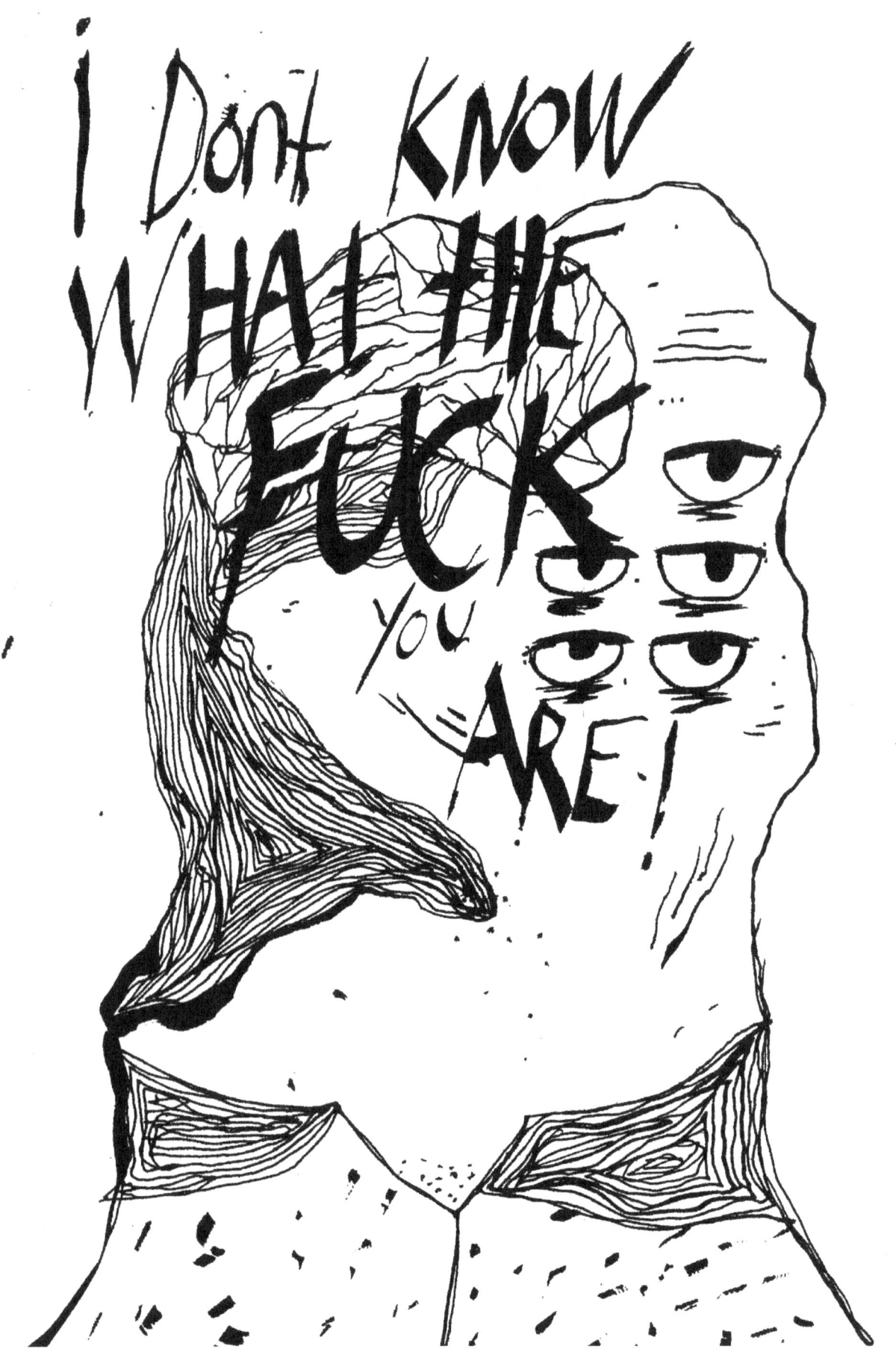

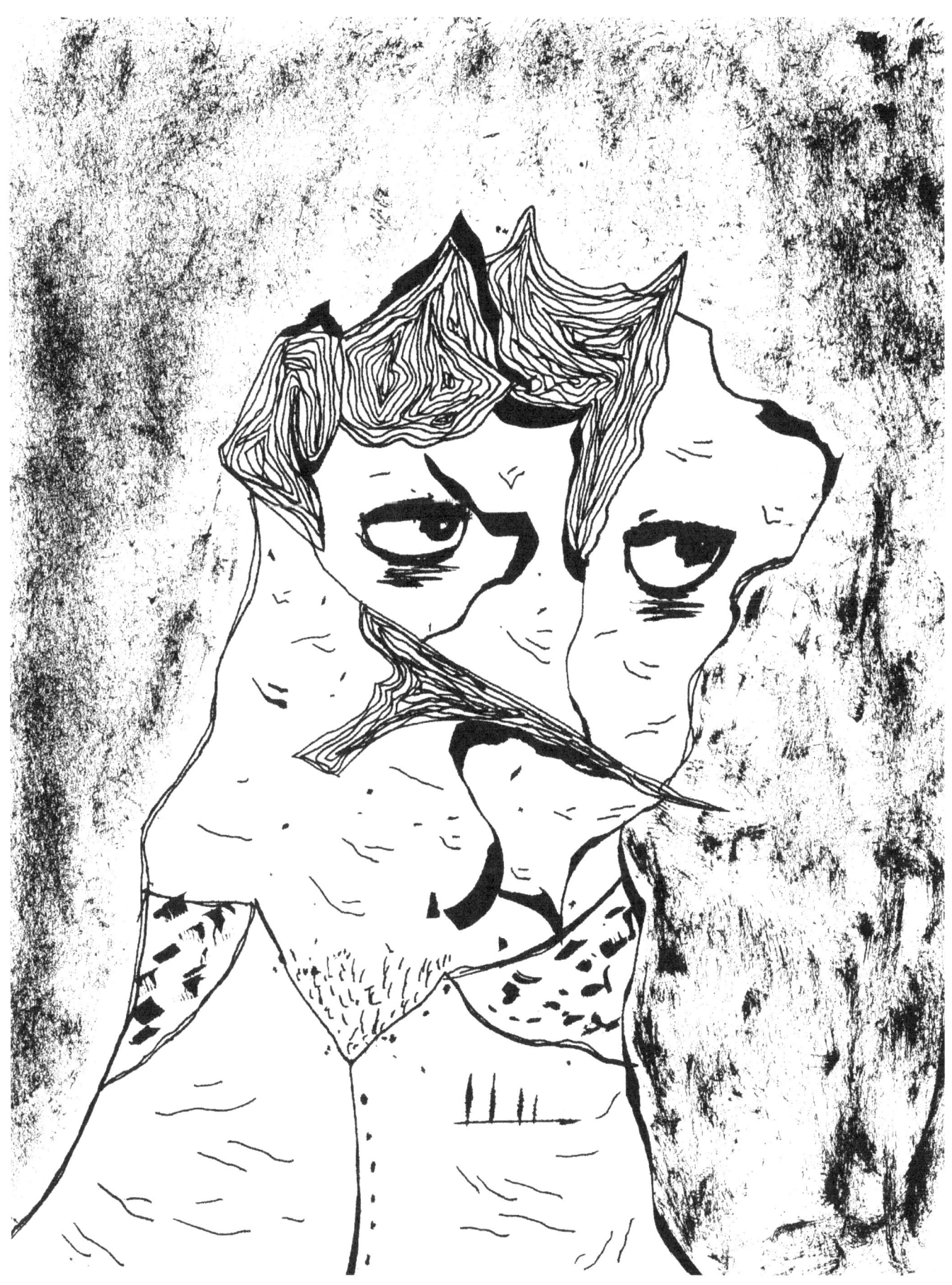

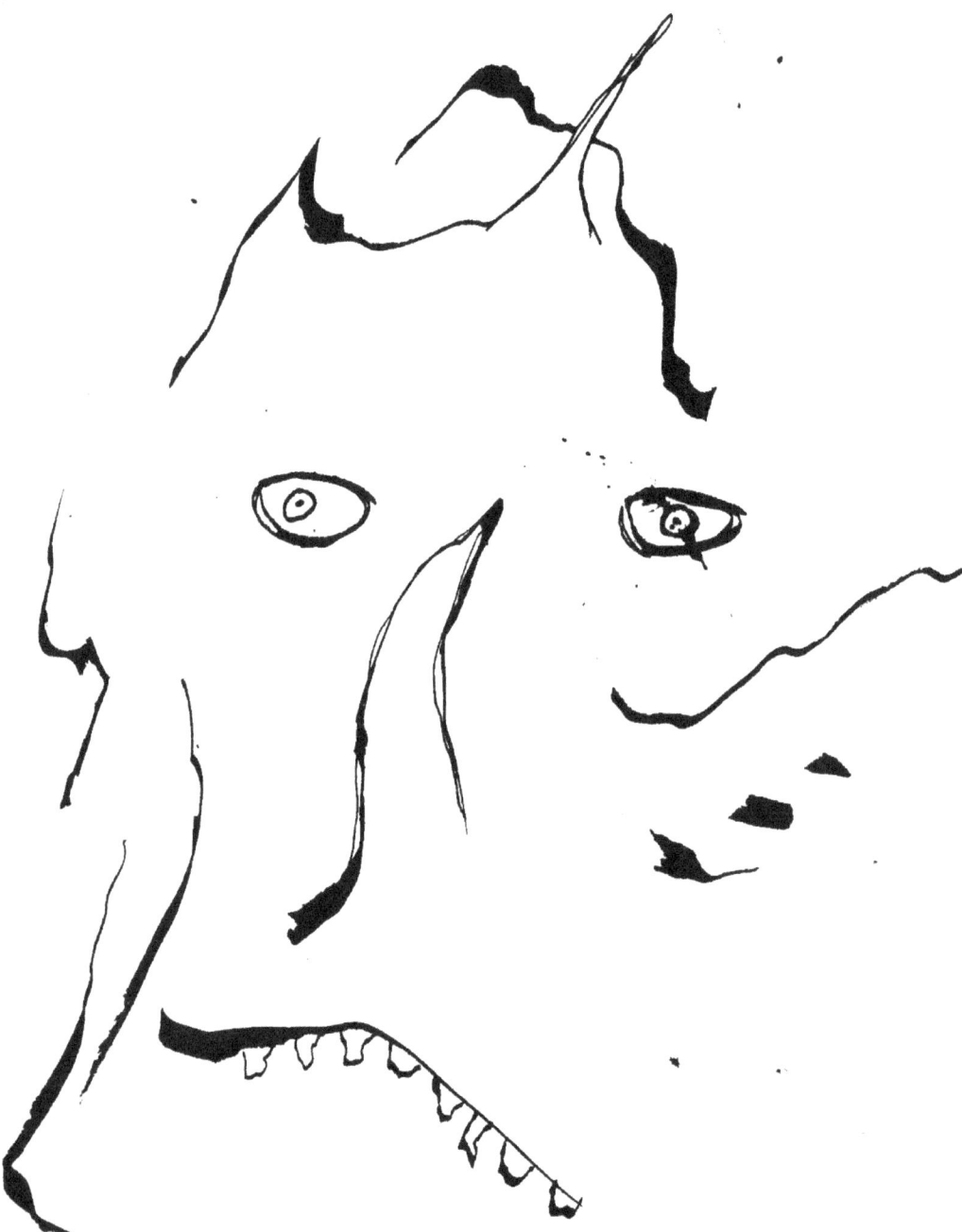

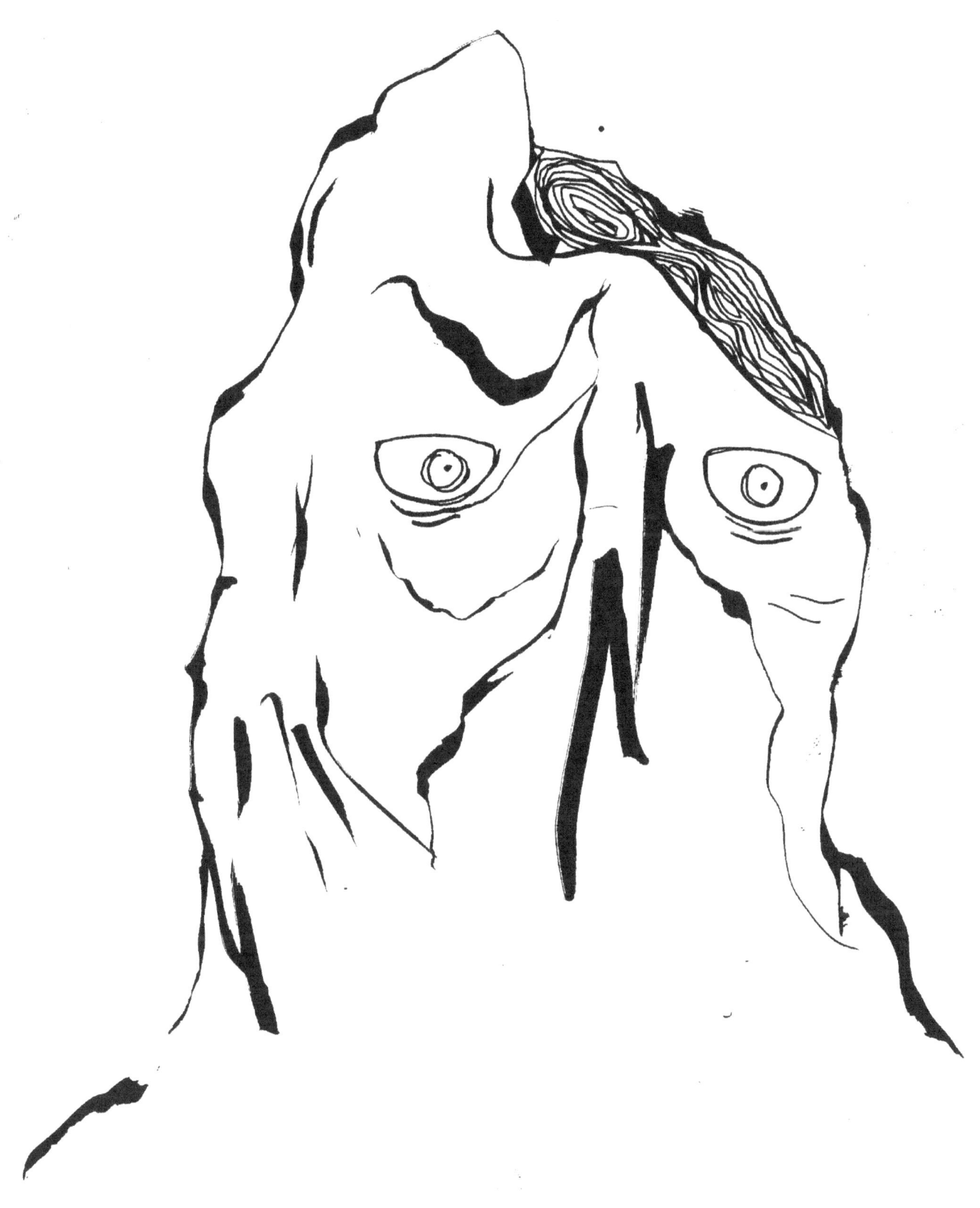

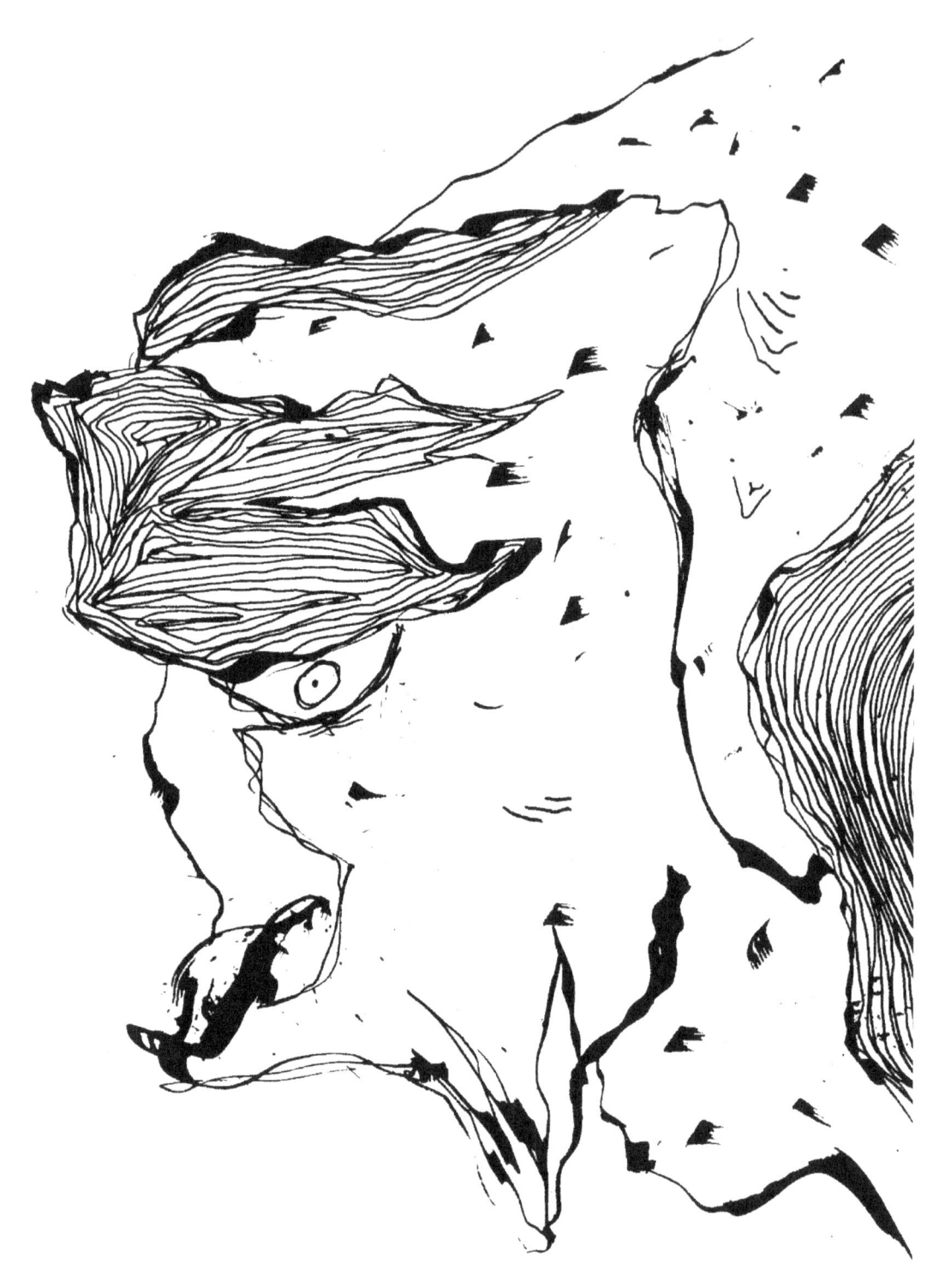

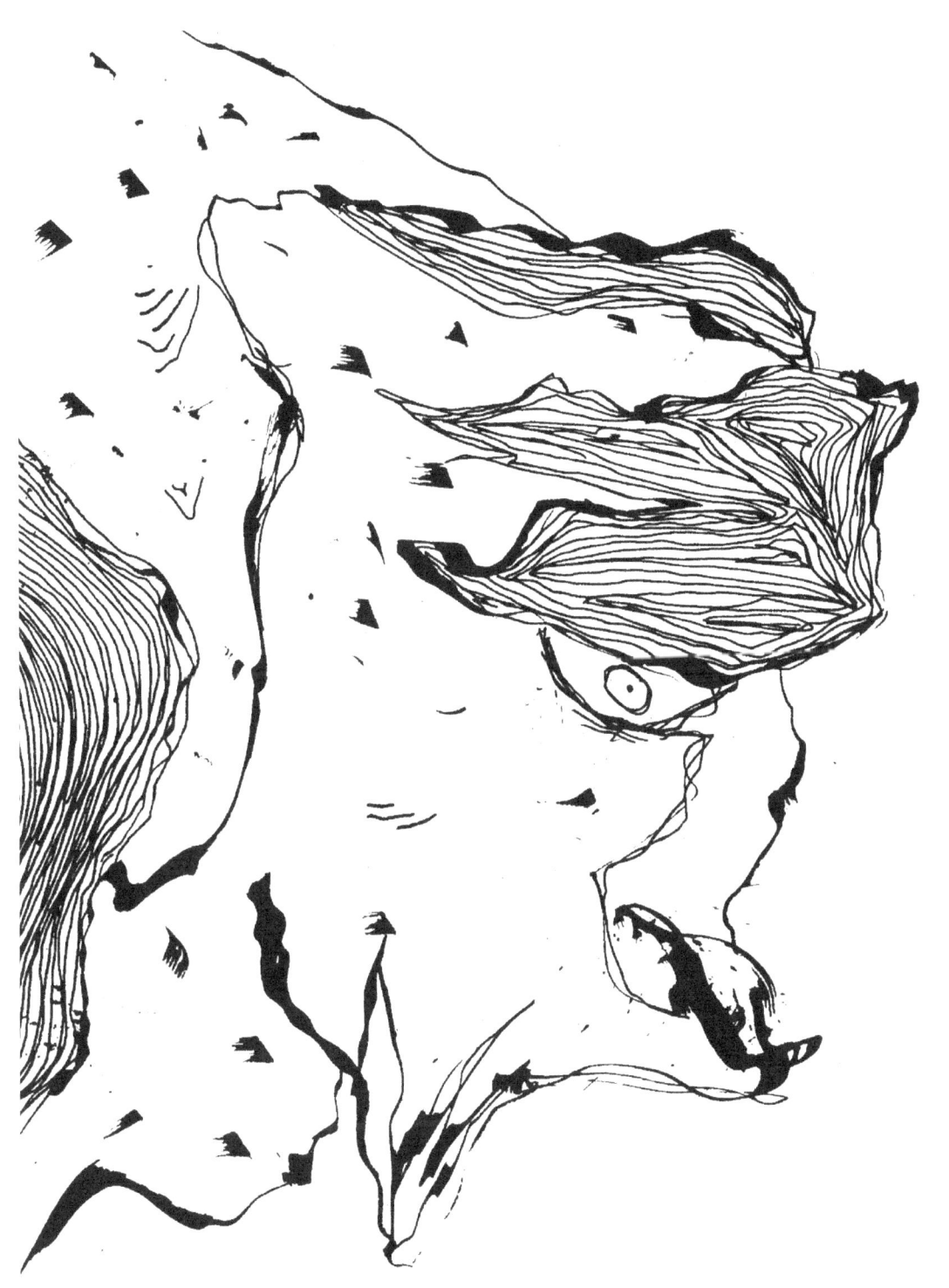

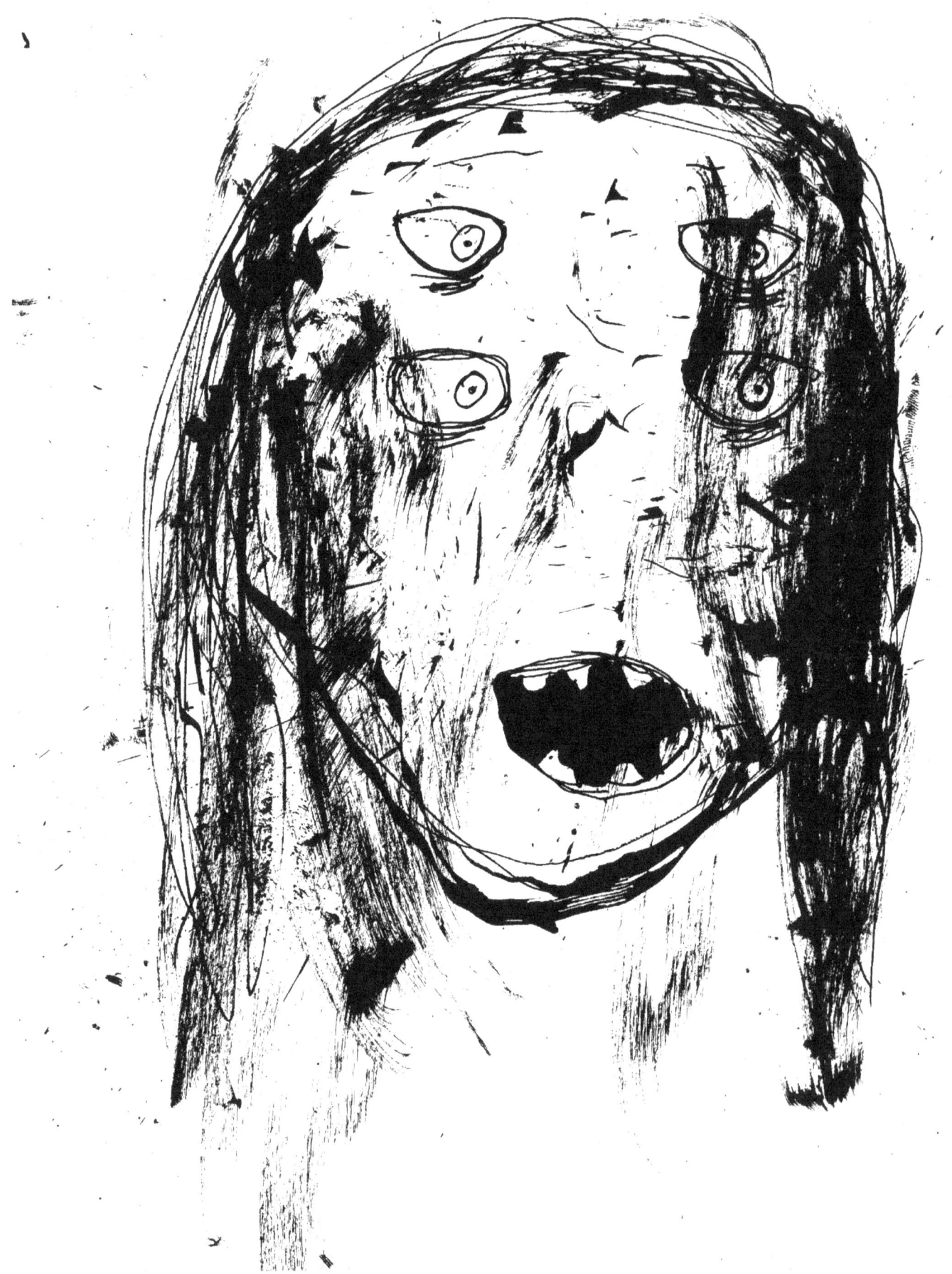

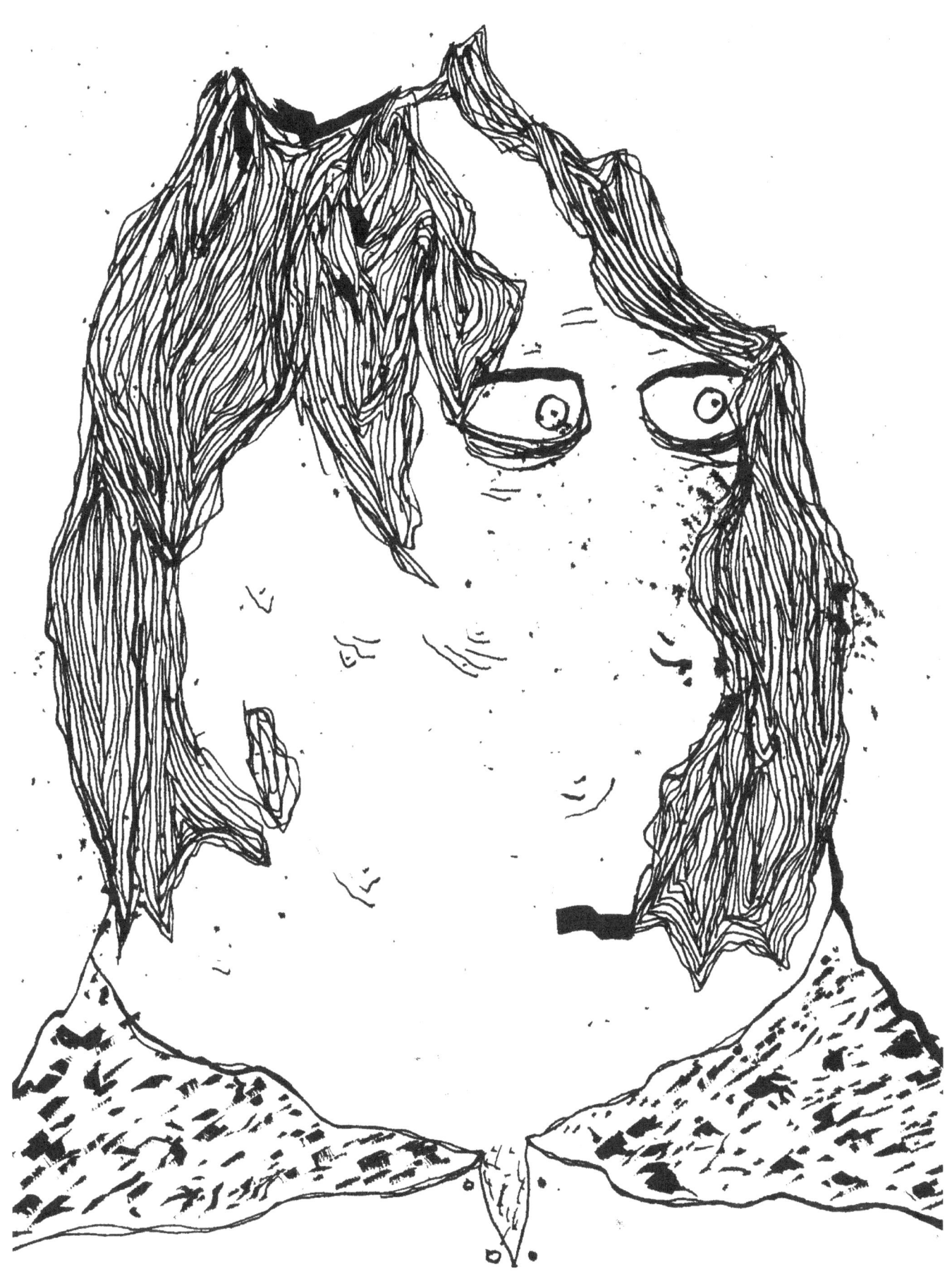

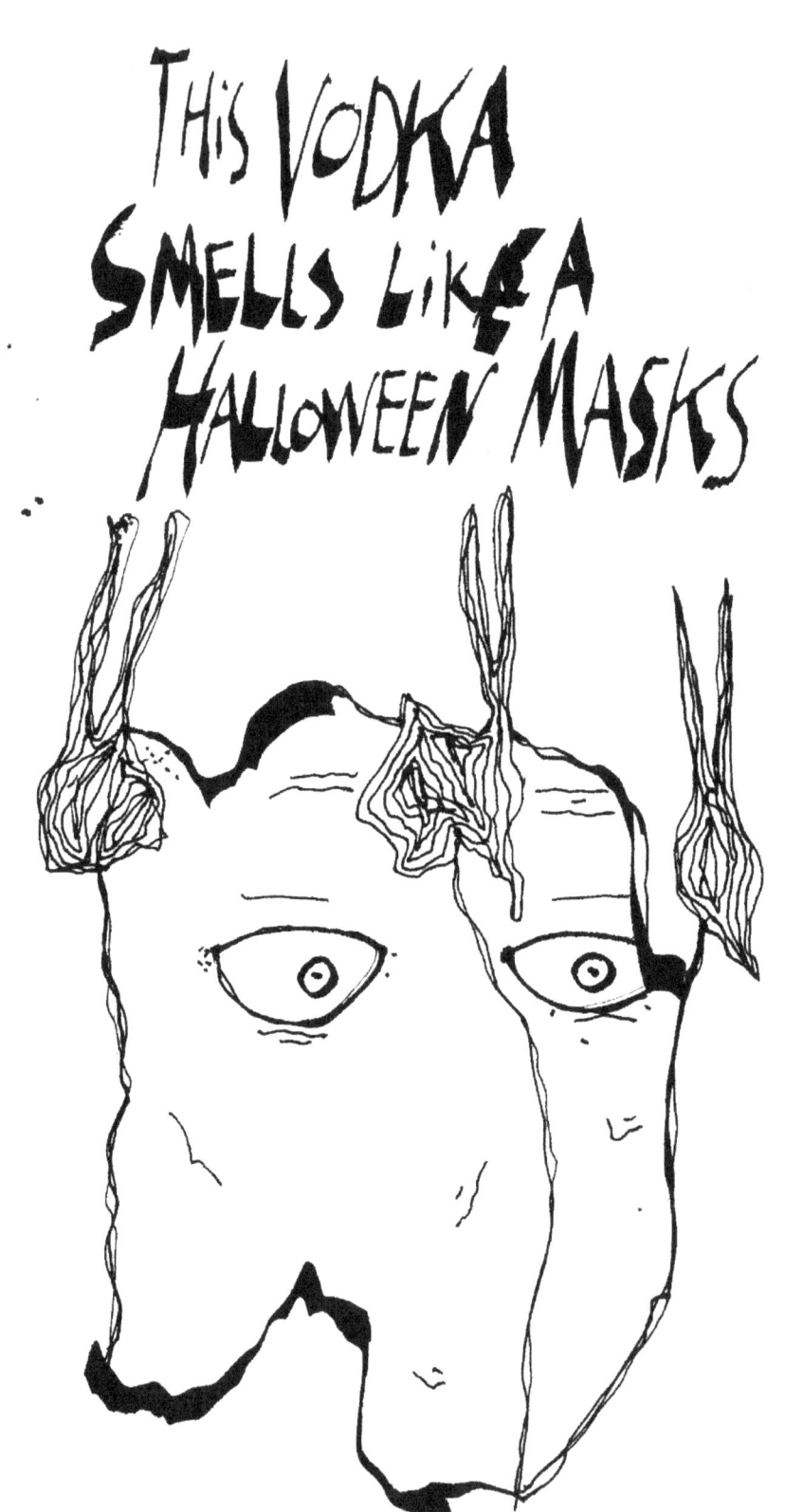

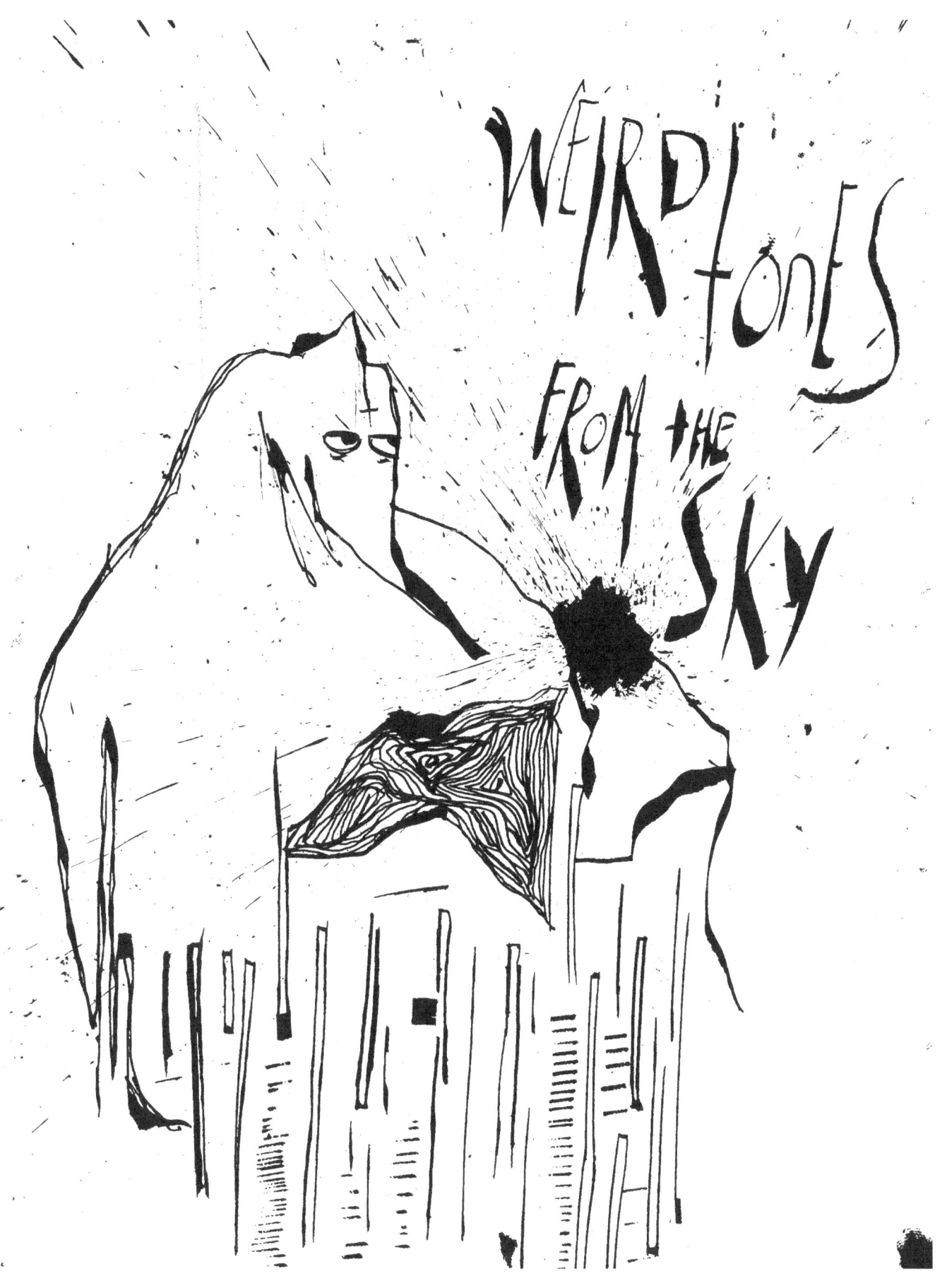

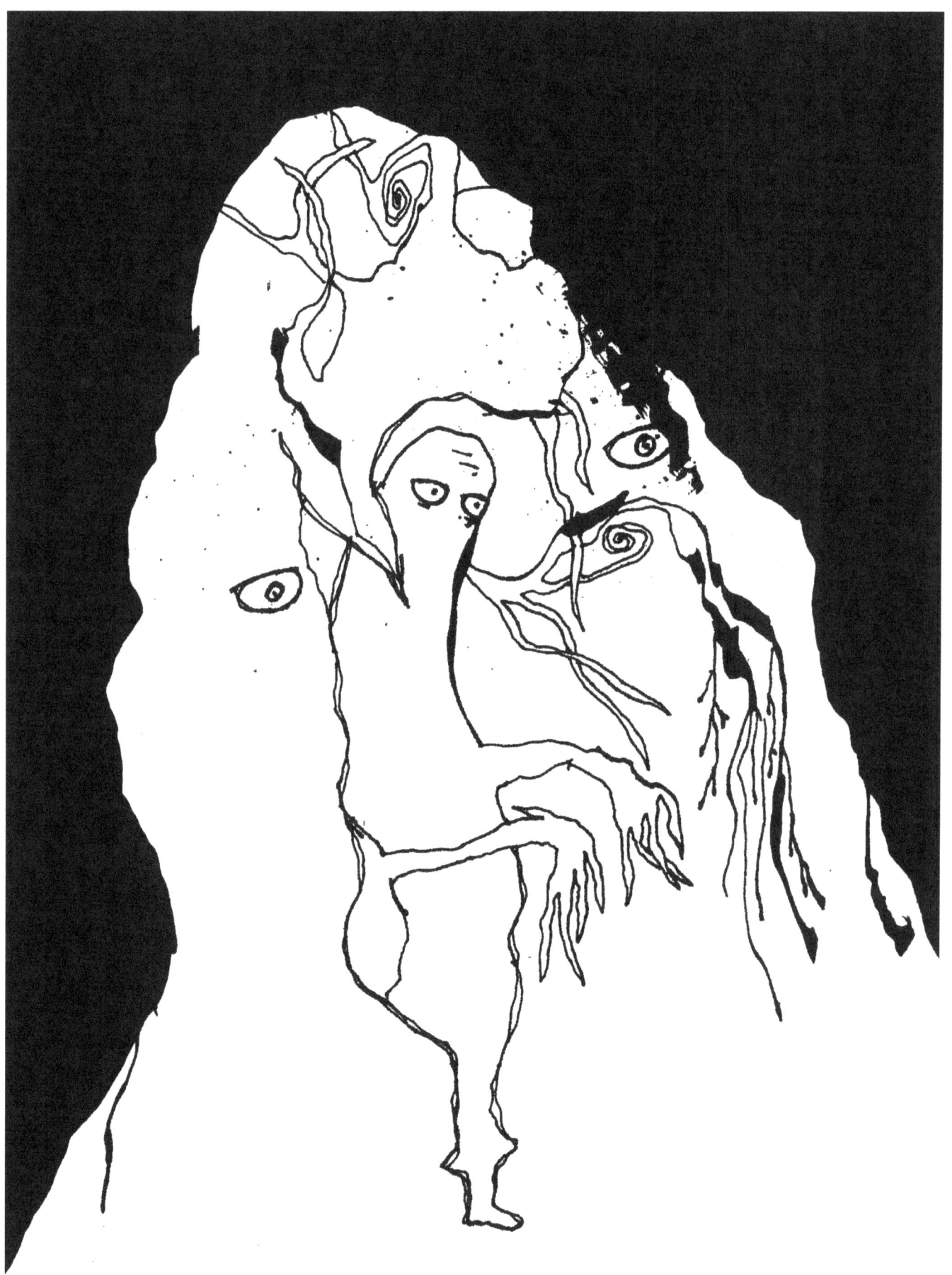

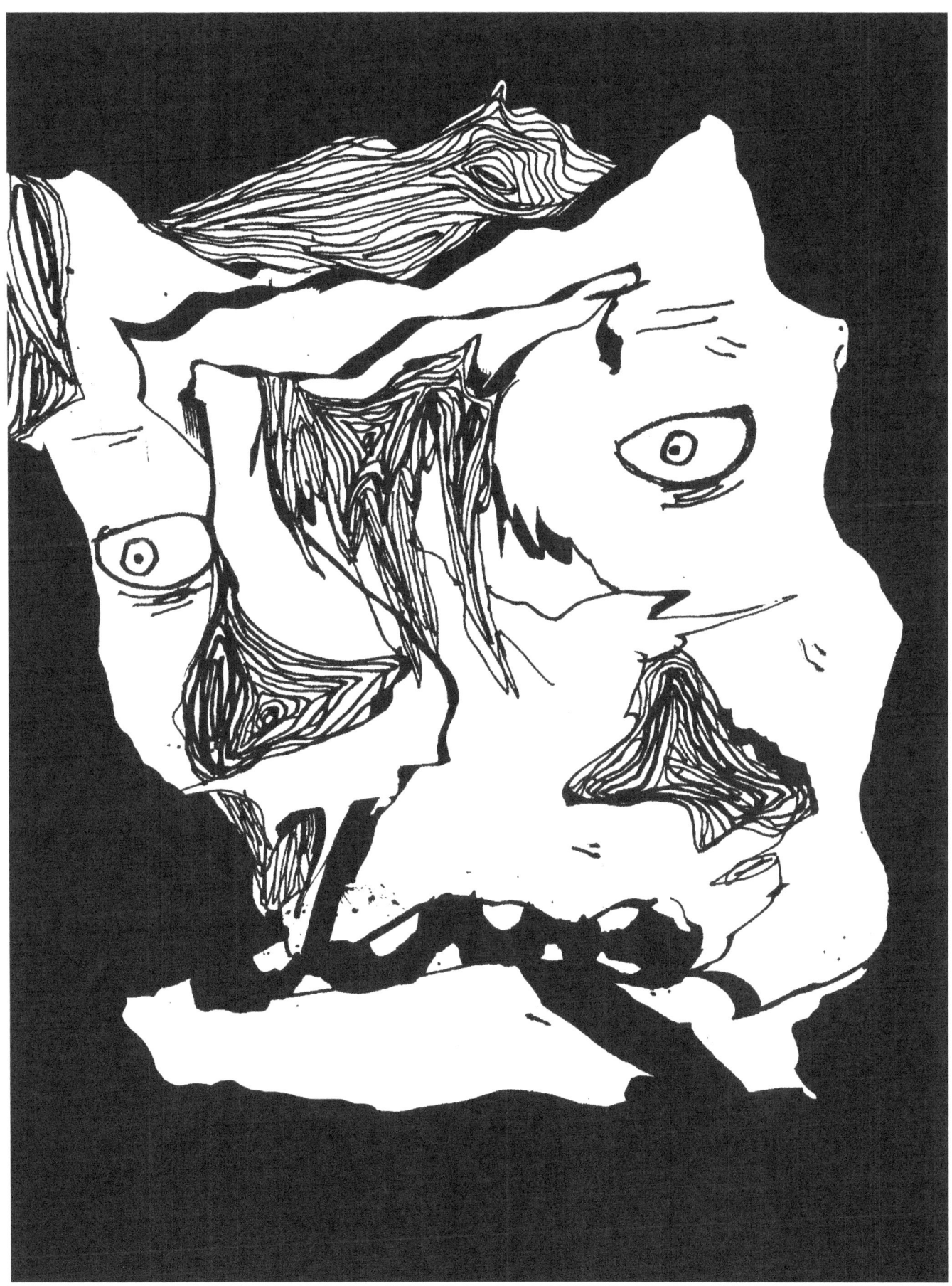

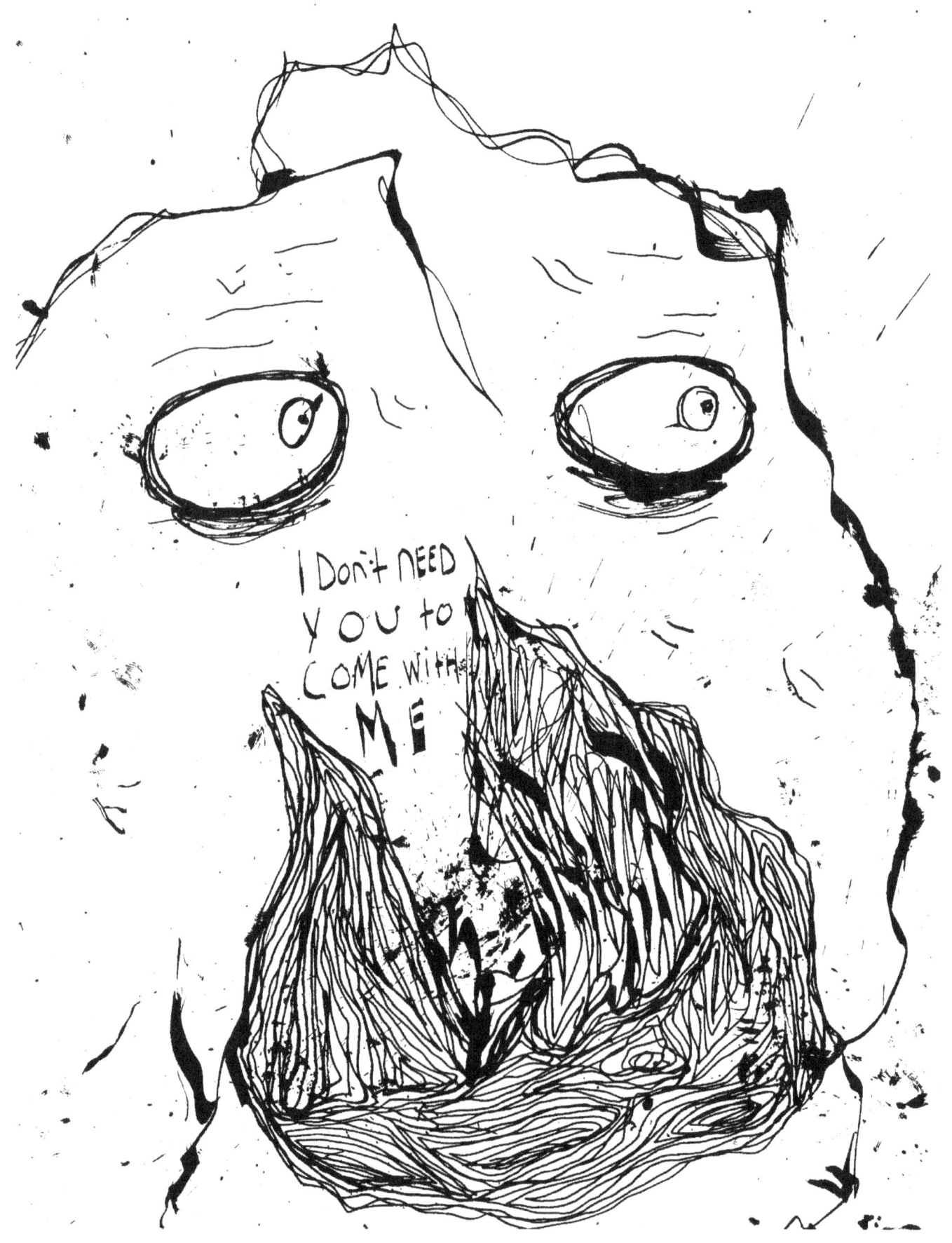

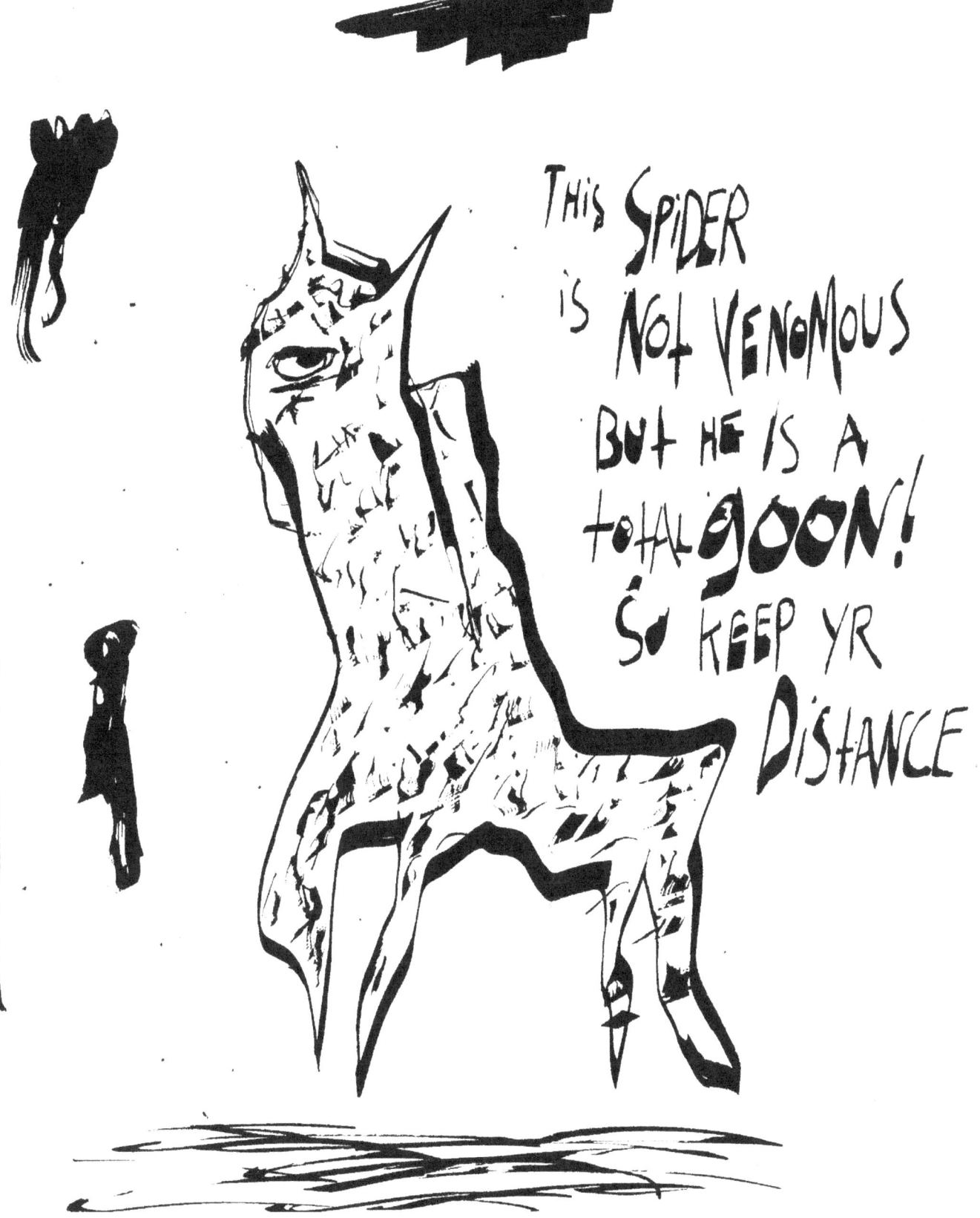

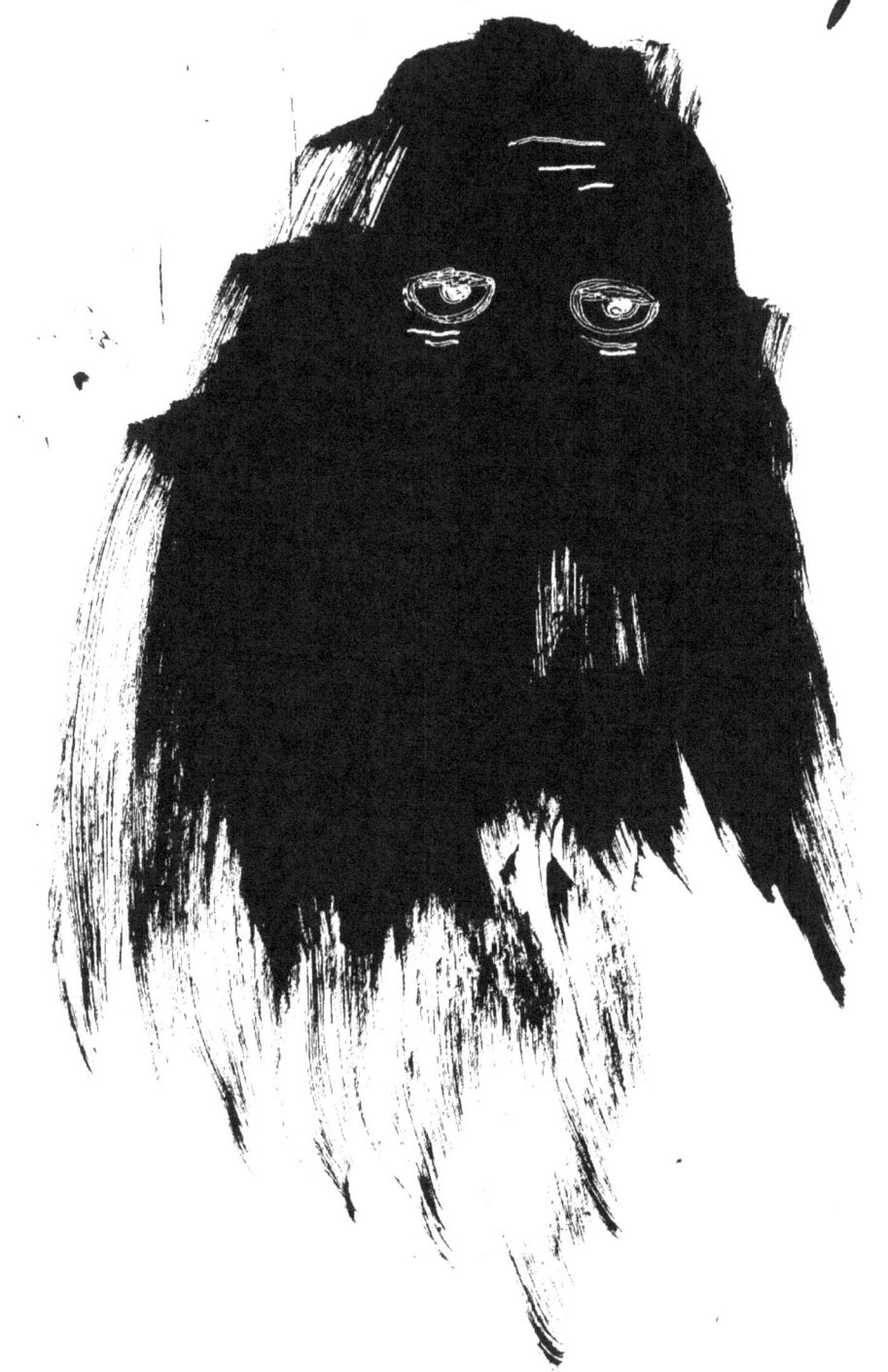

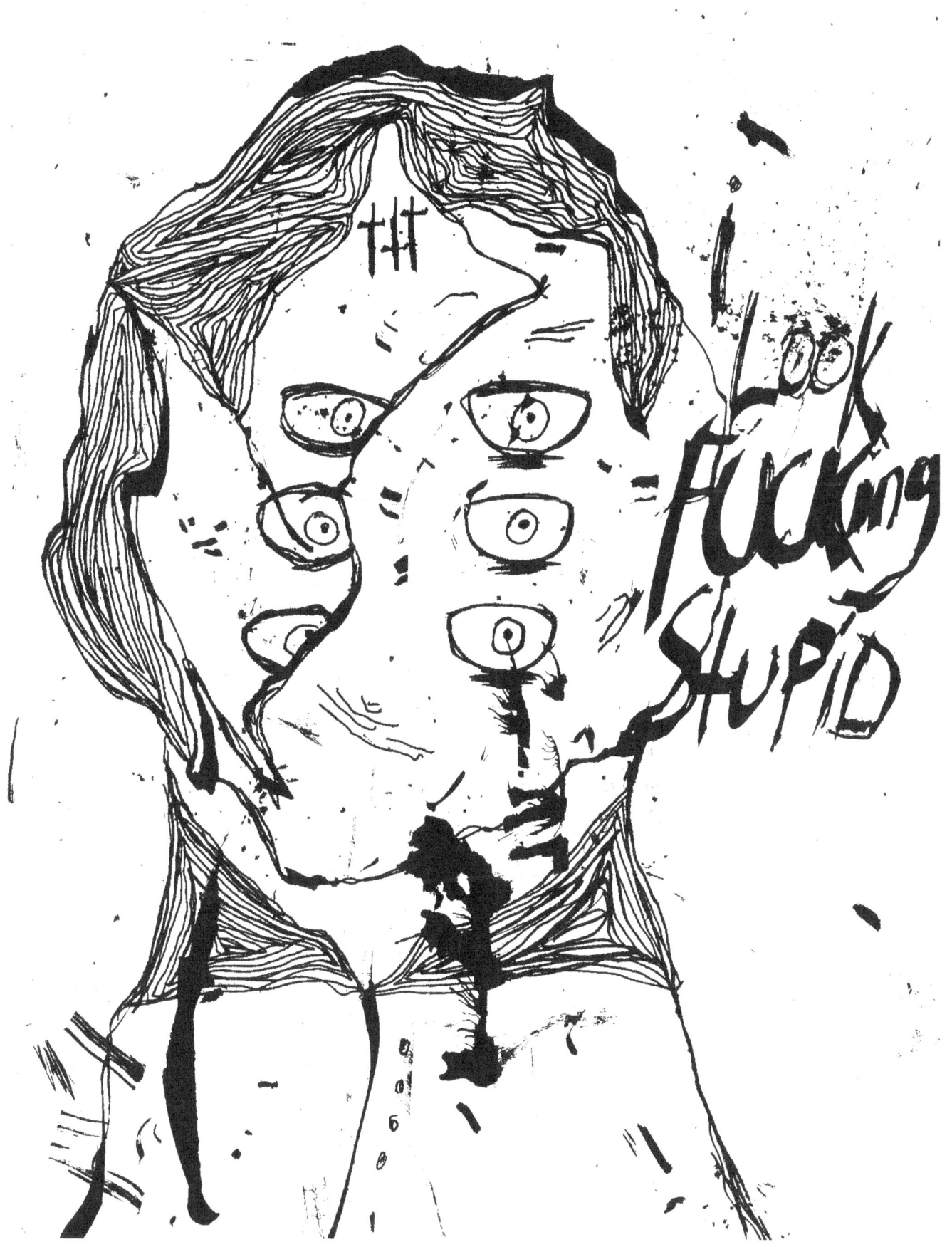

(MY) FIRST SEA BIRTH

Decades have passed. My cubed tongue body inevitably cobbles itself together in the rough surf. I am a jellified approximation of a man. I am tossed out of the waves in front of a lighthouse shaped like a fang. The building is humid; the stairs are carved stone and overgrown. At the top of the structure is tent caterpillar nest. The webbing is immense. I can hear the scurrying of legs inside. I knock on the nest, and my mangled paw rips the webbing open.

THE FIRST MISCARRIAGE

Some odd breed of caterpillars spill out
onto the floor at my feet
A torrent of malformed tubes, half gestated
slinging limbs and torn wings.
An alarm rings through the lighthouse.
The insects are screaming, or singing, or chanting.
So much noise.
The sound of the door downstairs being kicked open.
The sound of combat boots on stone.
The sound of heavy breathing.
The sound of armed militia men bursting into the room.
The sound of them taking aim.

i often have a different body

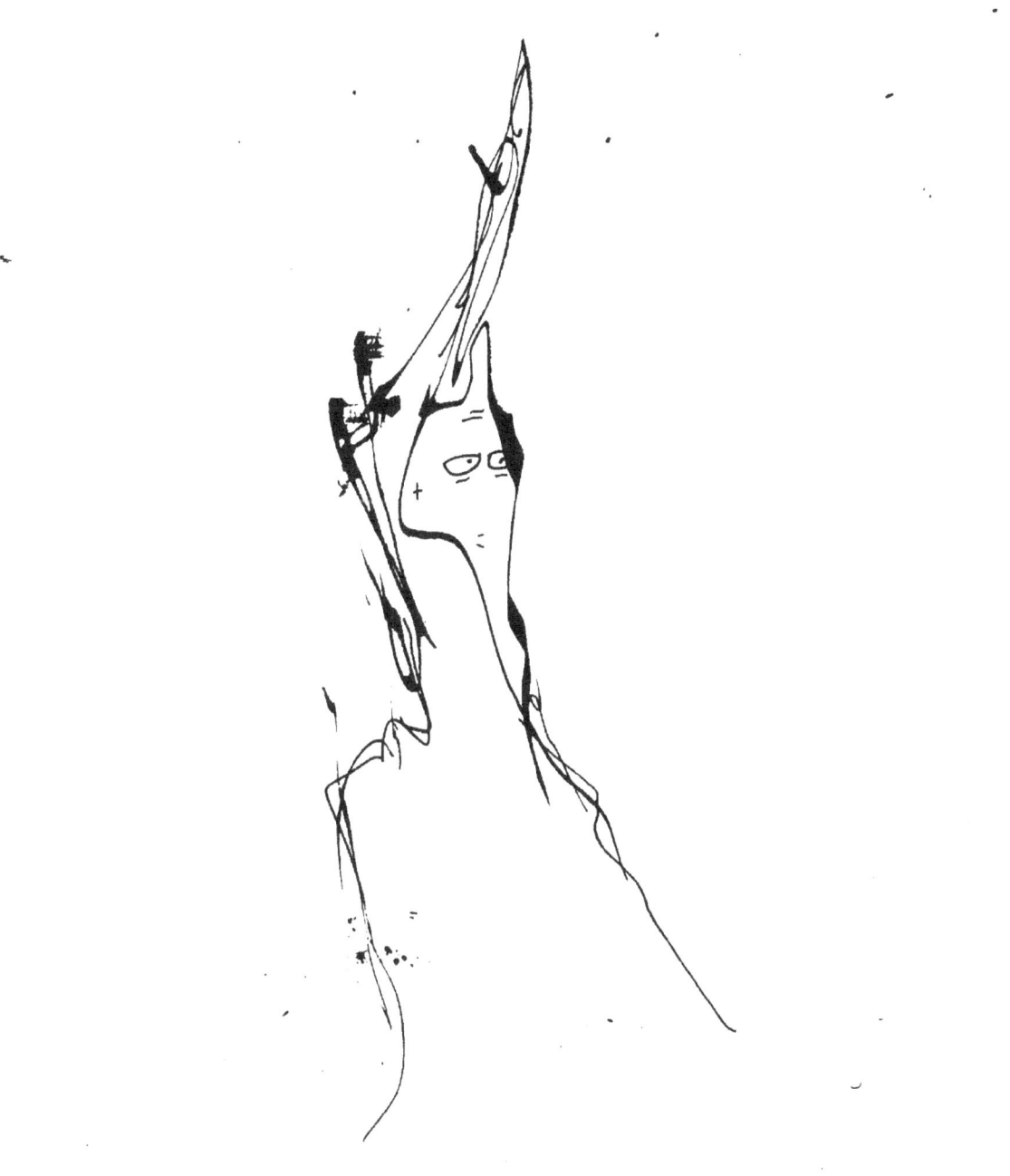

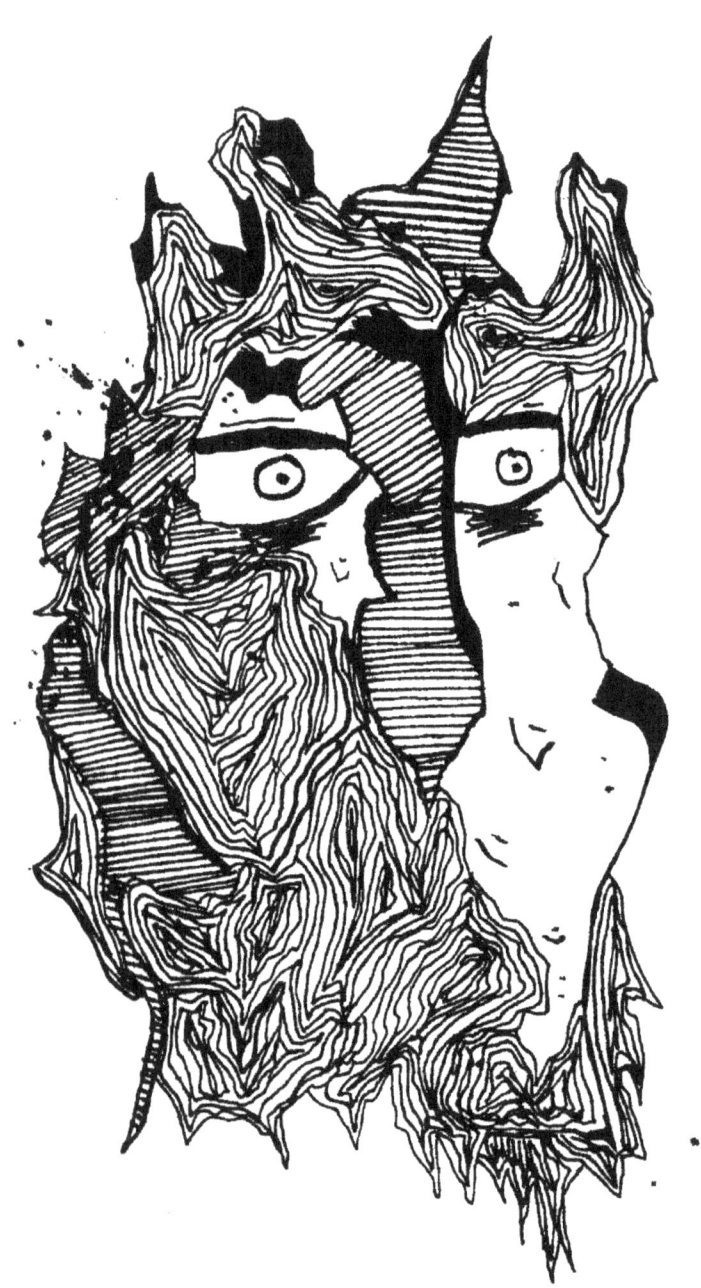

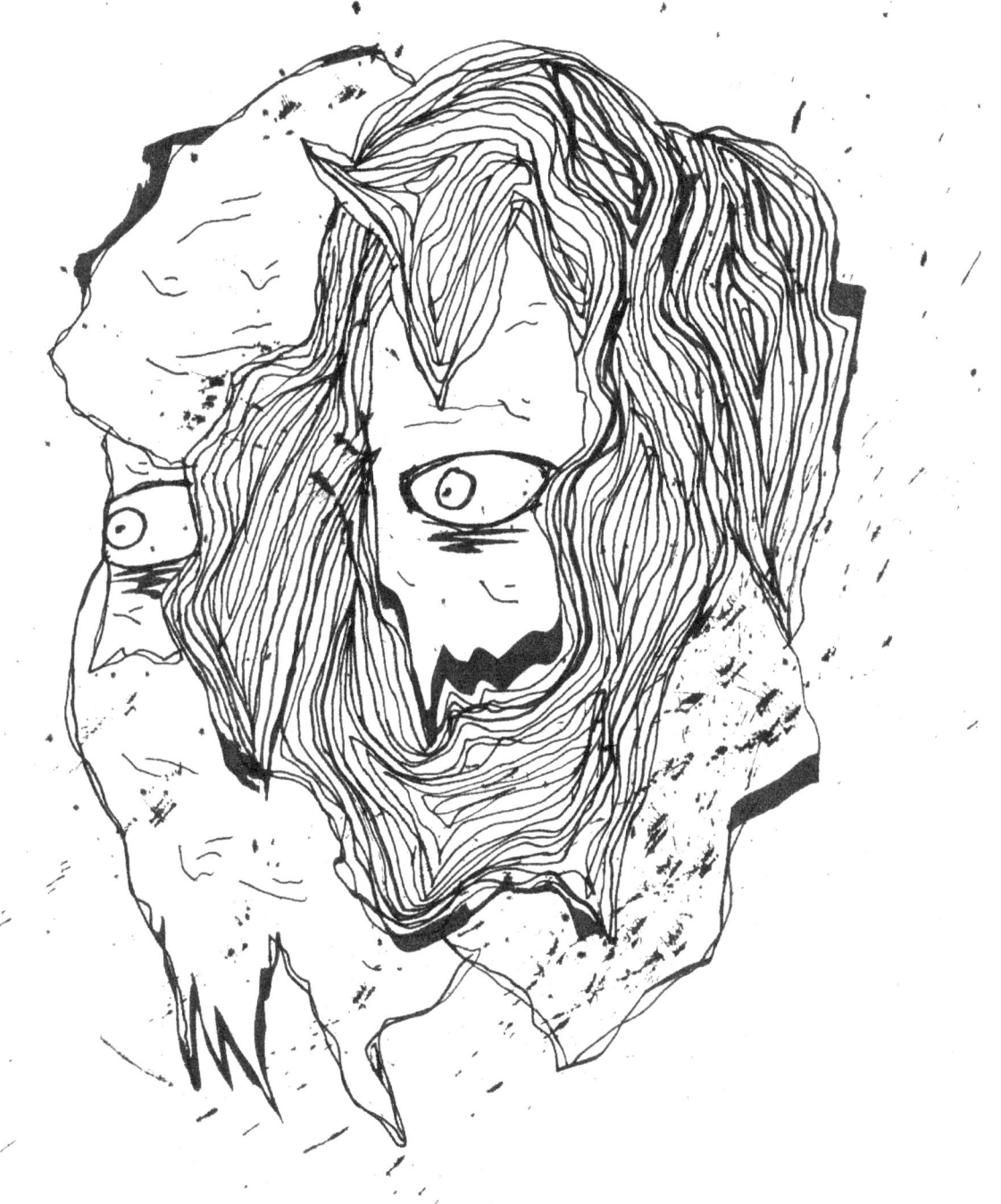

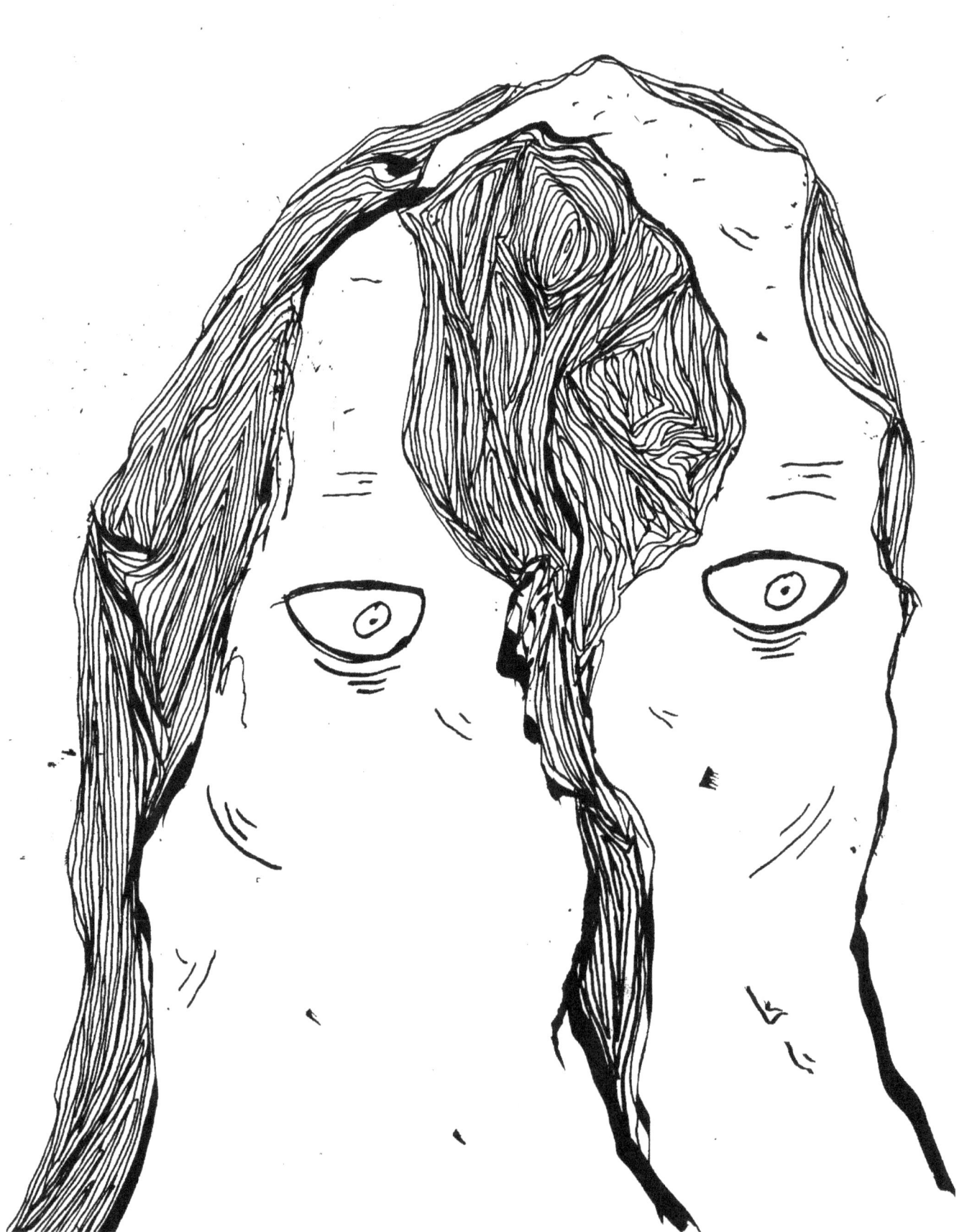

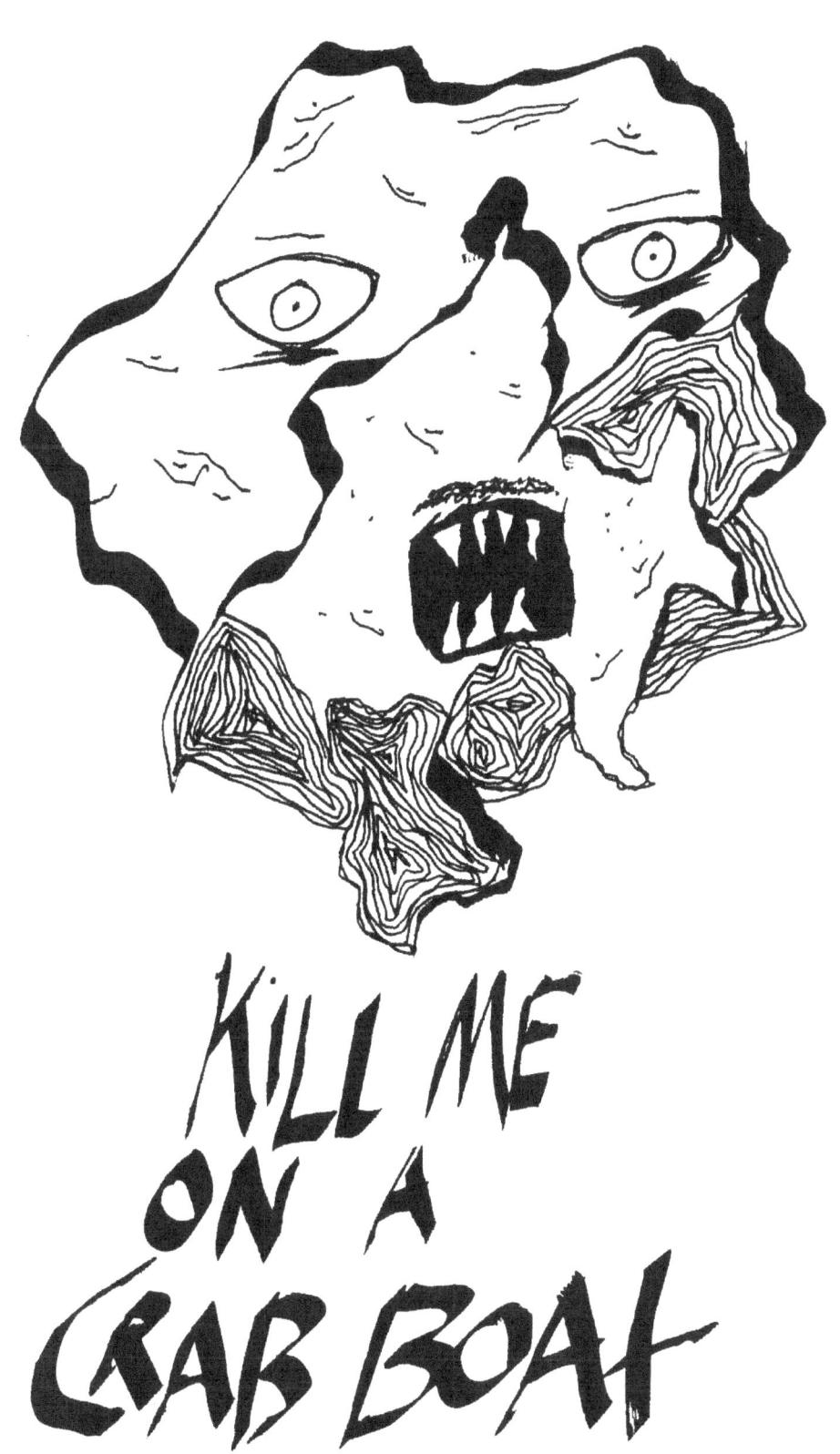

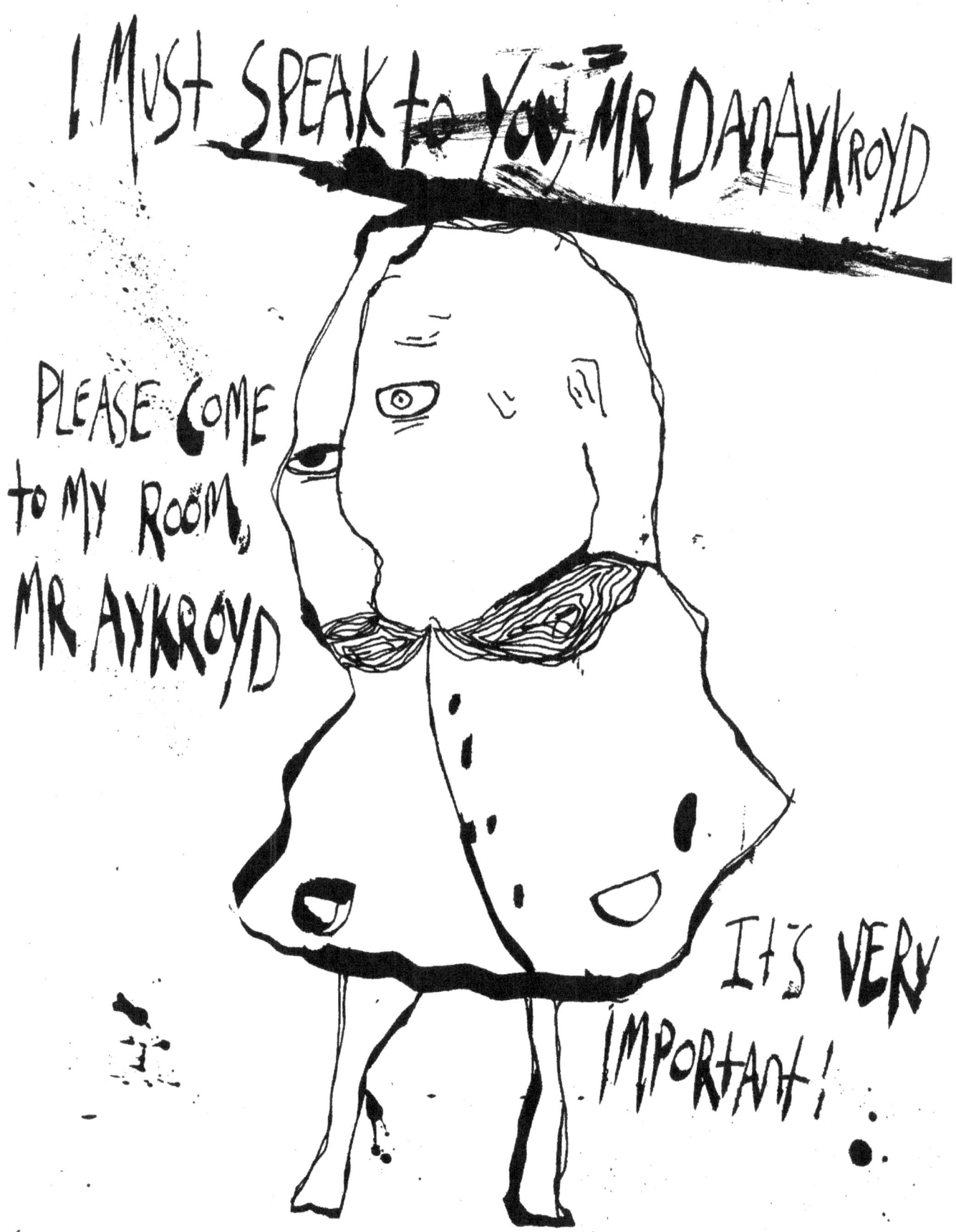

gut FRIEND

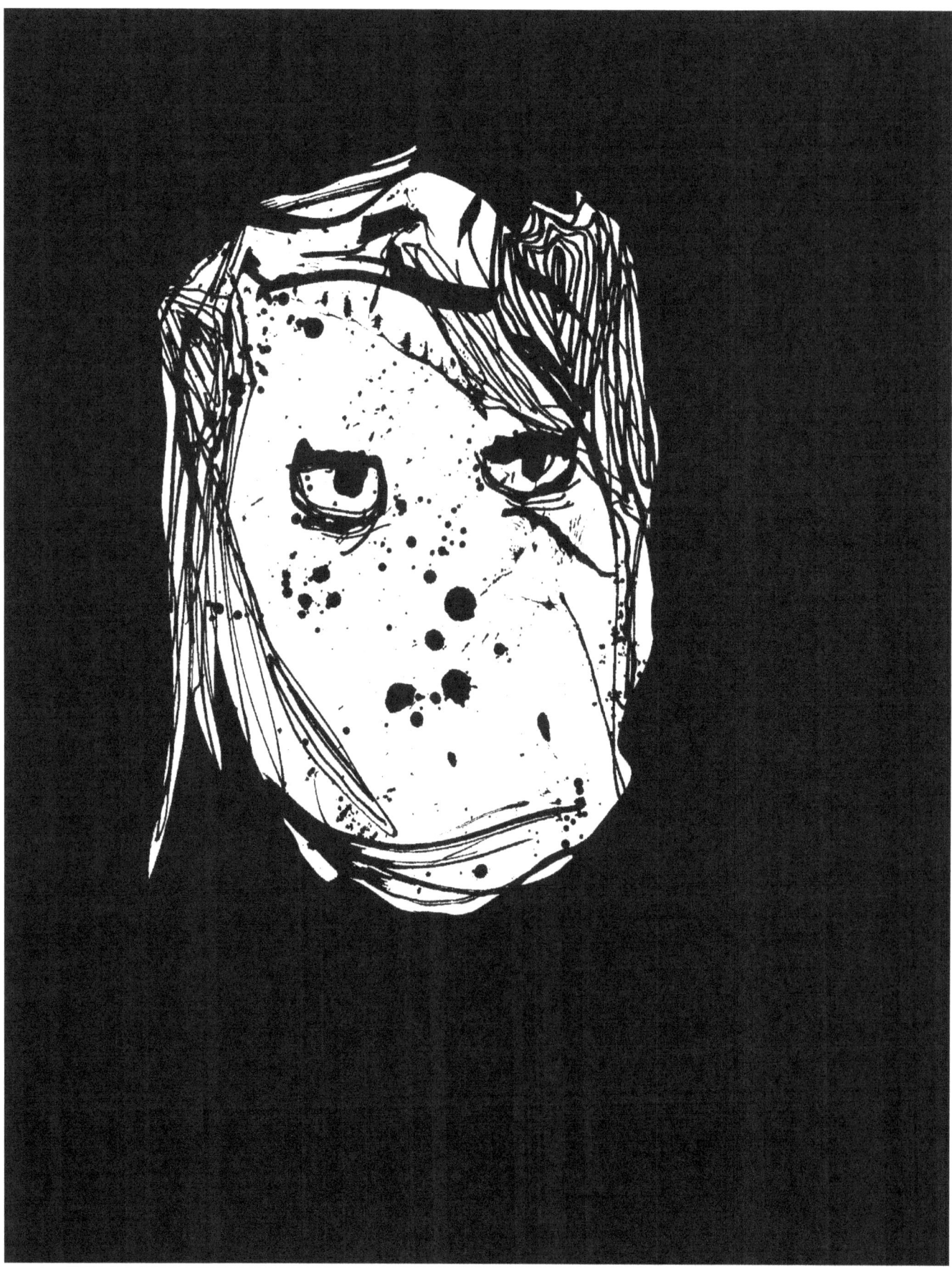

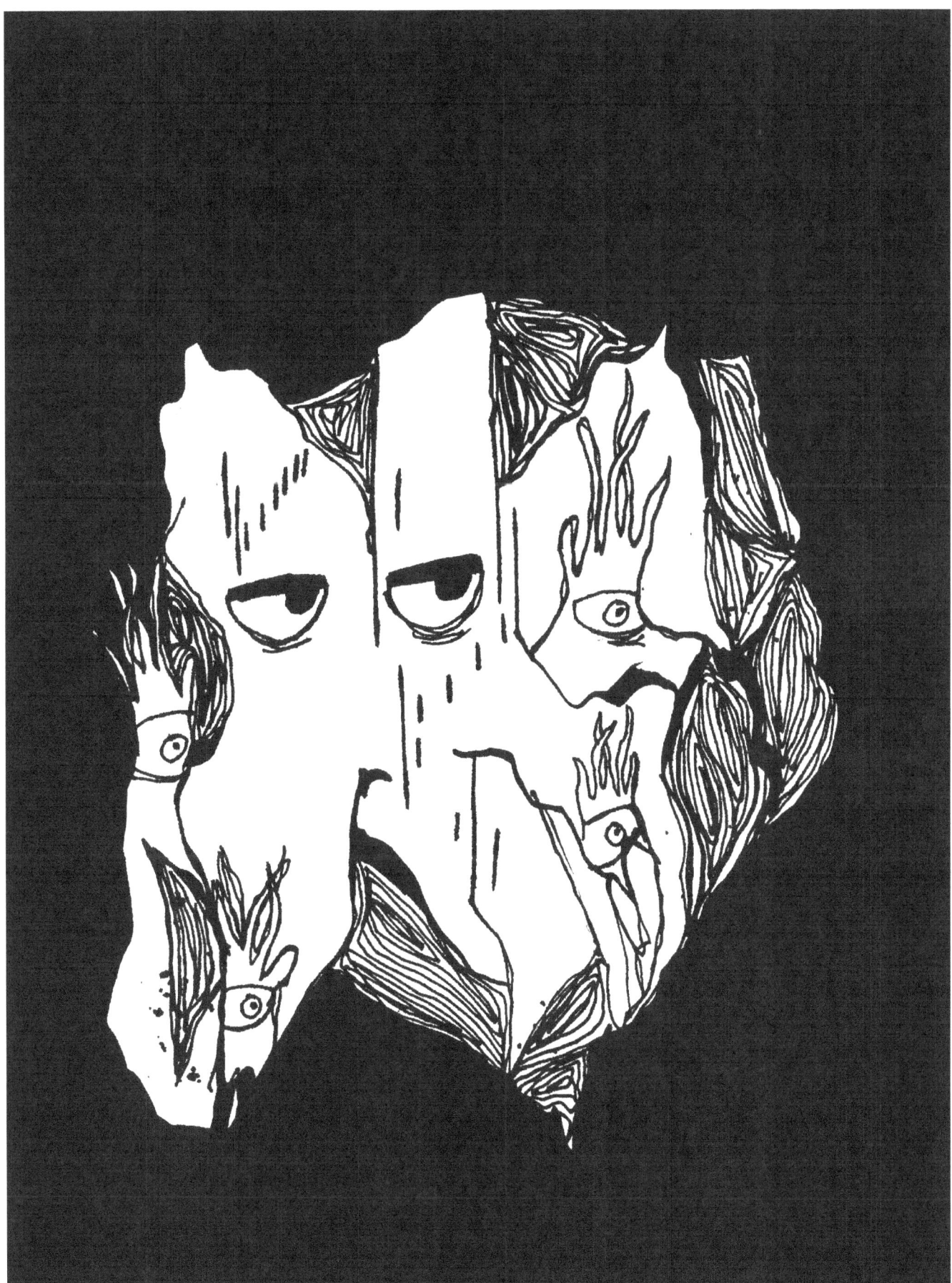

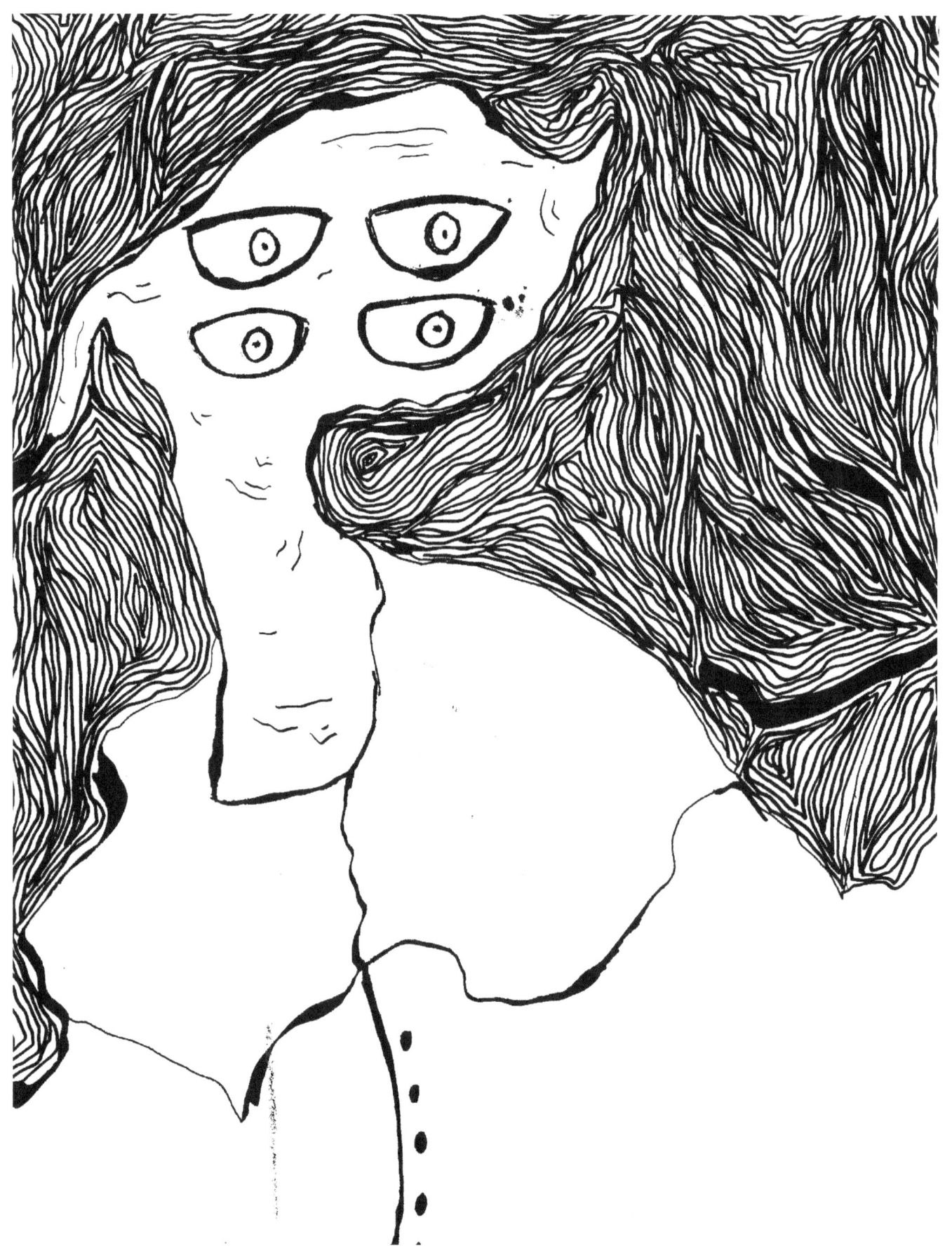

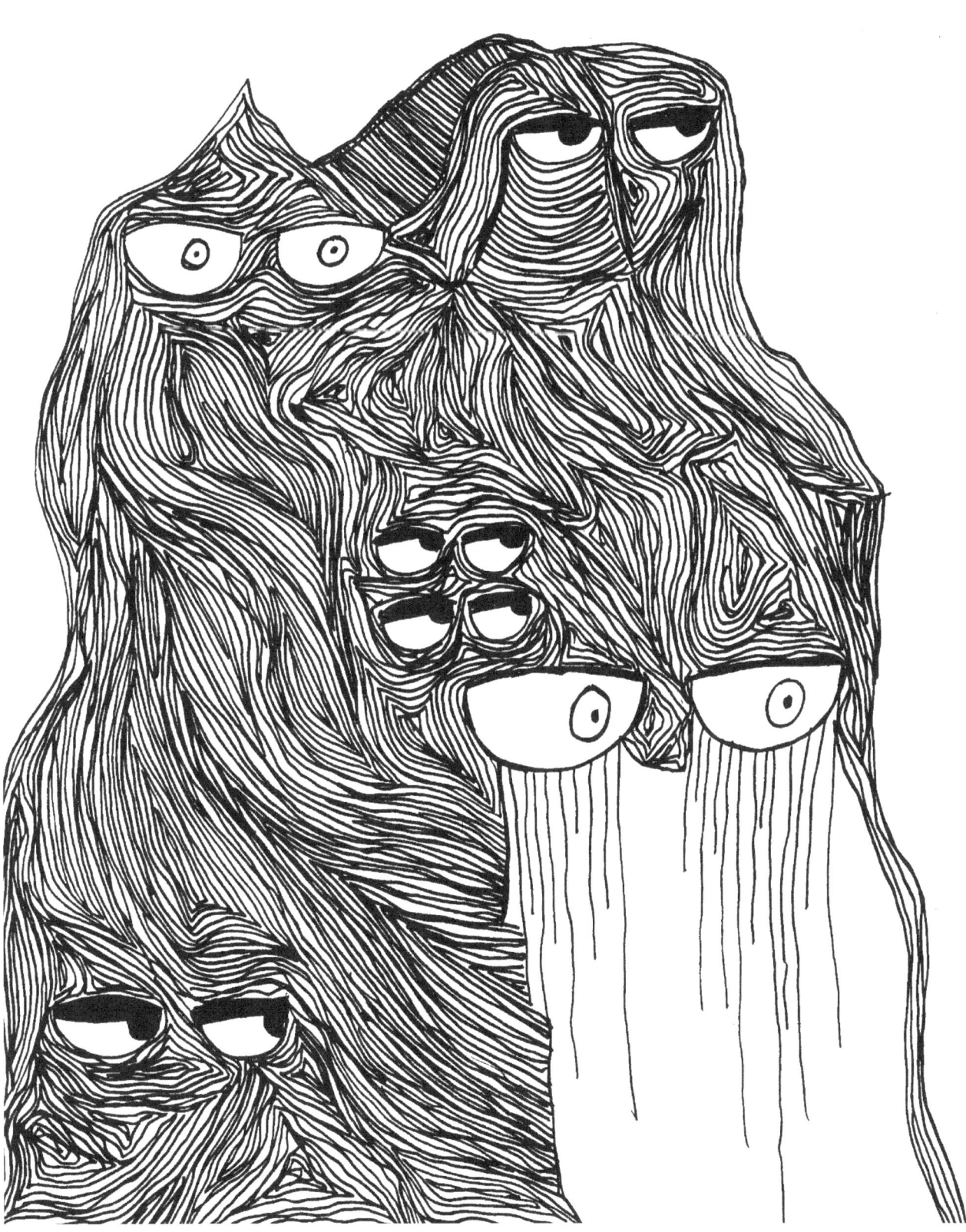

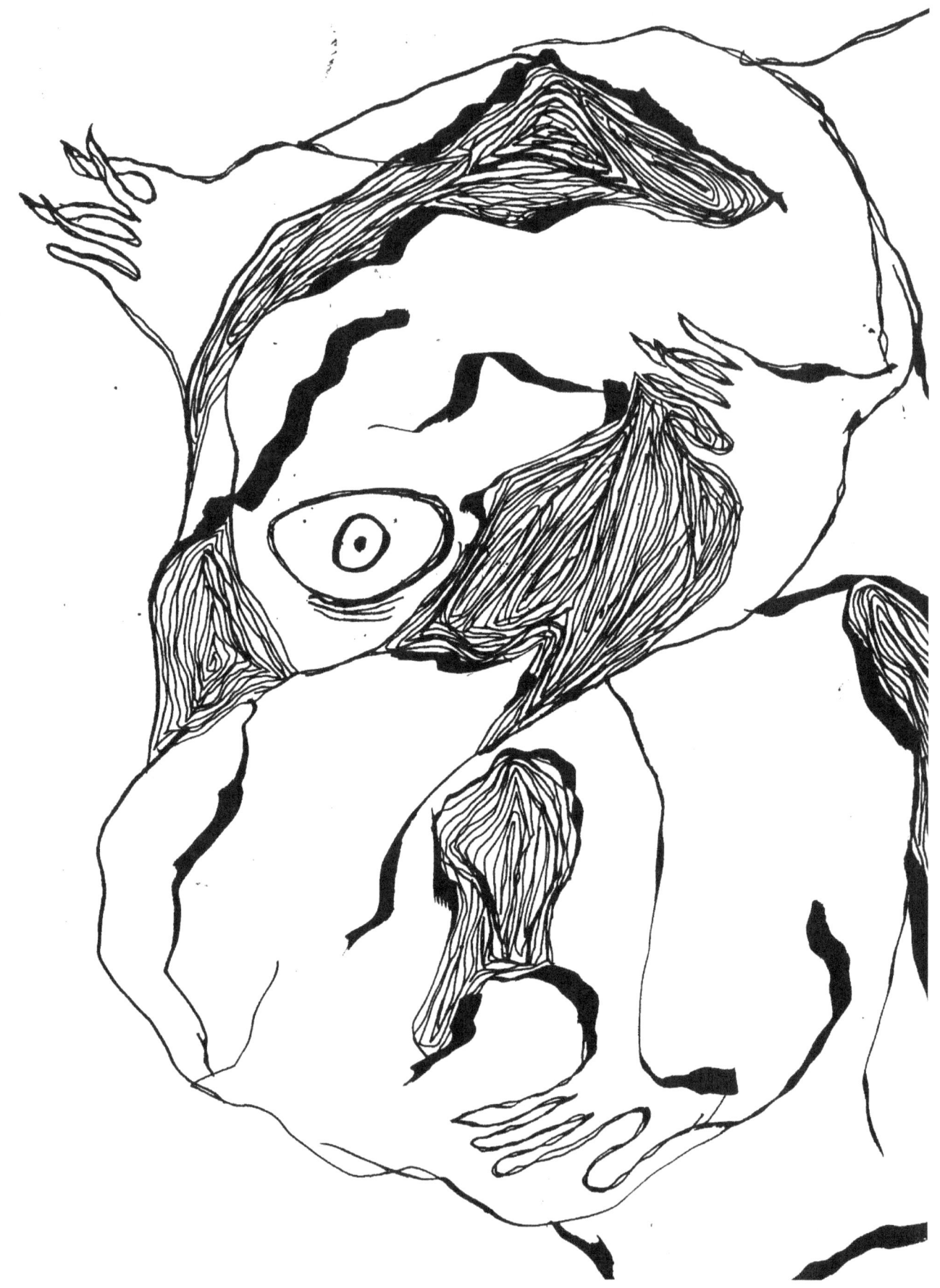

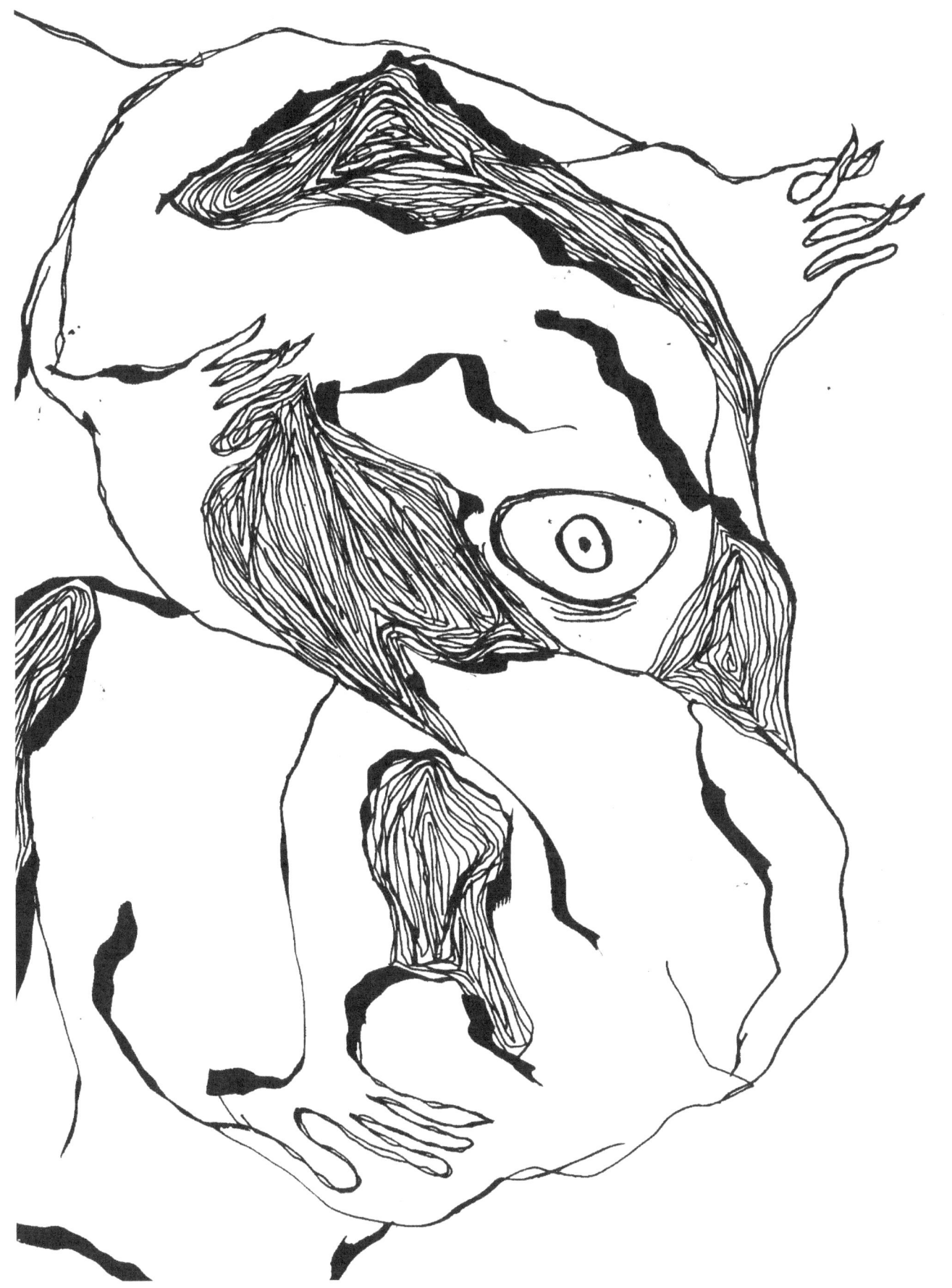

Guy falls off a thing, but it's very funny

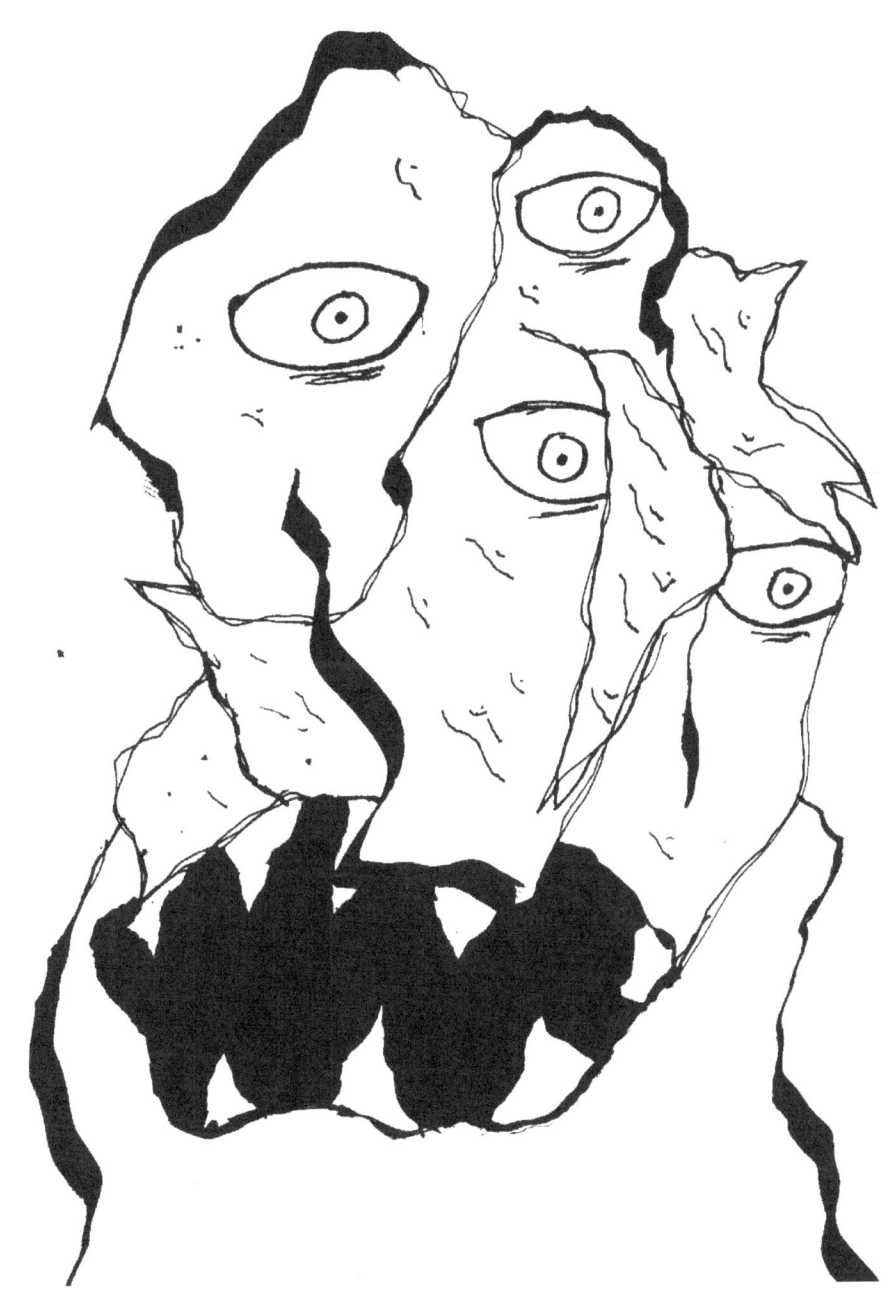

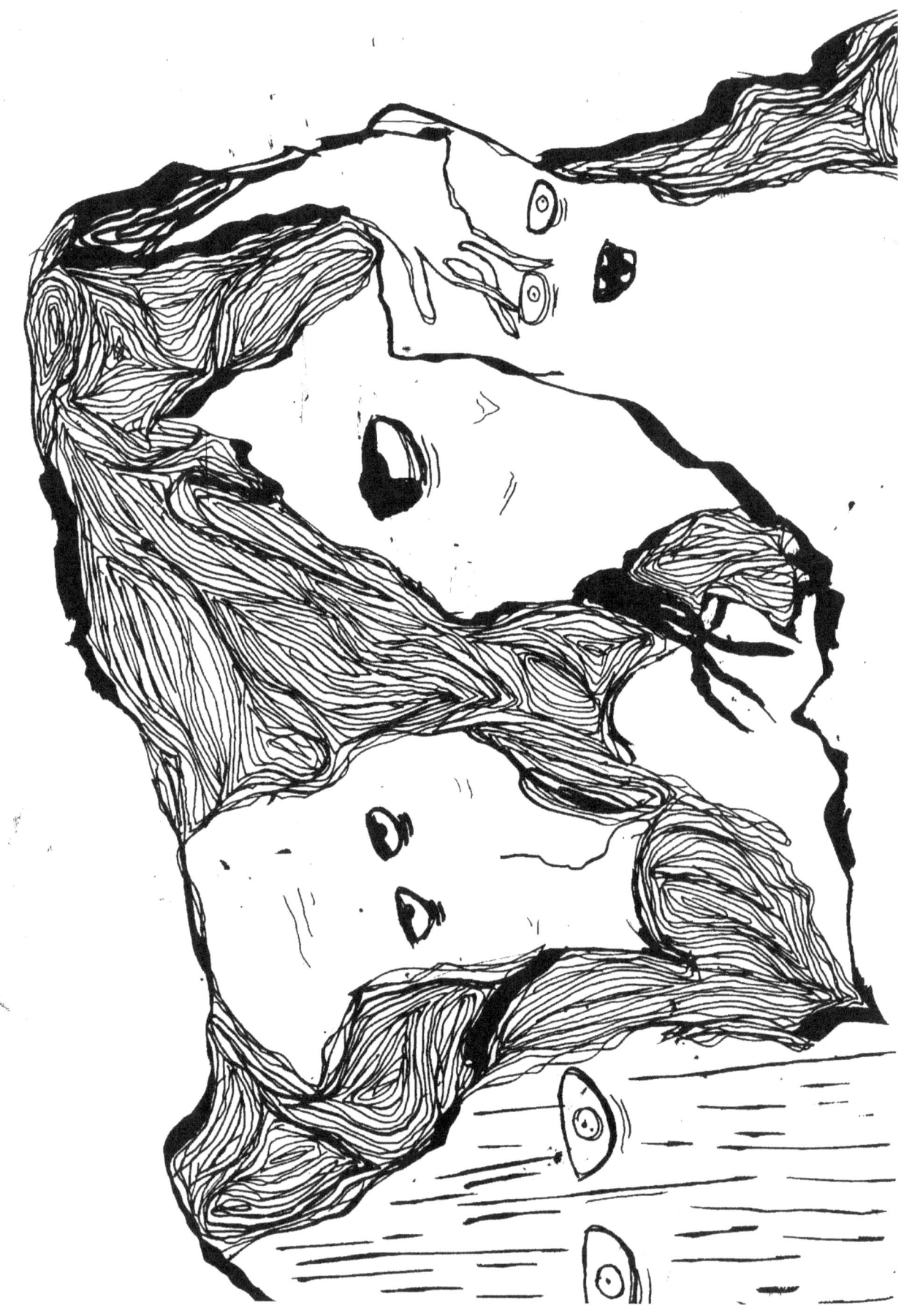

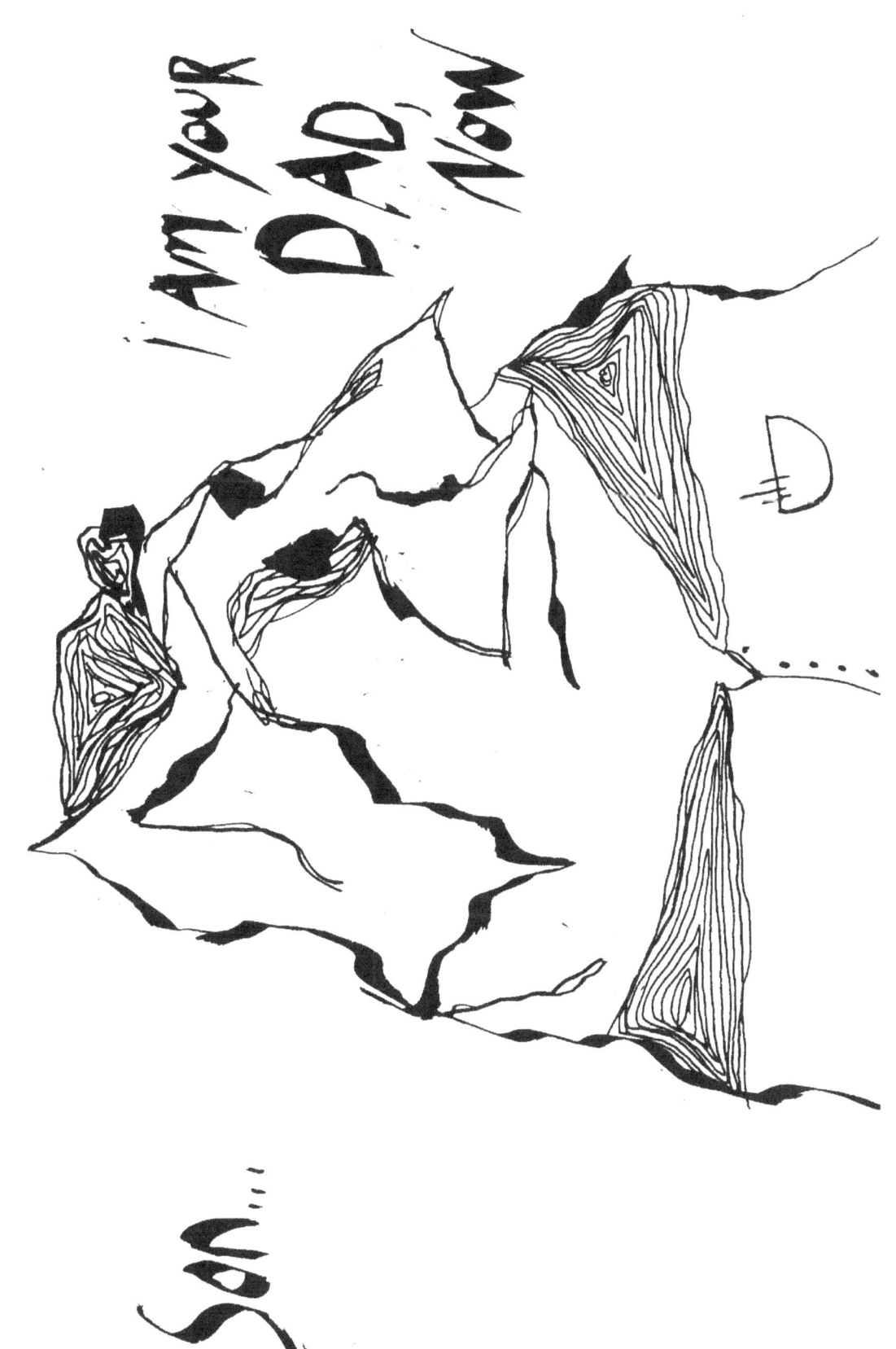

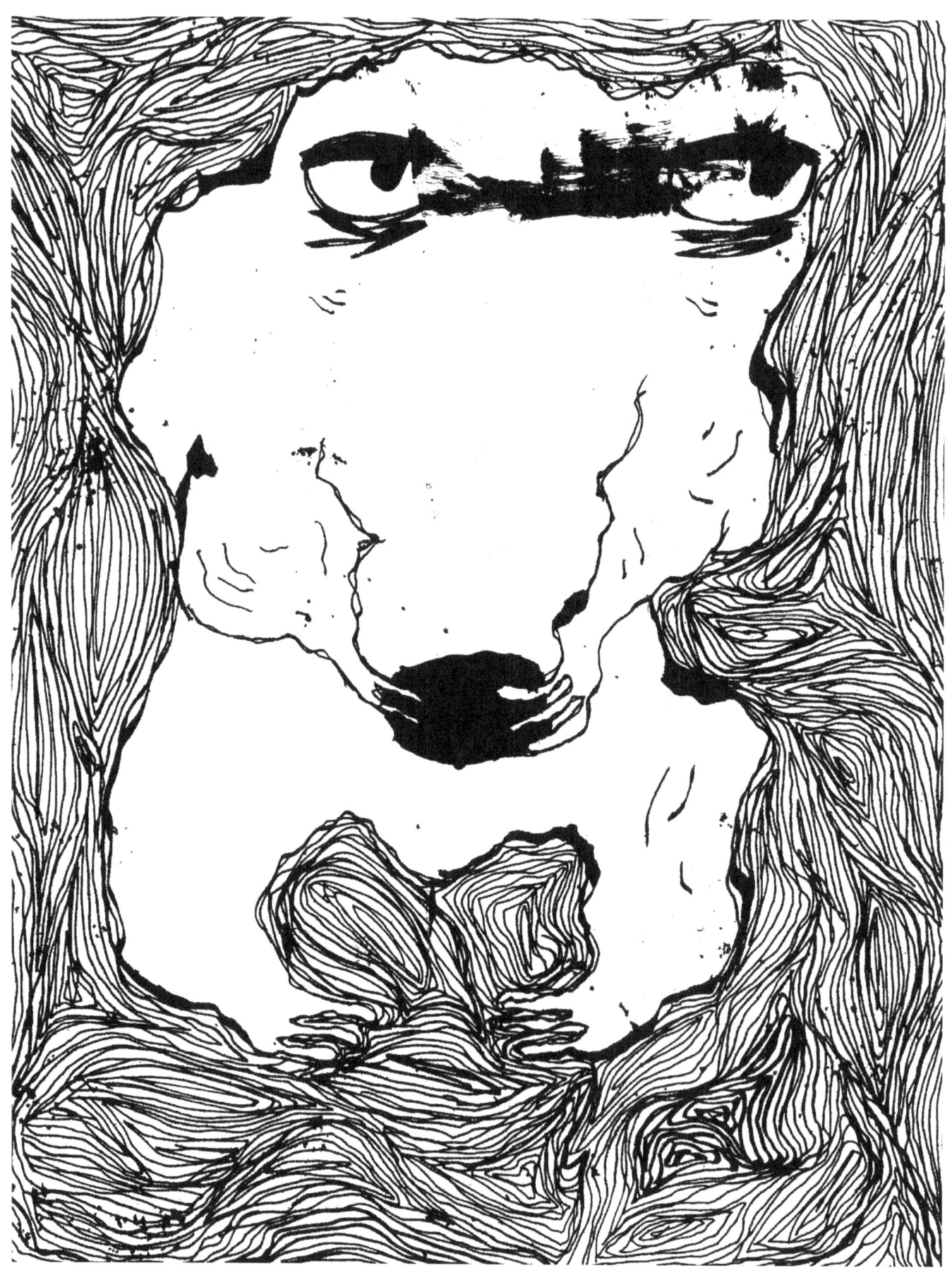

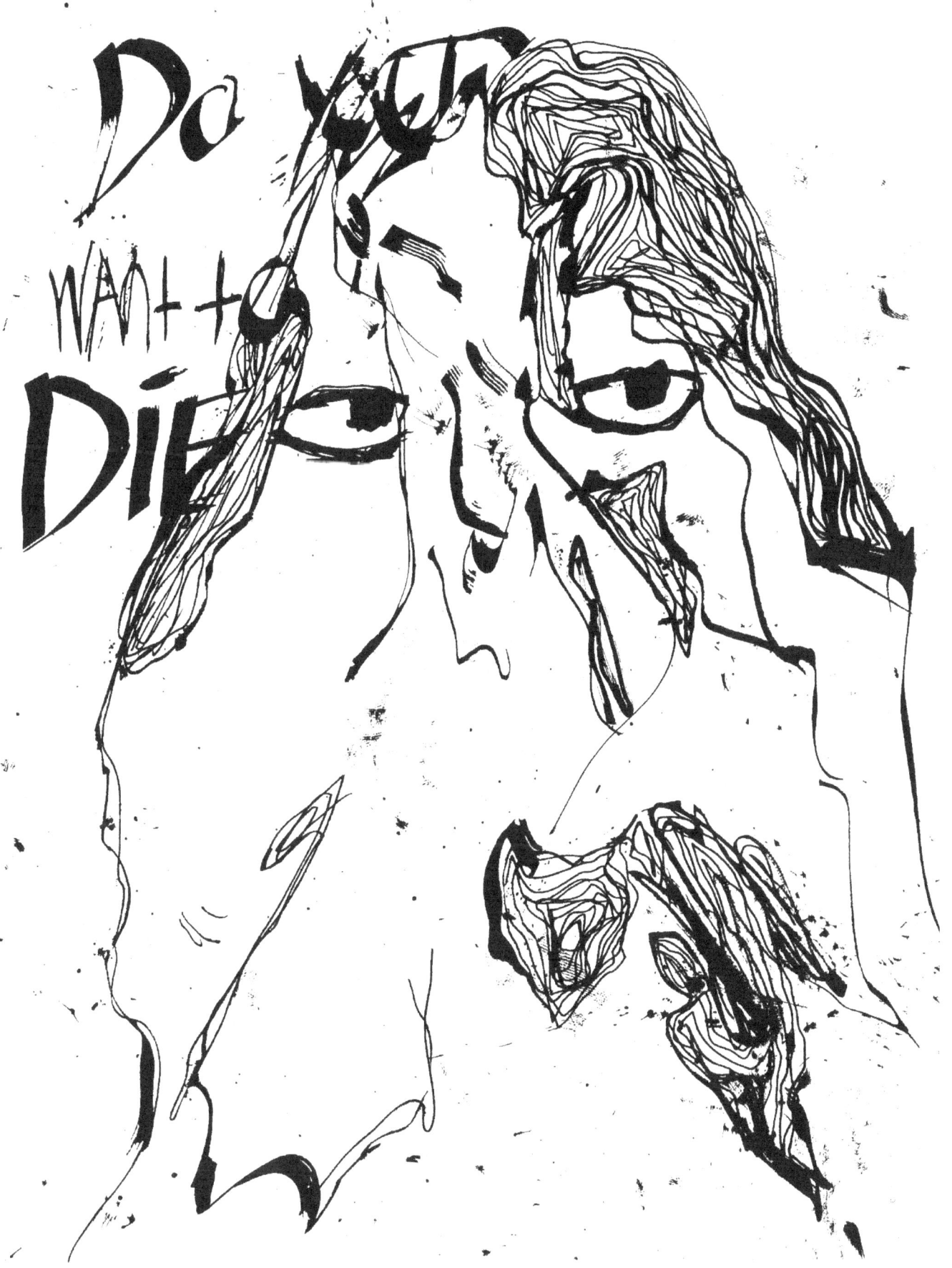

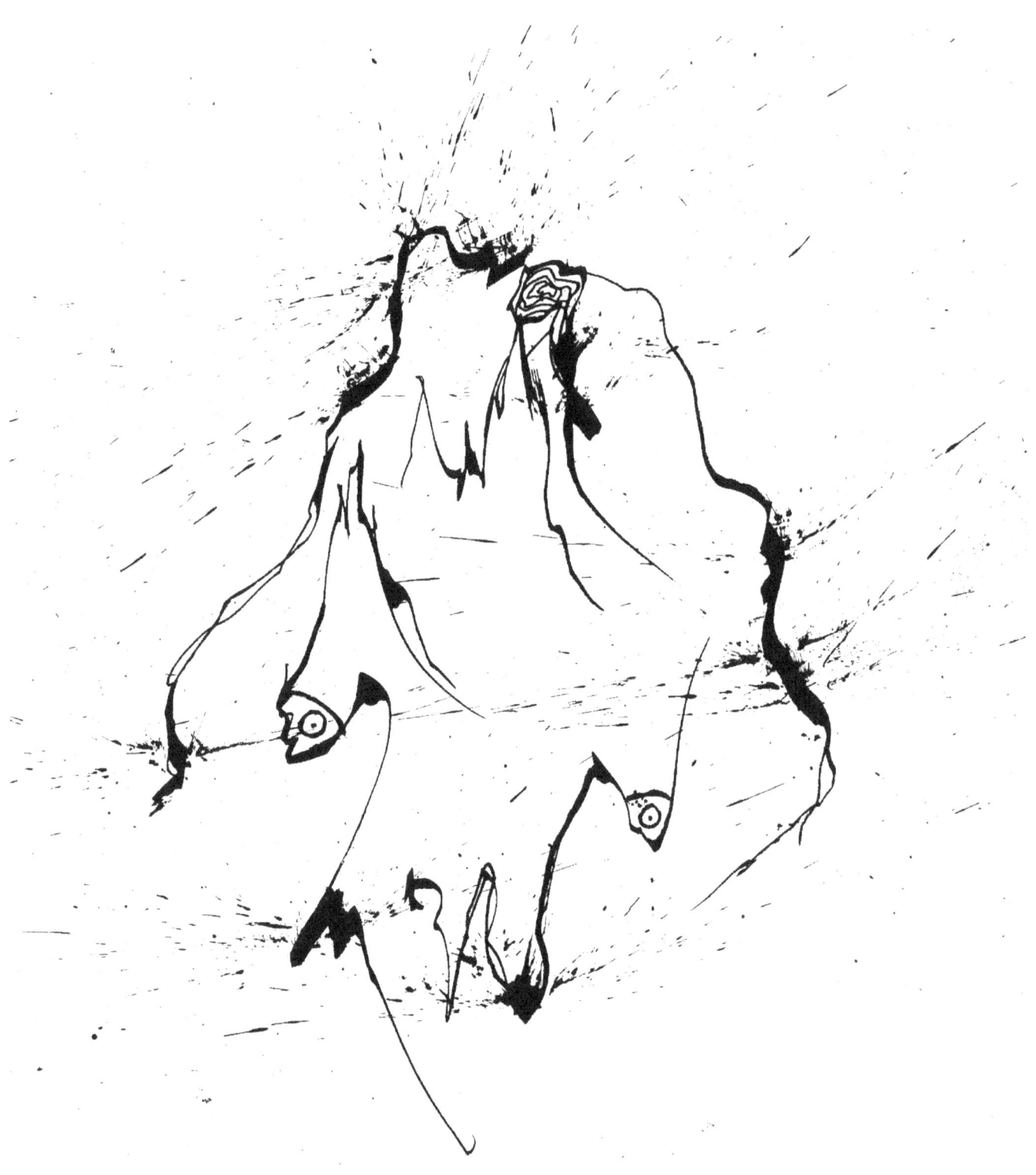

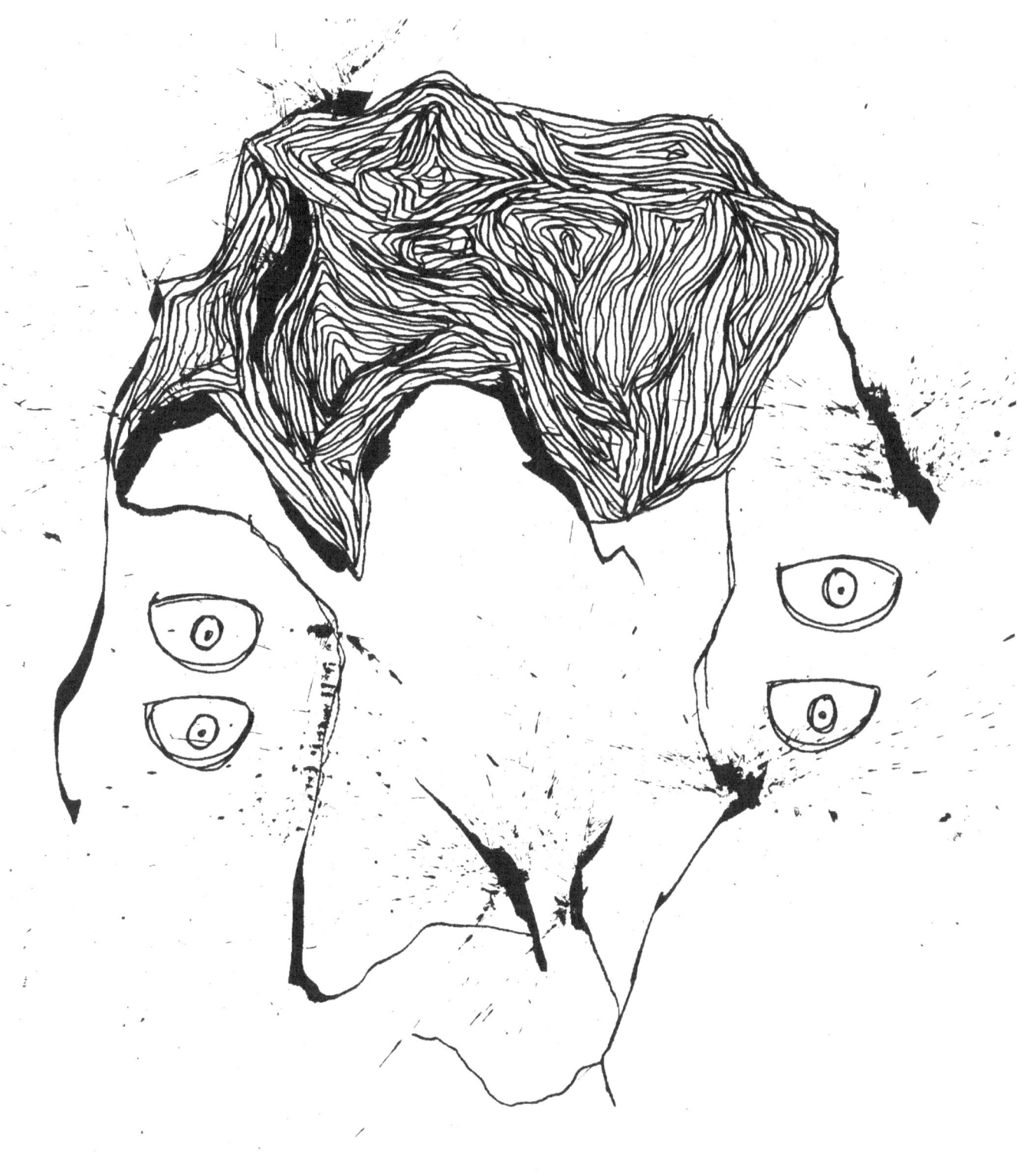

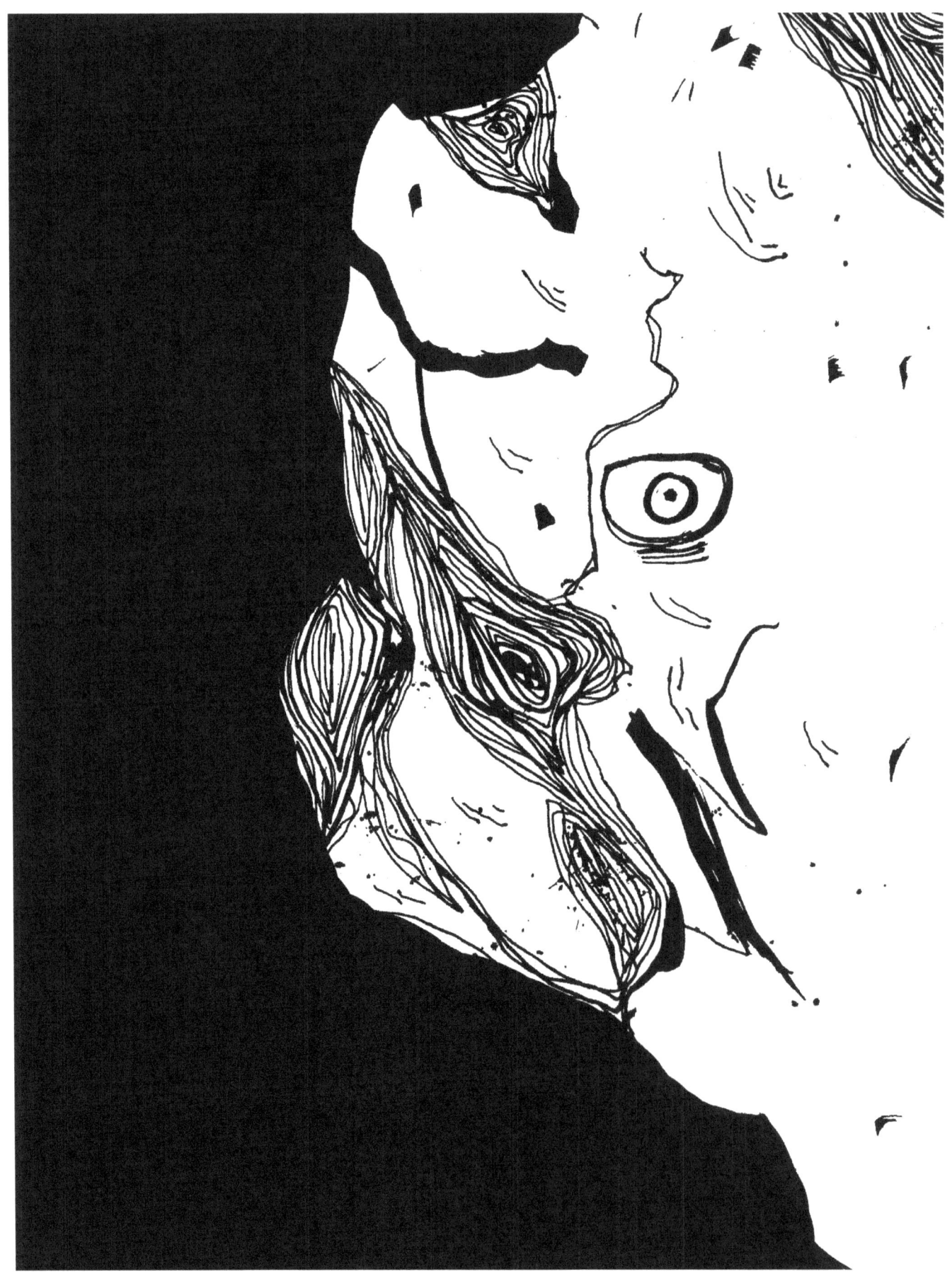

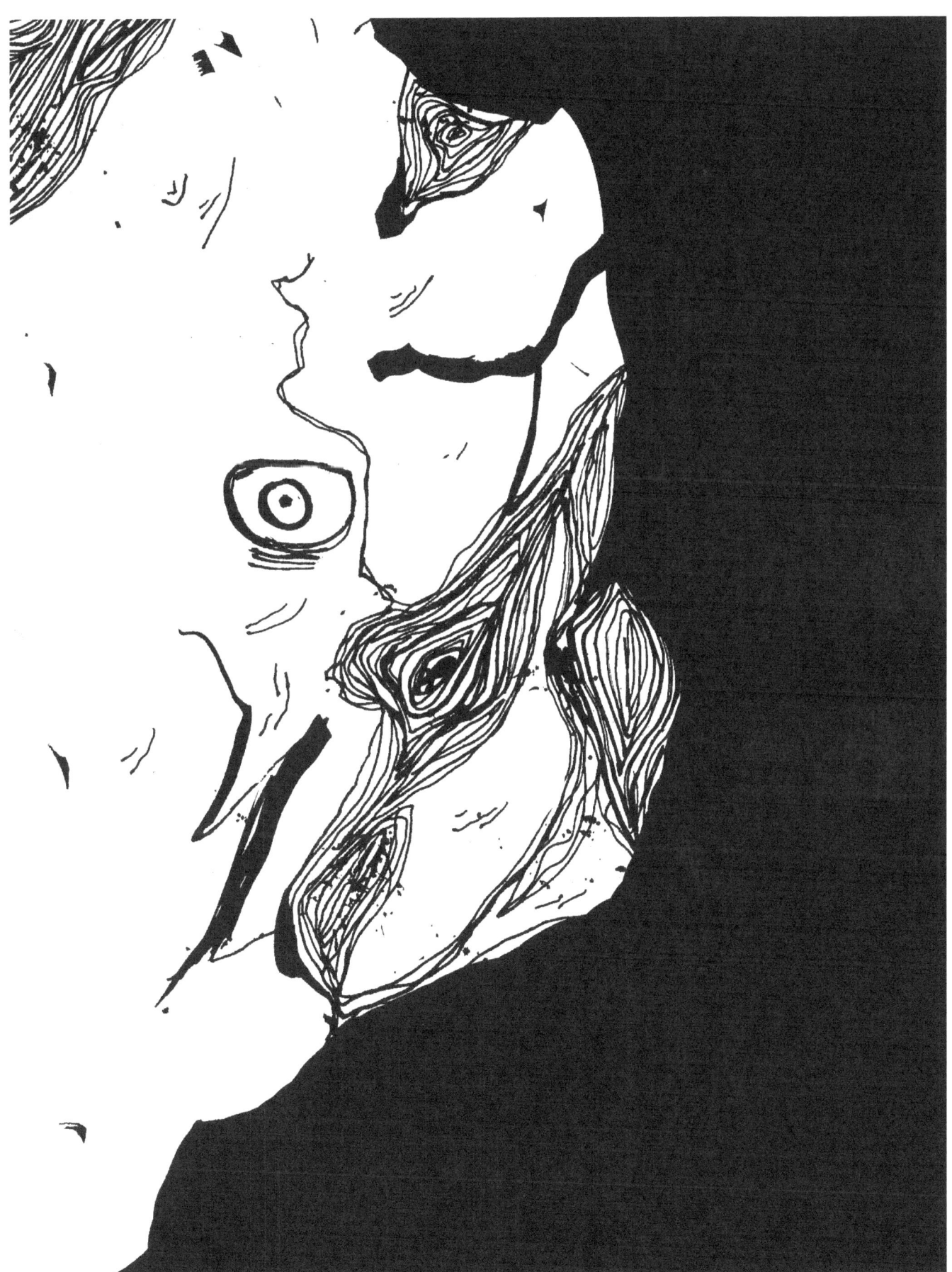

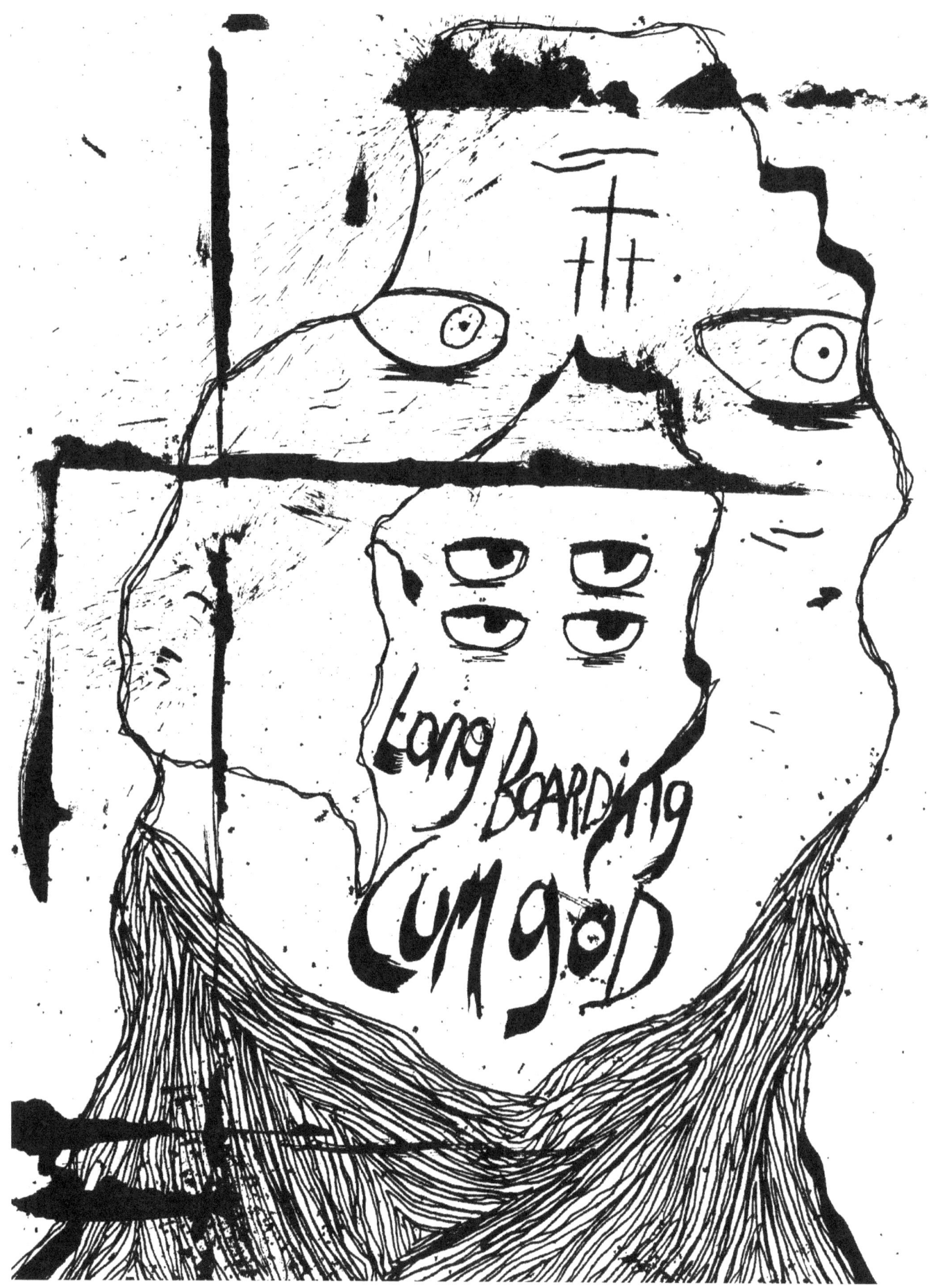

JACK KNIFE into the WHACK LIFE

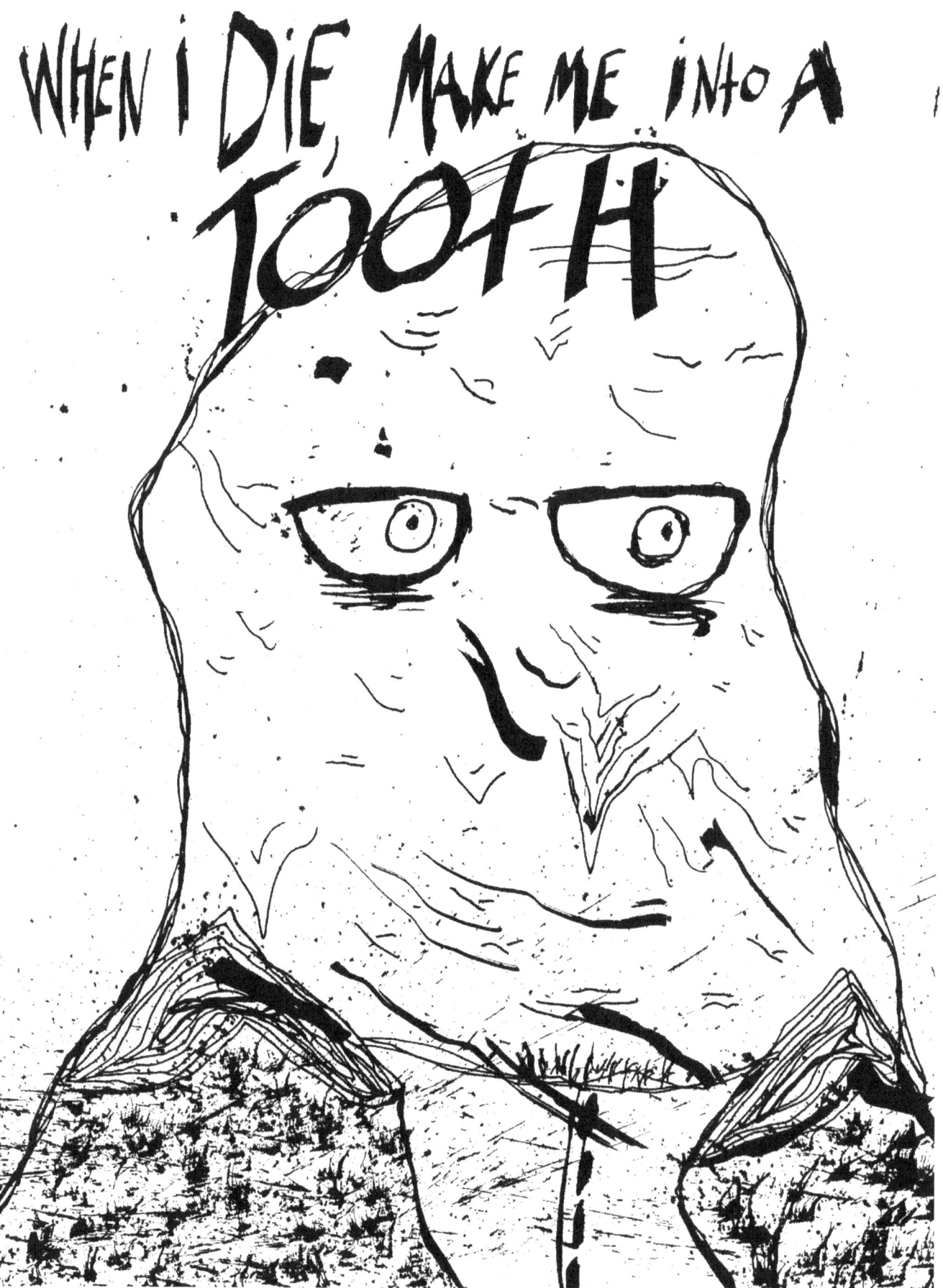

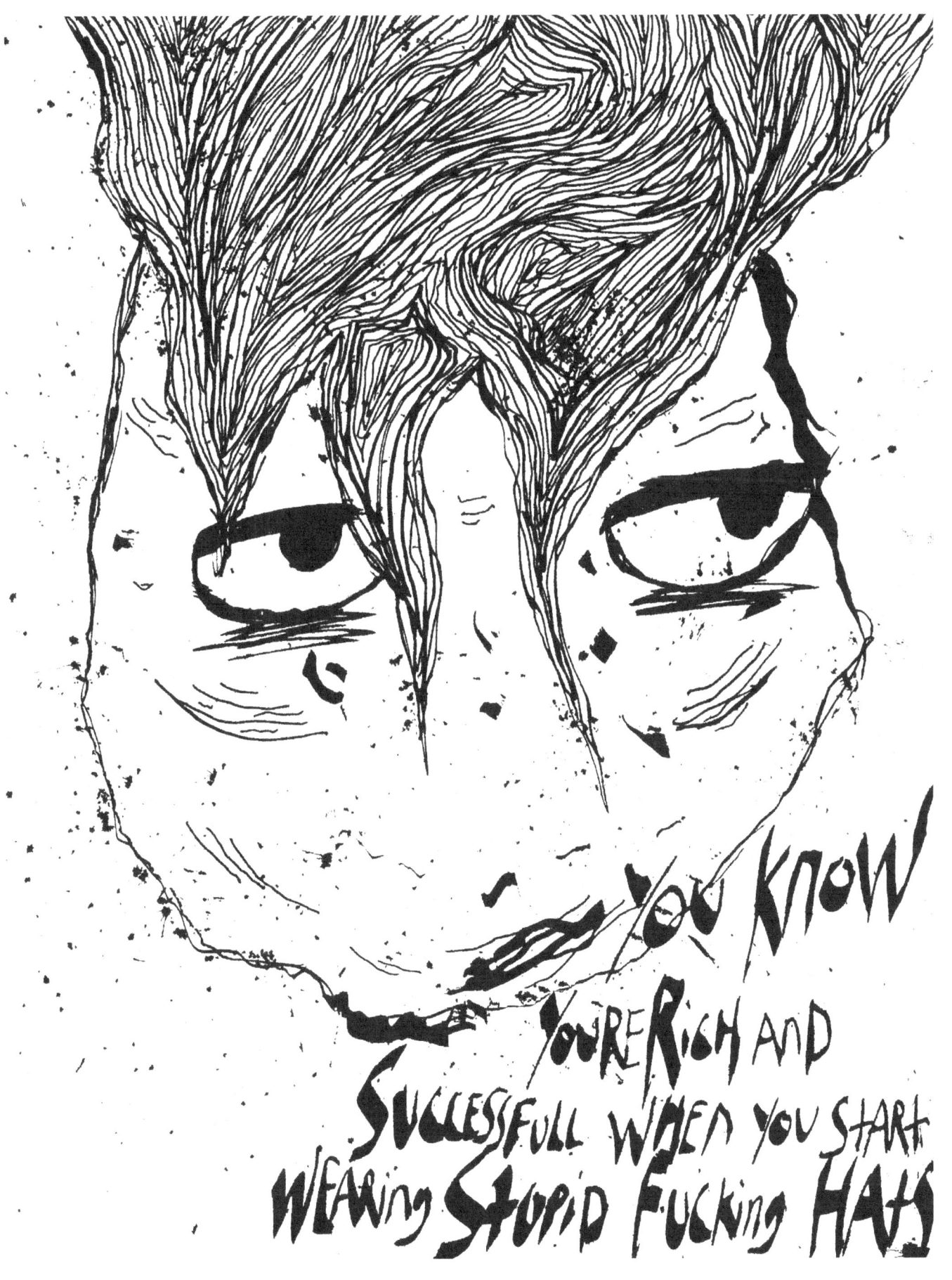

WE ALL KNOW THAT MUMMYS WOULD BE THE SEXIEST DUDES IN THE AFTERLIFE

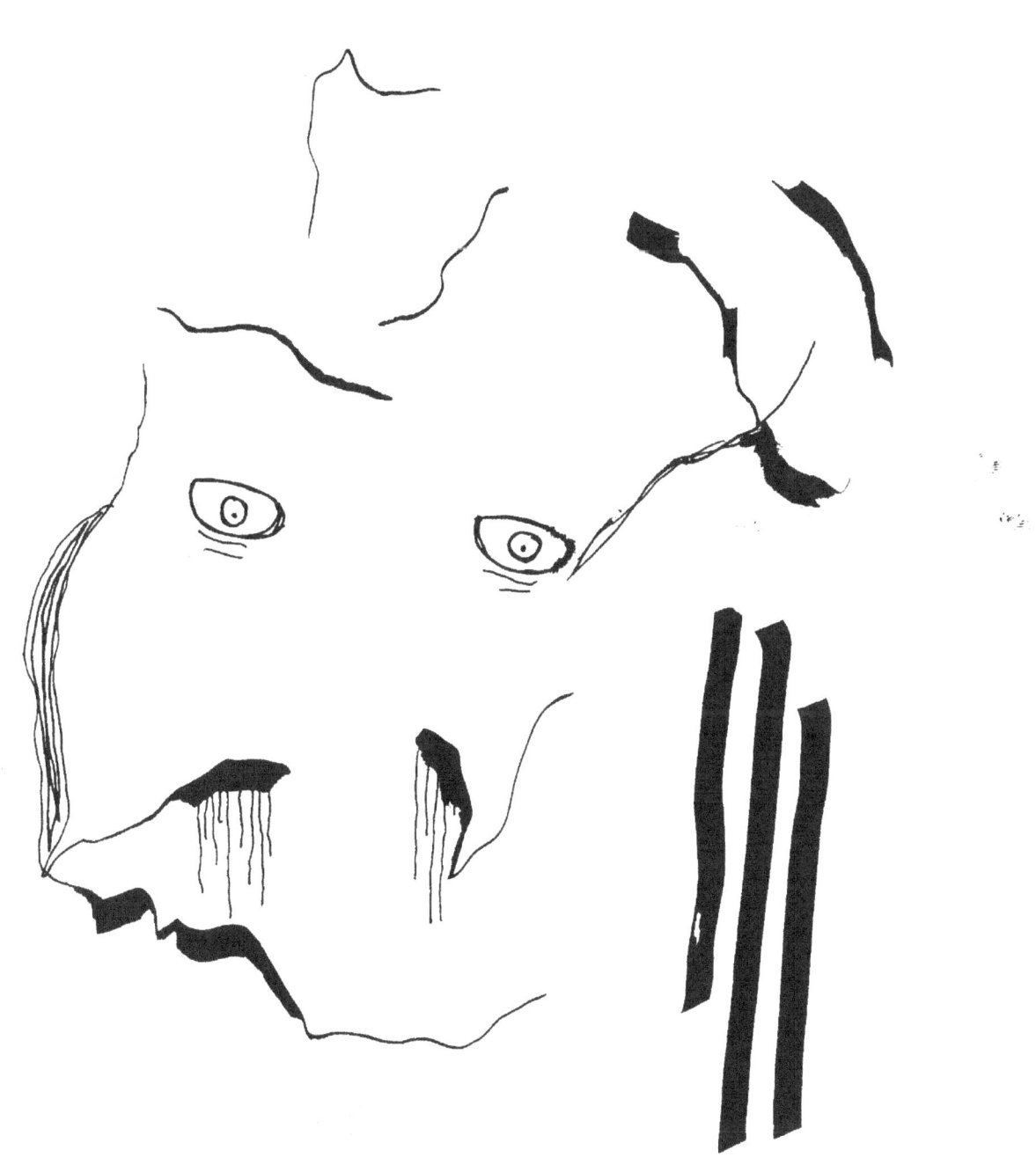

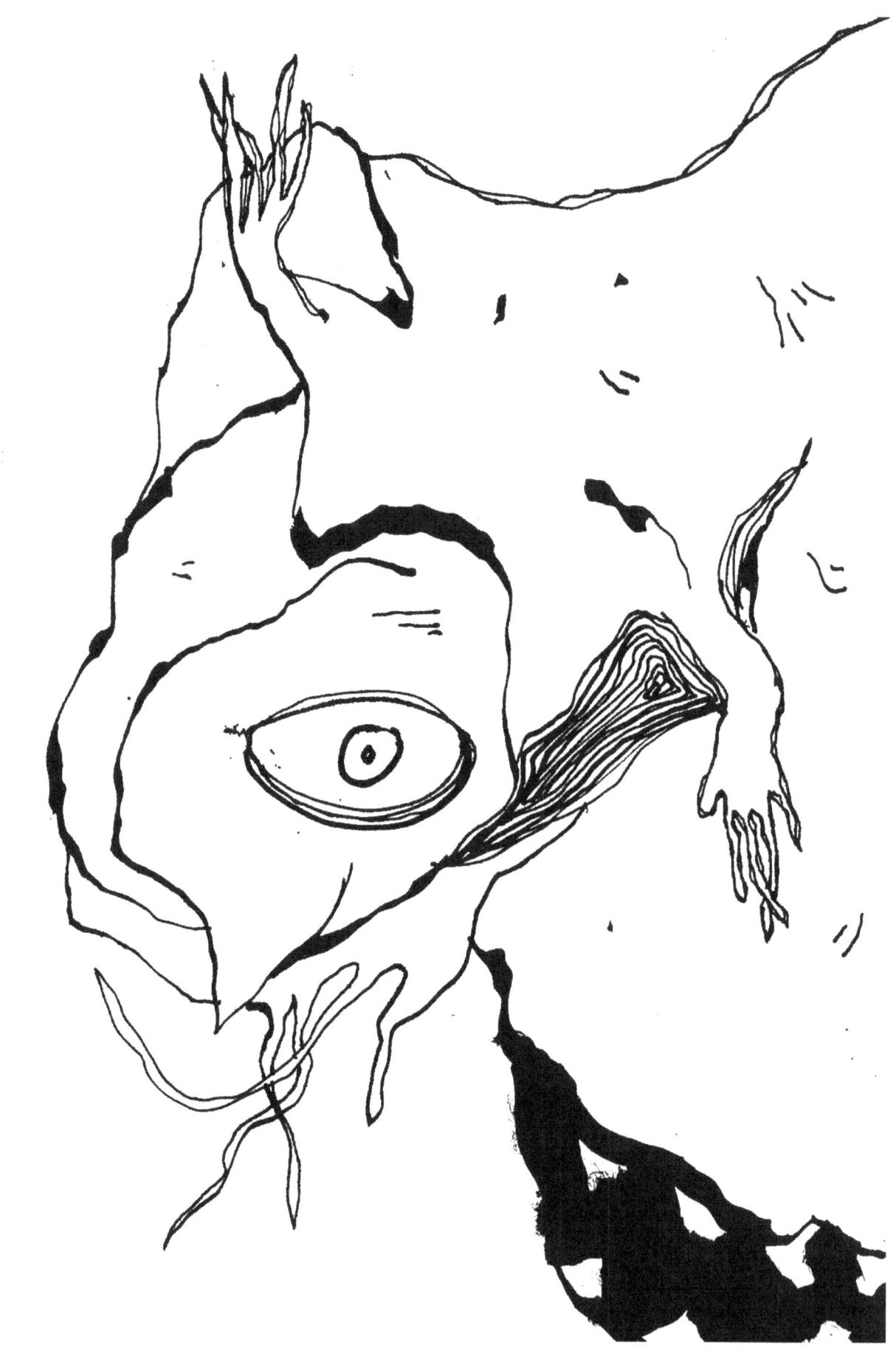

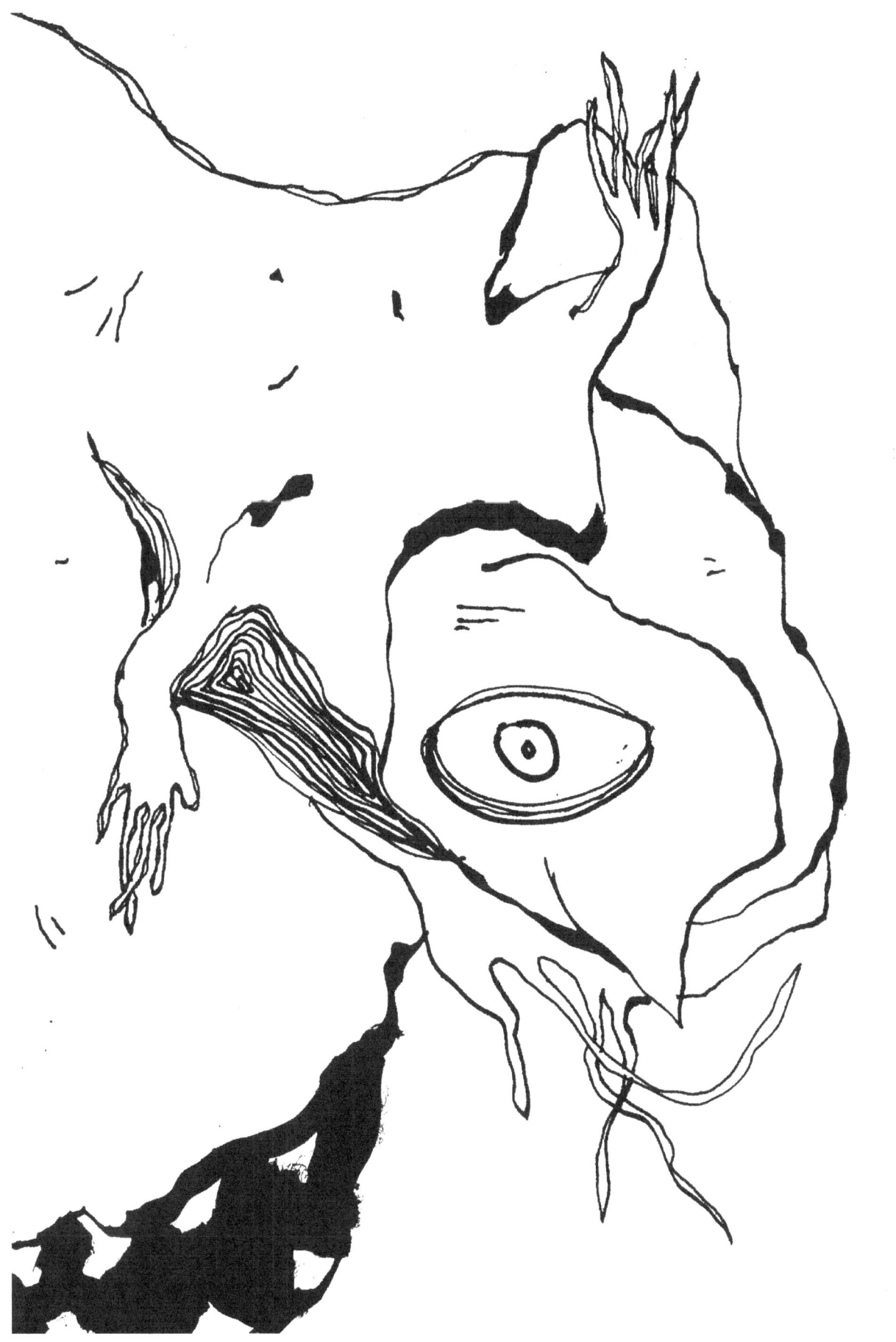

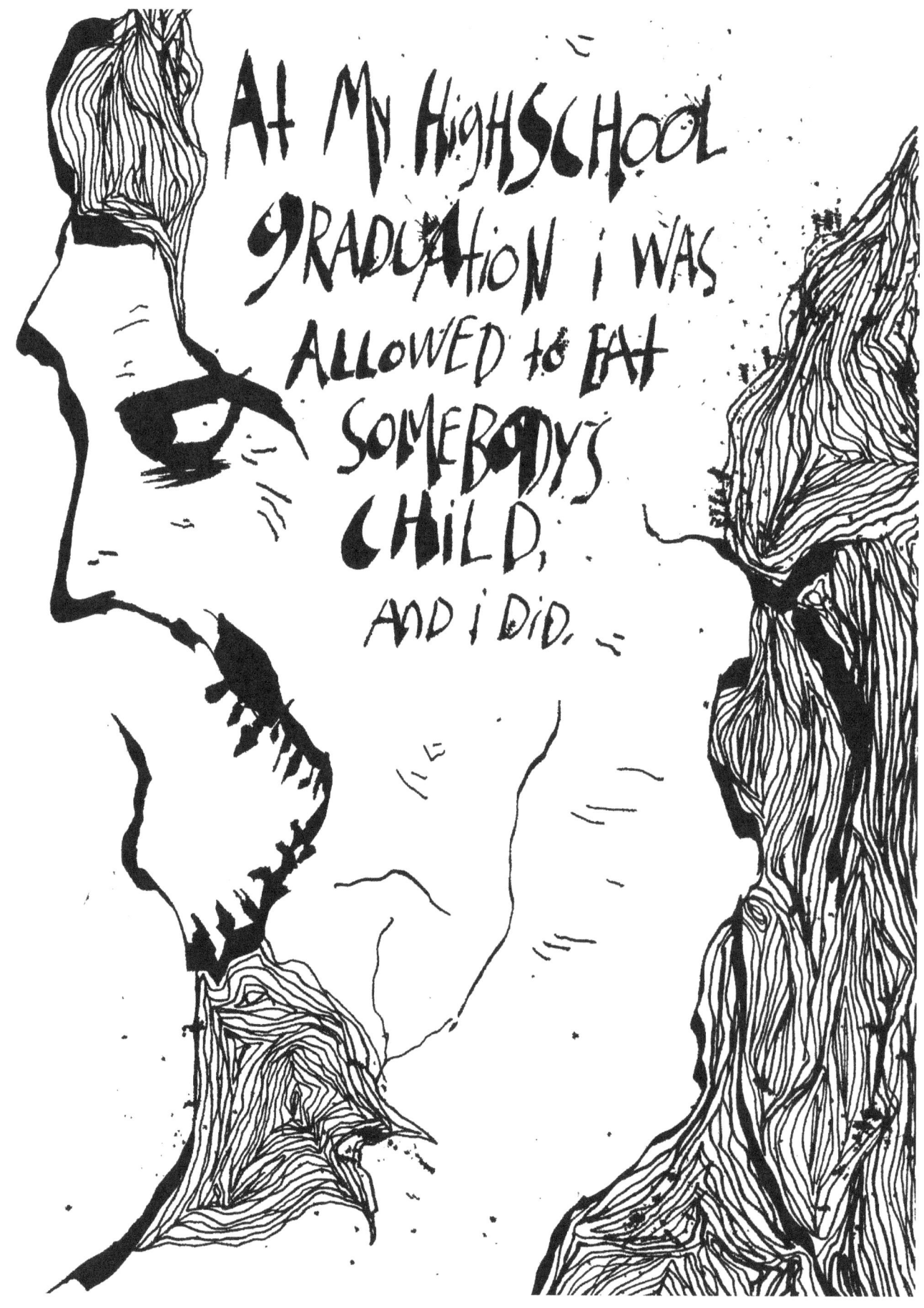

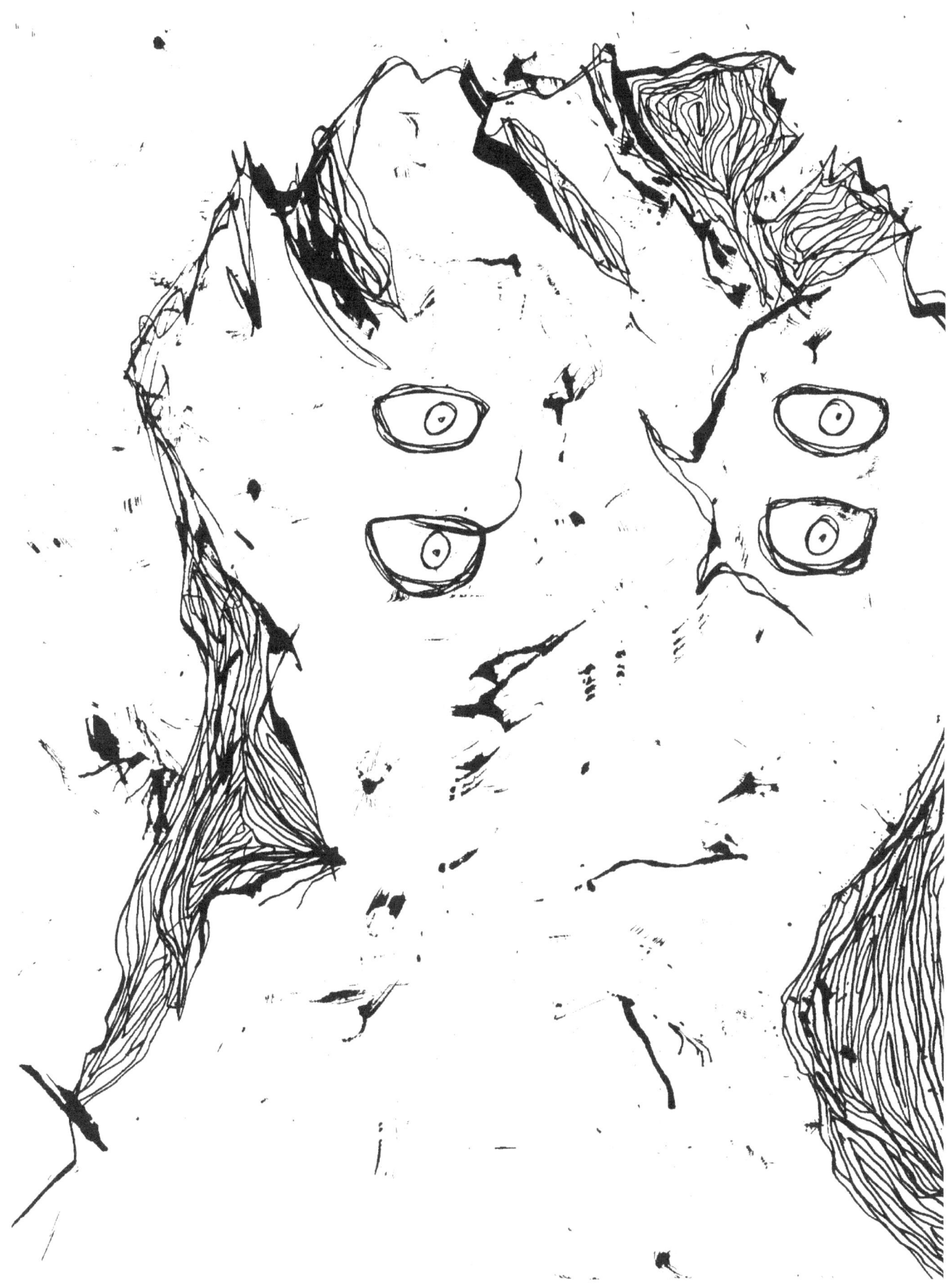

YOU CAN NOT RECORD MY VOICE.
IT IS IMPOSSIBLE. THE SOUND YOU HEAR ON YOUR DICTAPHONE IS NOT MY VOICE

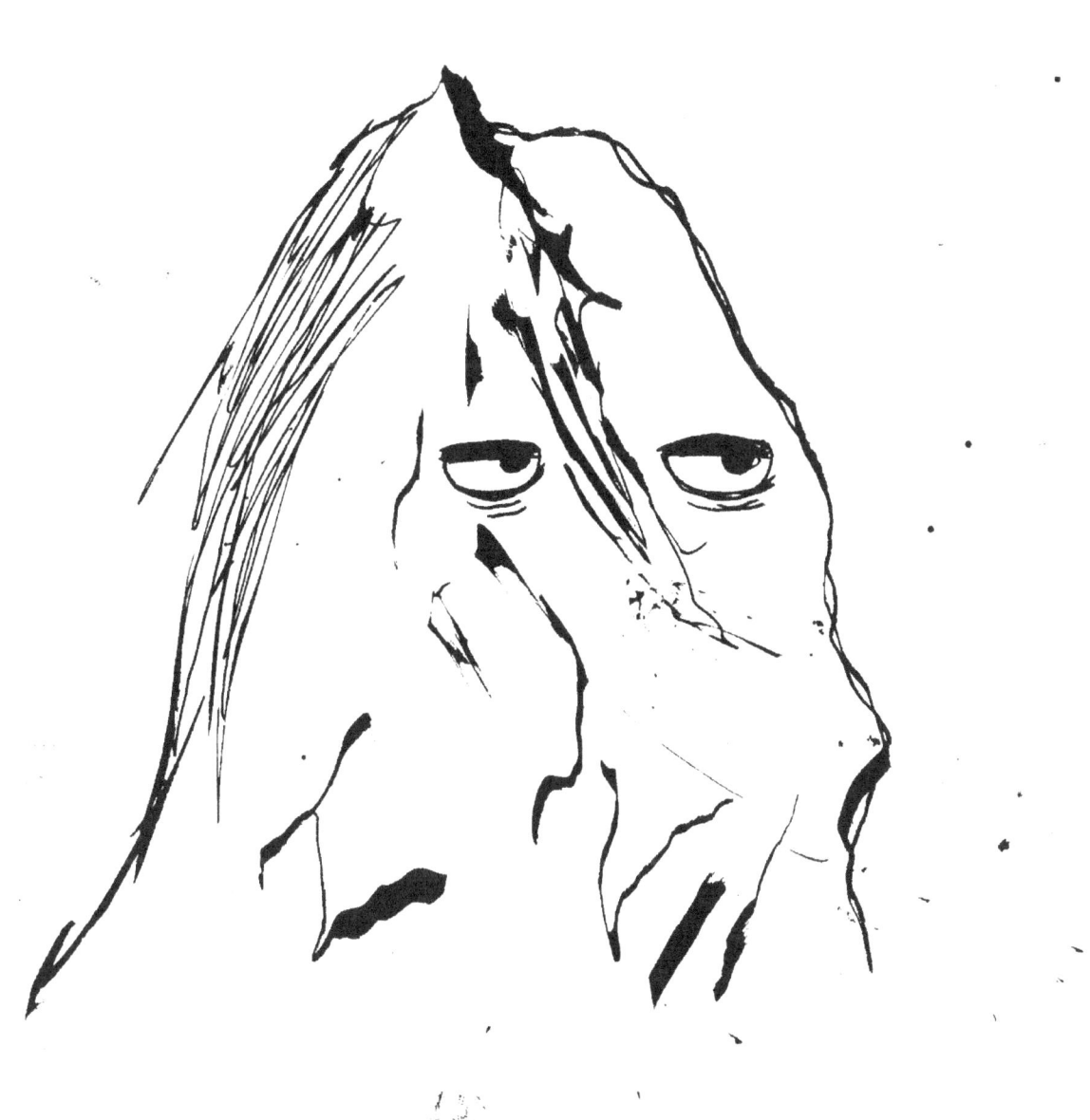

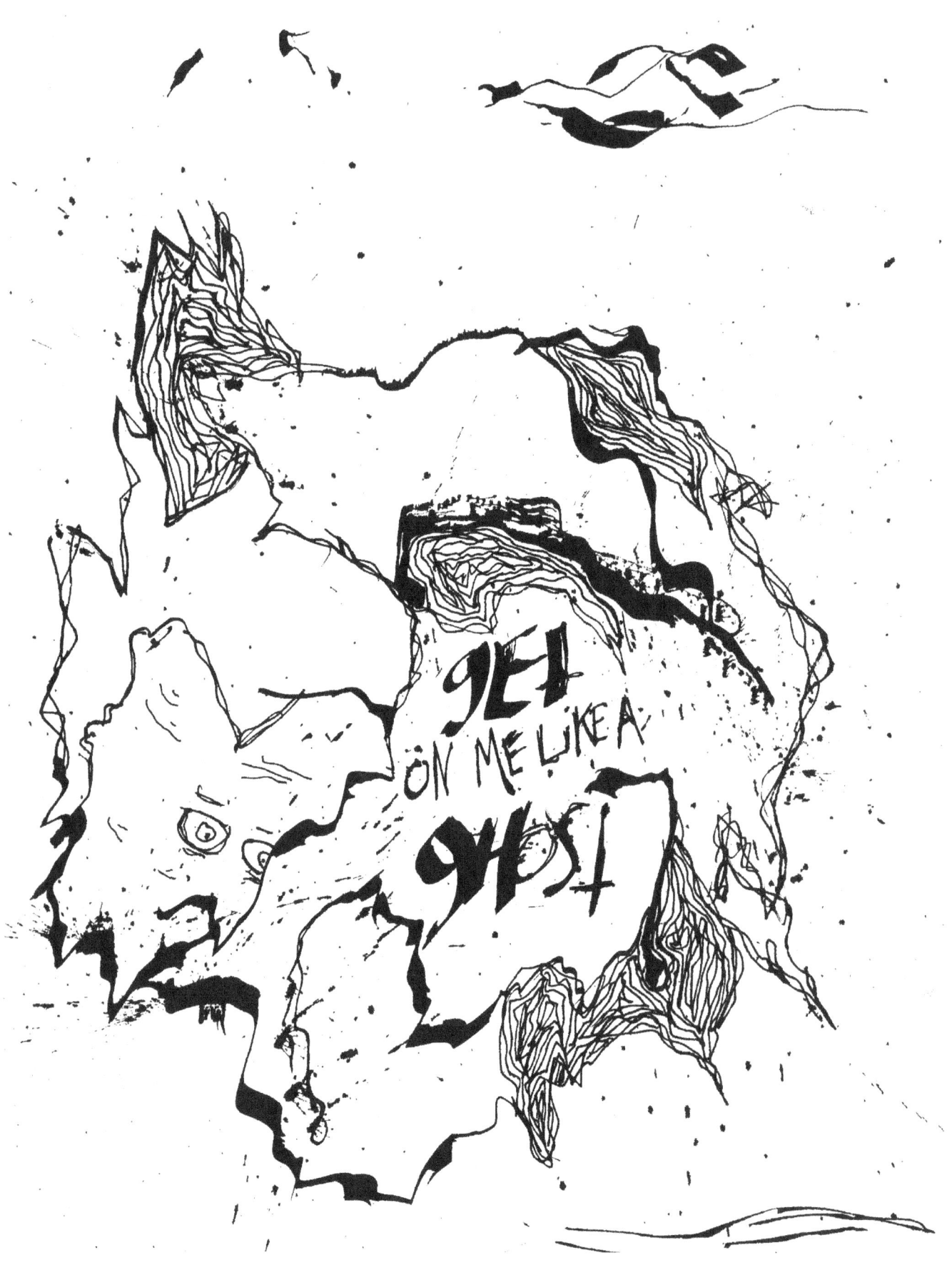

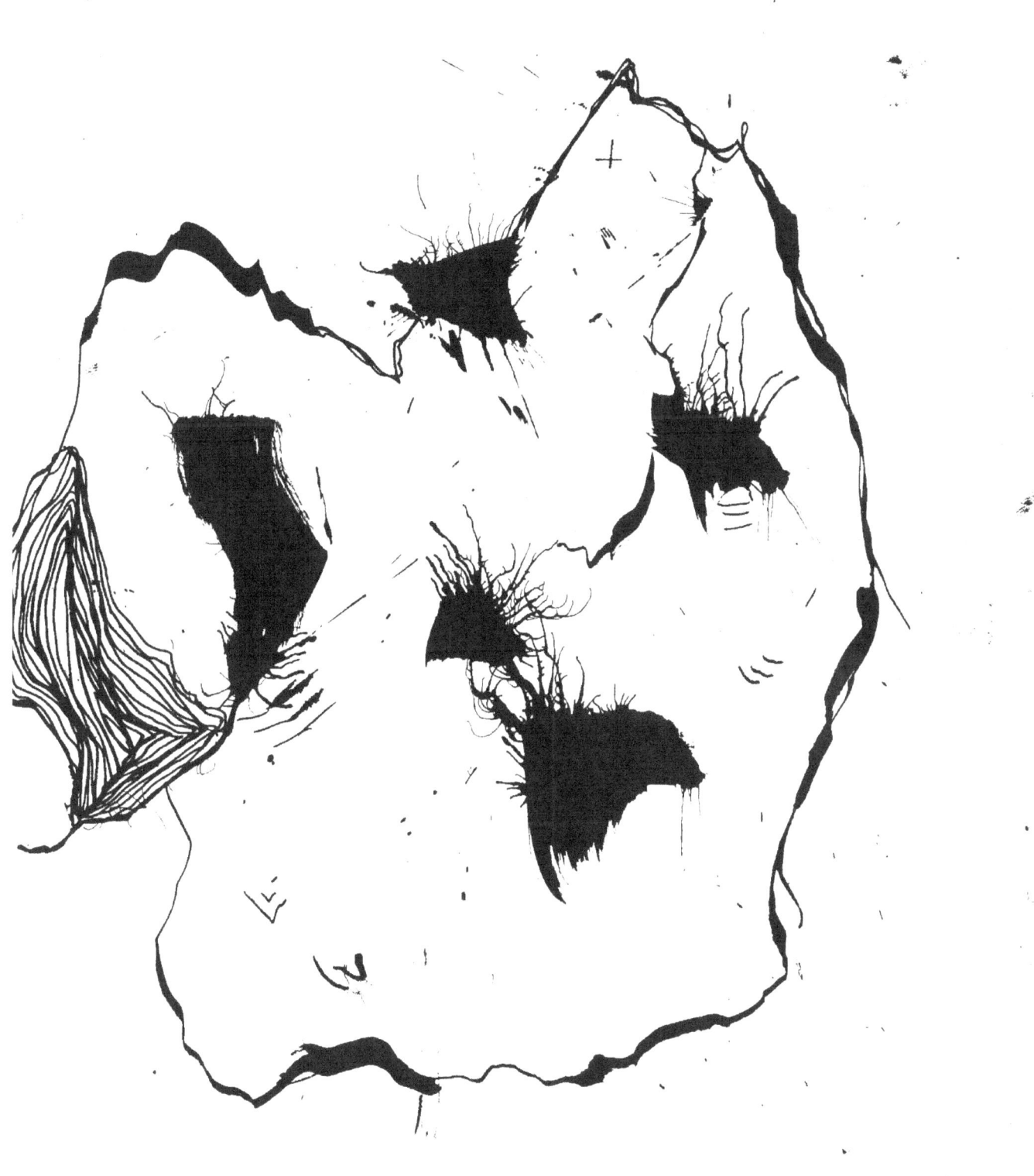

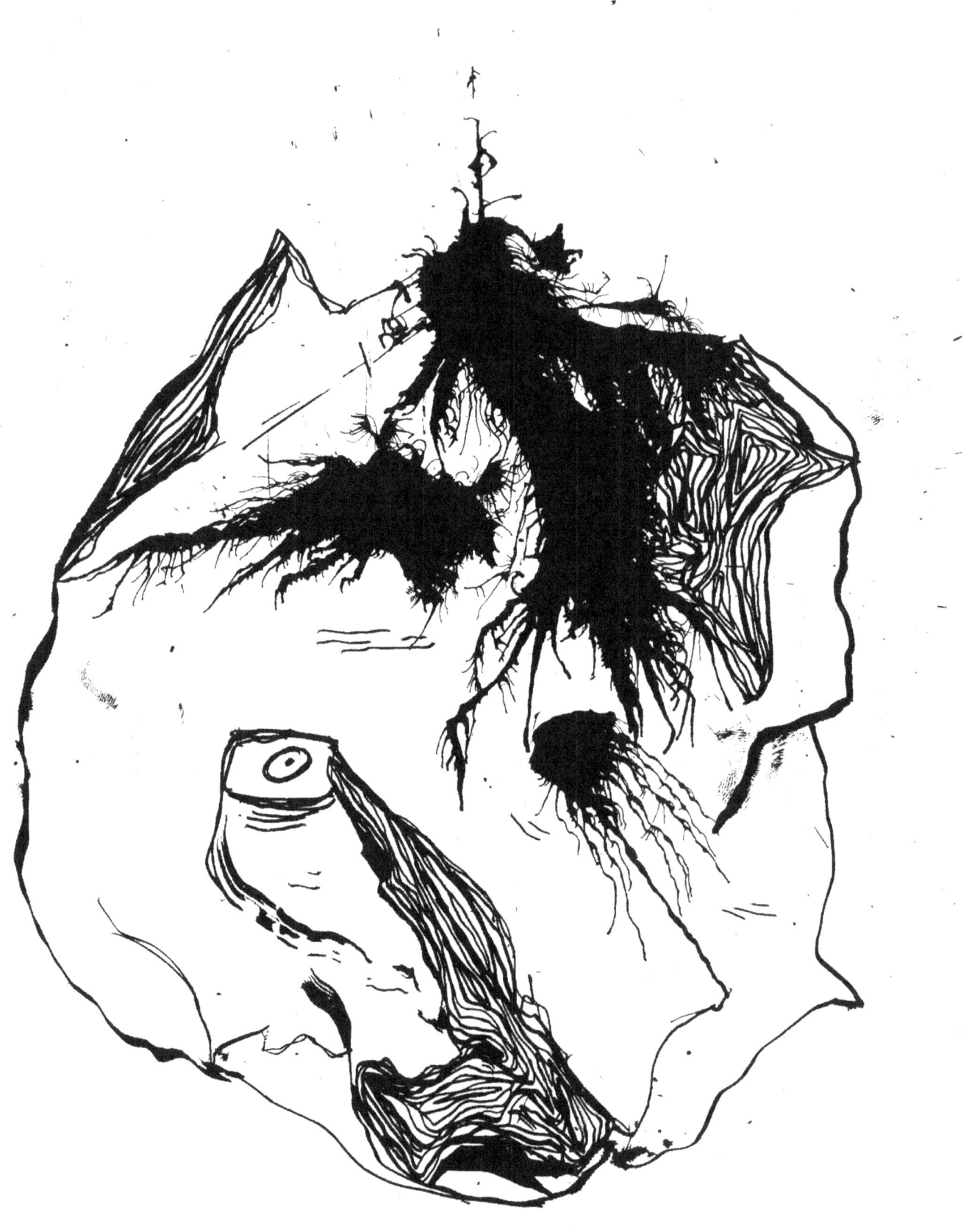

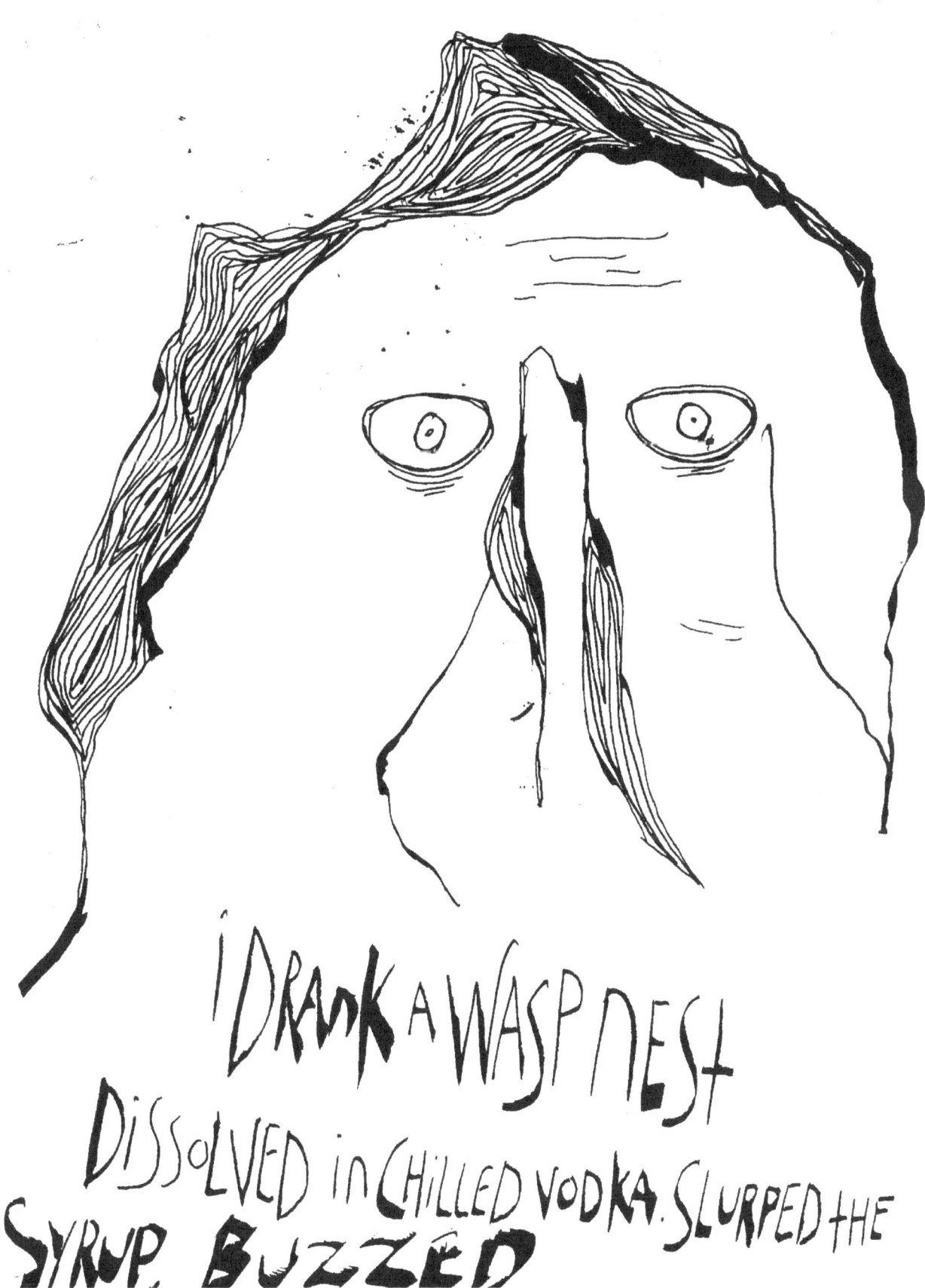

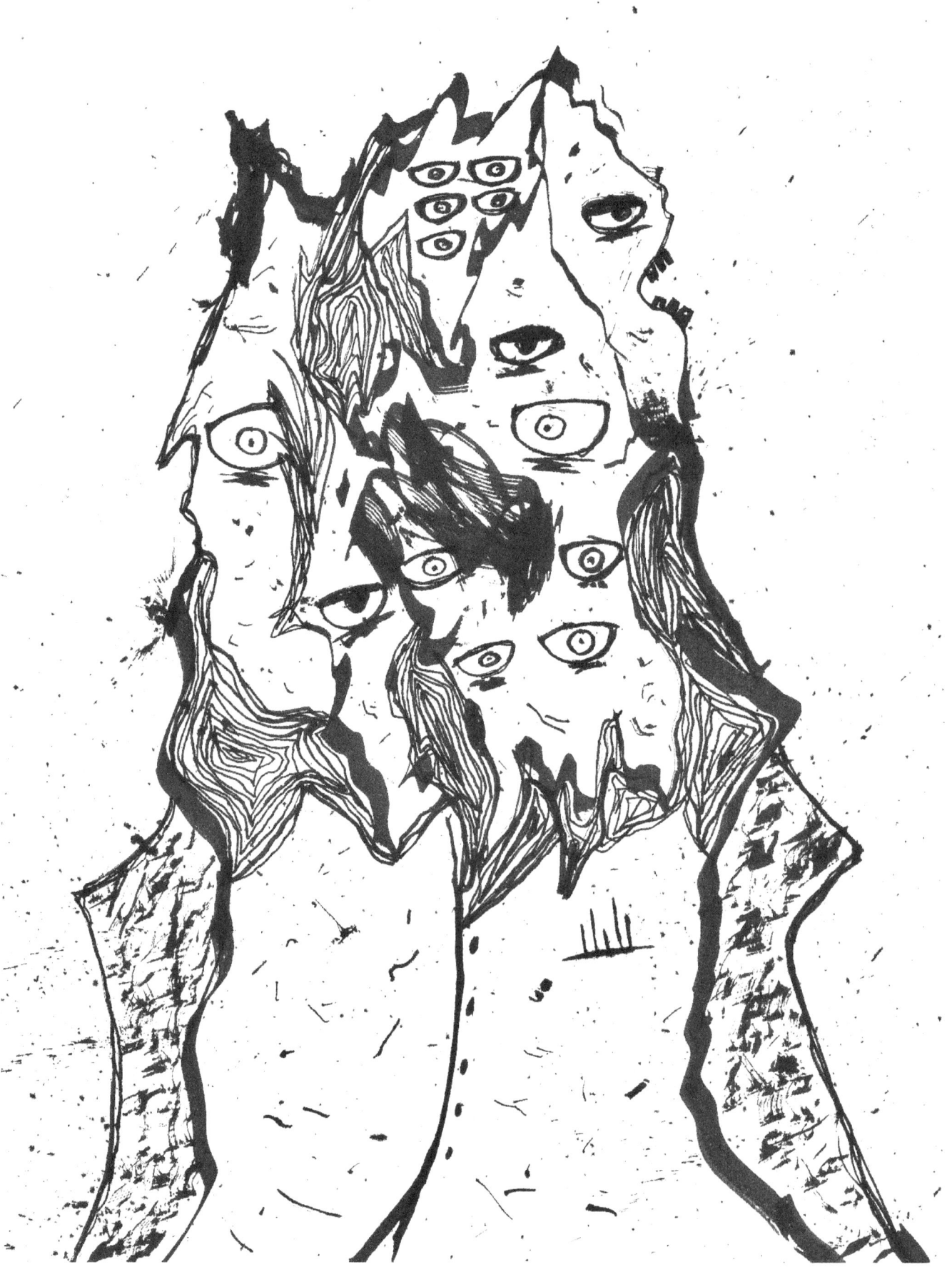

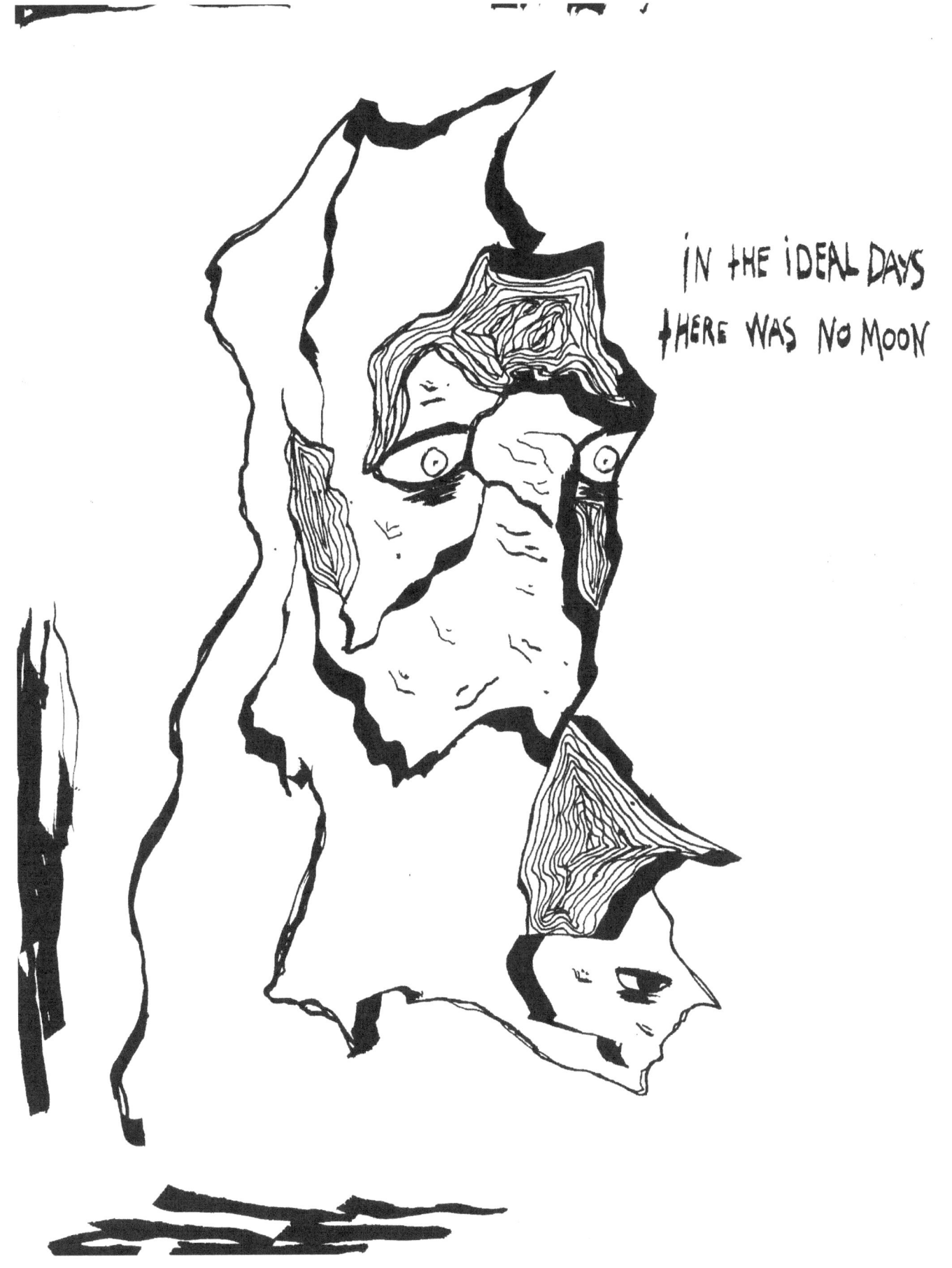

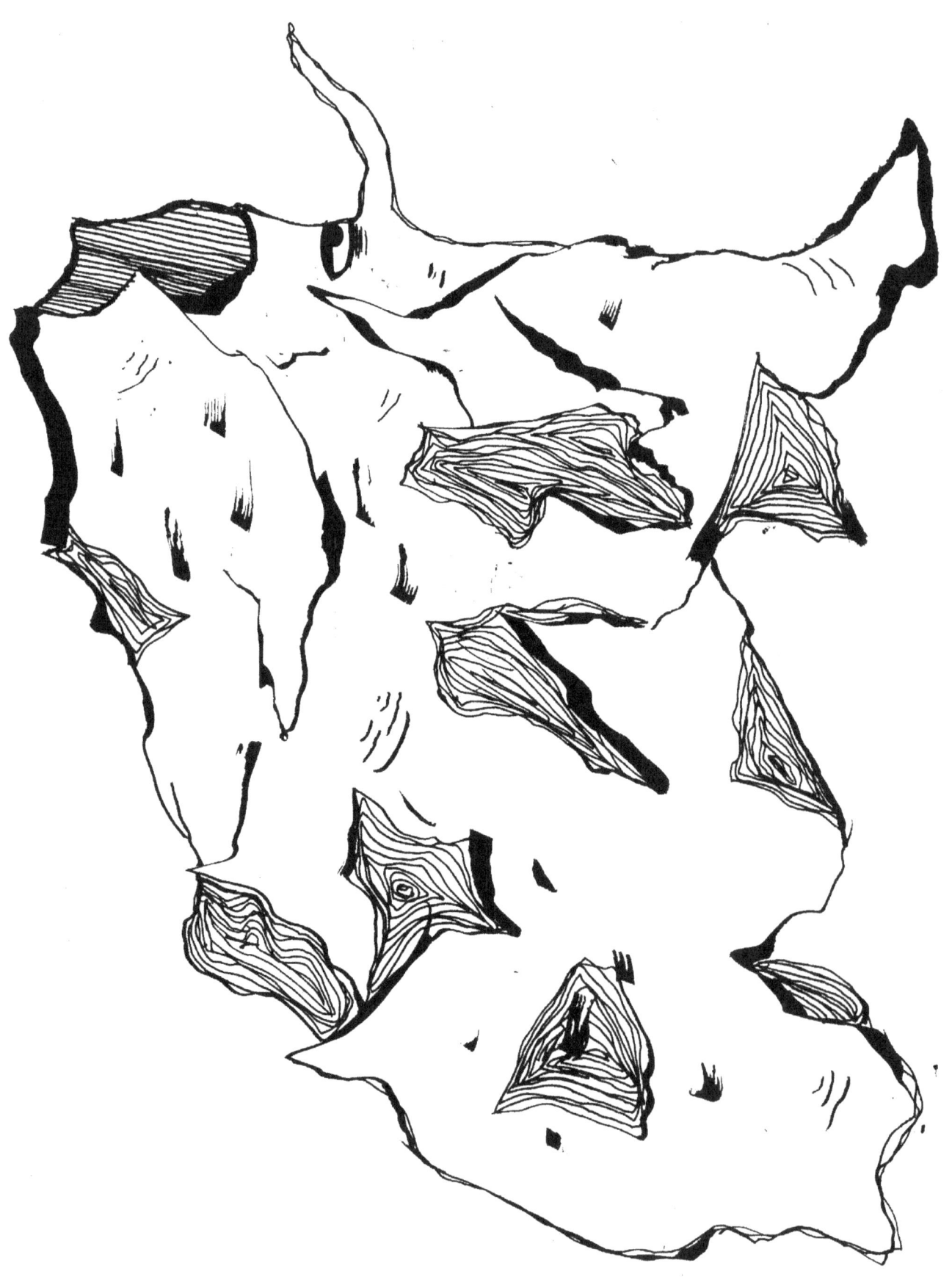

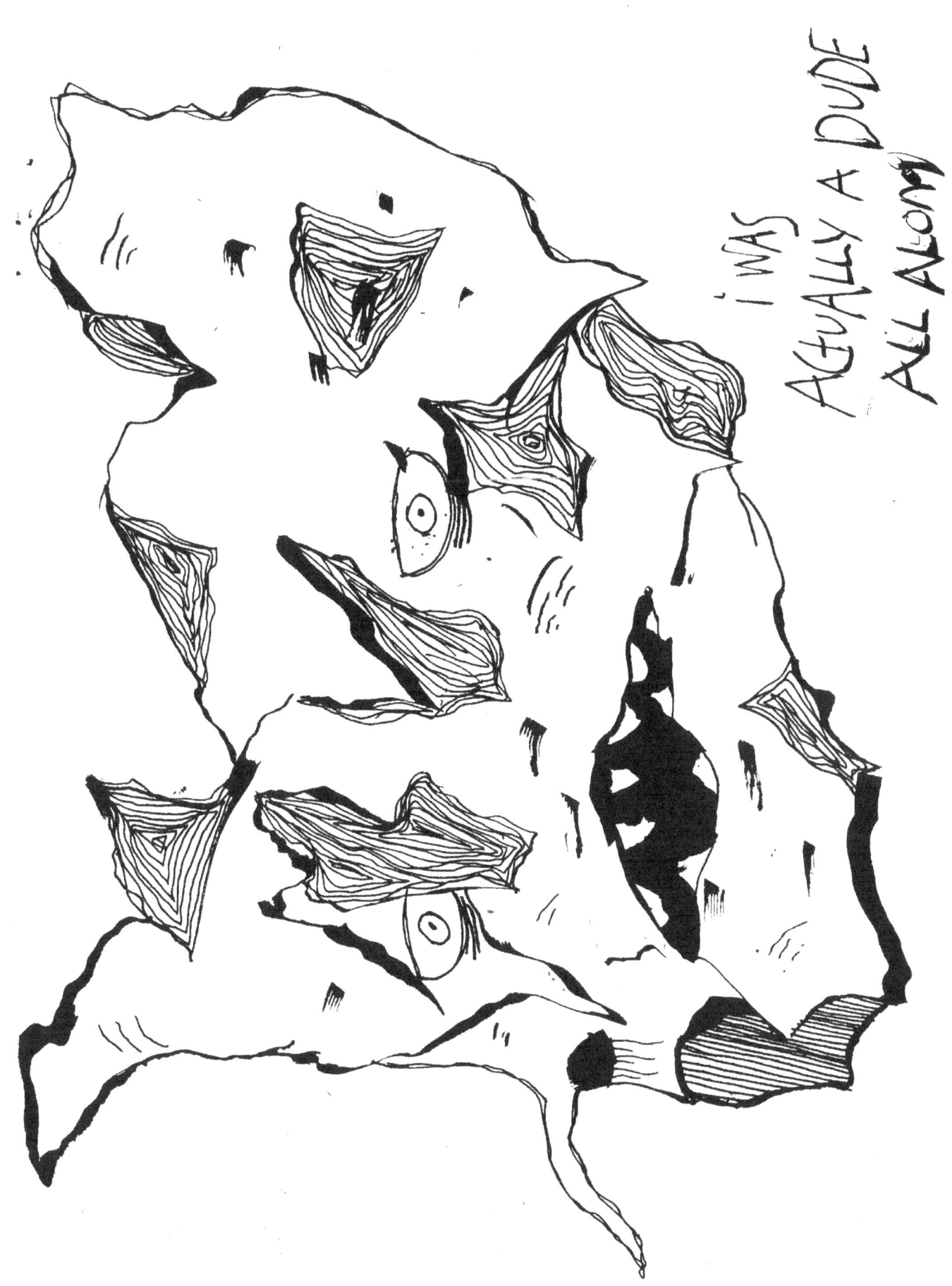

THE LAST EARTH DEATH

I am gunned down.
I am gunned down.
I am gunned down.
I am surely, entirely, and powerfully gunned down.

My lacerated flesh and destroyed bones are set on fire before the insects can chew and recycle me.
The ash is swept up into a wet rag, and that too is set on fire
The smoke is collected into plastic bags and deposited into heavy armored briefcases.
The briefcases are tied to enormous balloons and floated into space

(MY) FIRST SPACE DEATH

The pressure in space is tremendous
The balloons pop, the cases are crushed
The plastic bags are punctured
and what is left of me is scattered in the vacuum.

It is agony.

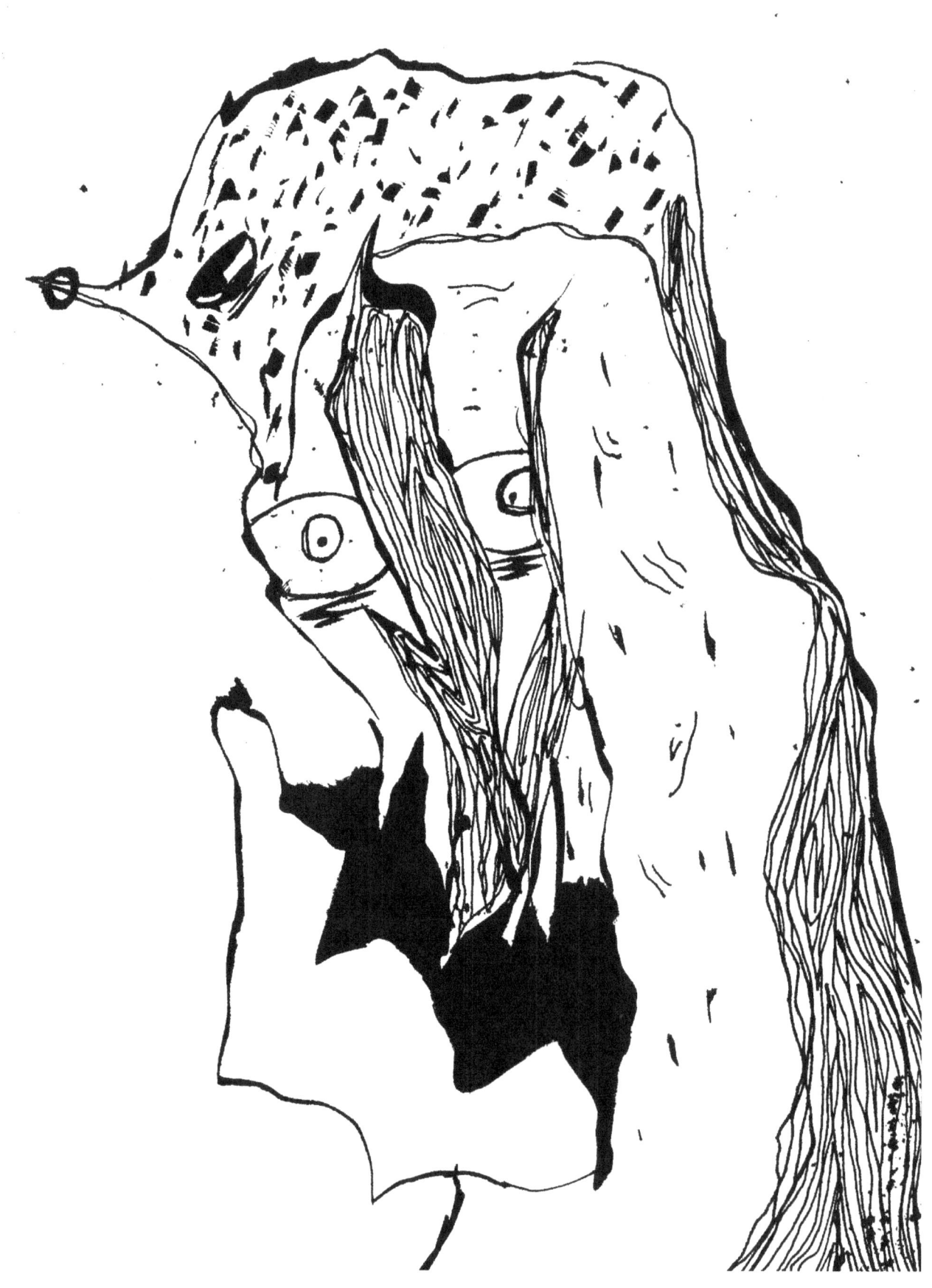

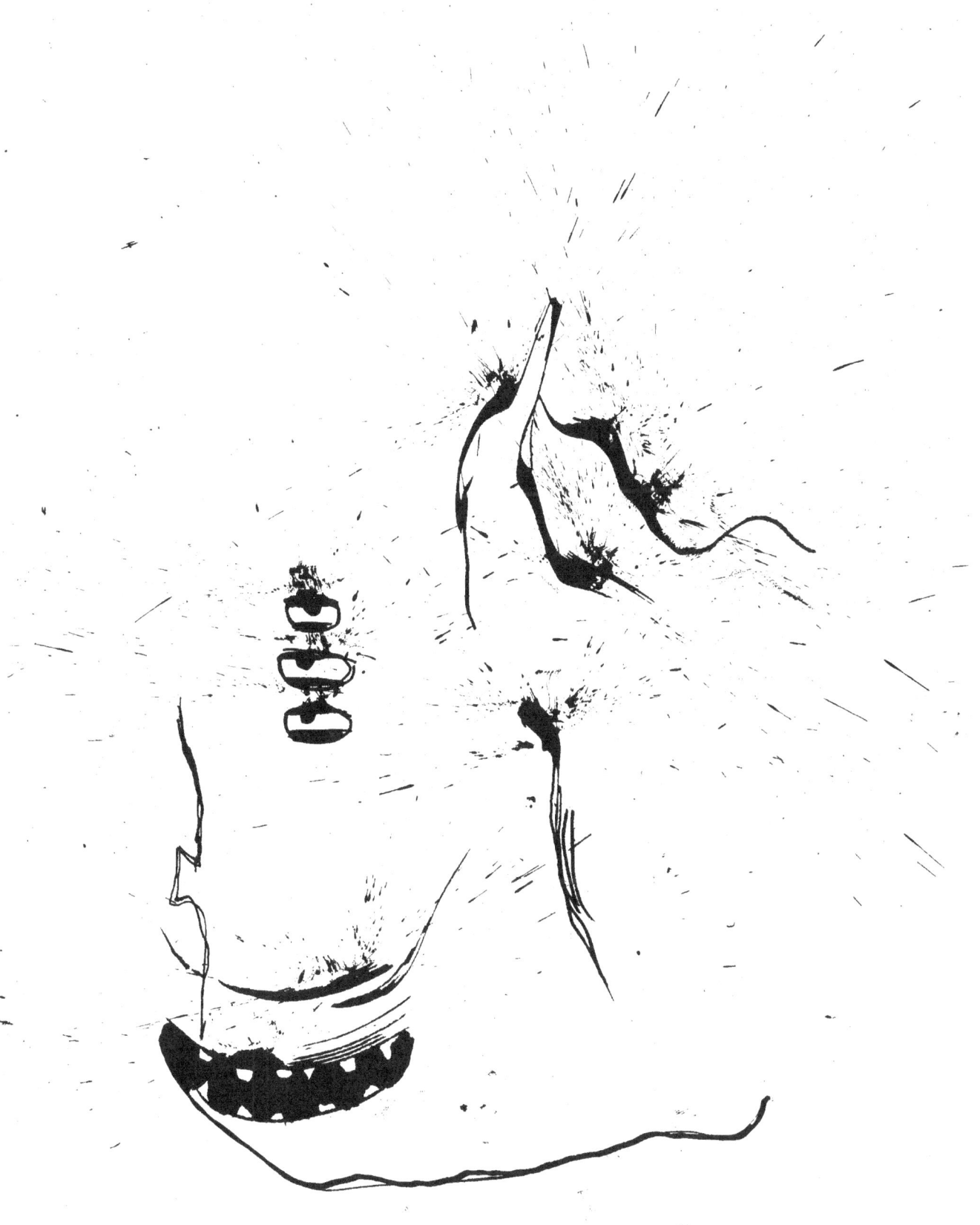

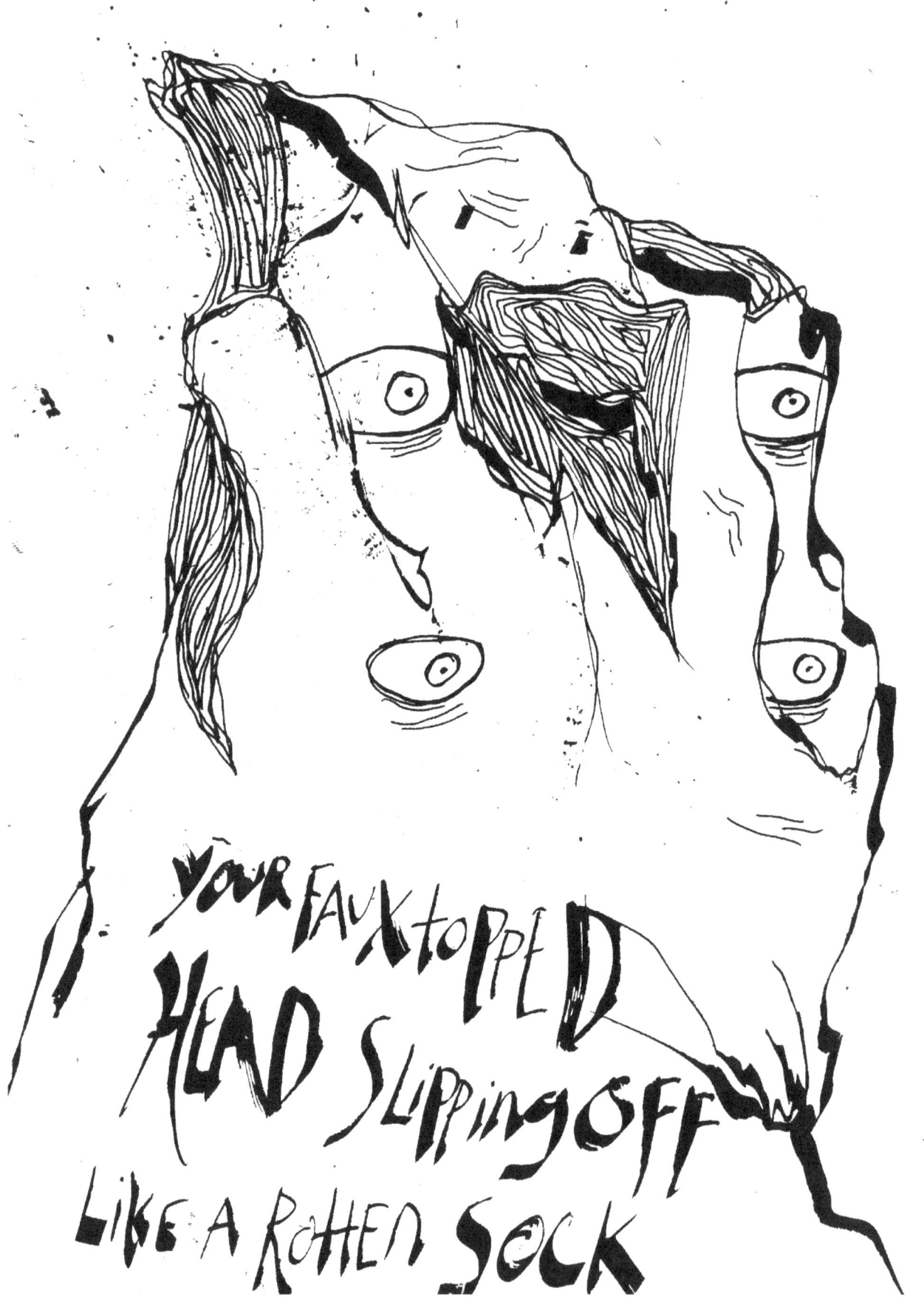

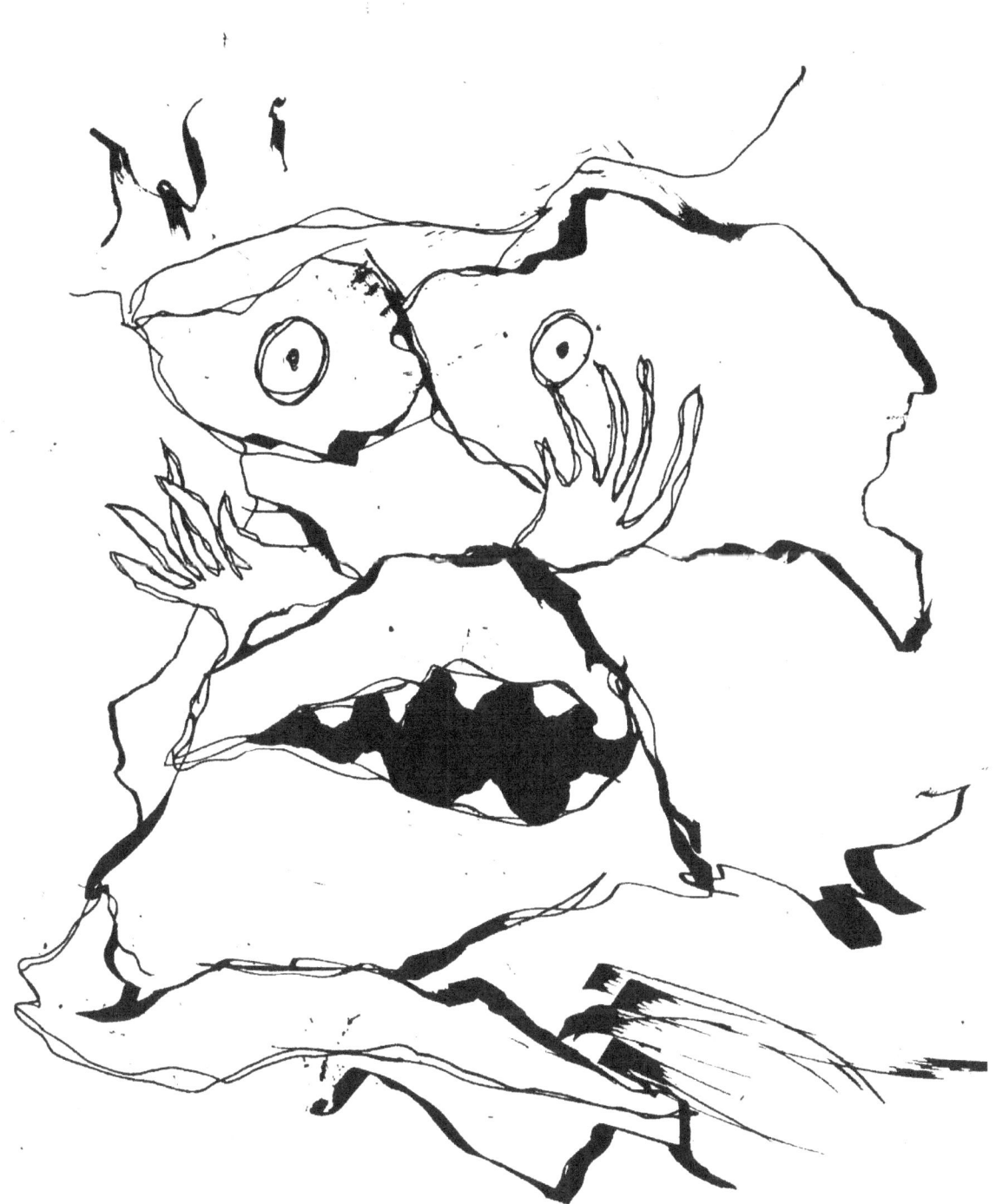

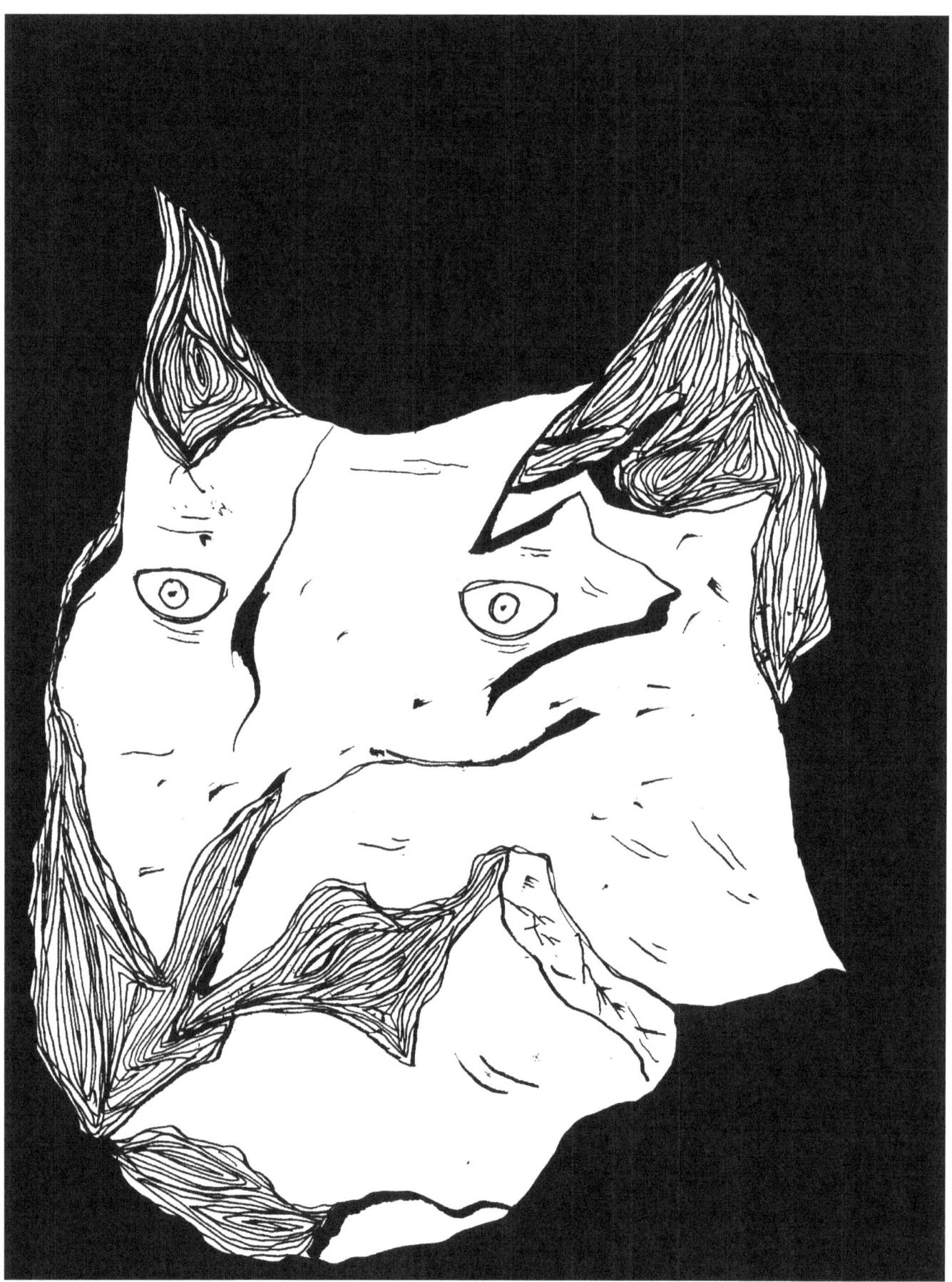

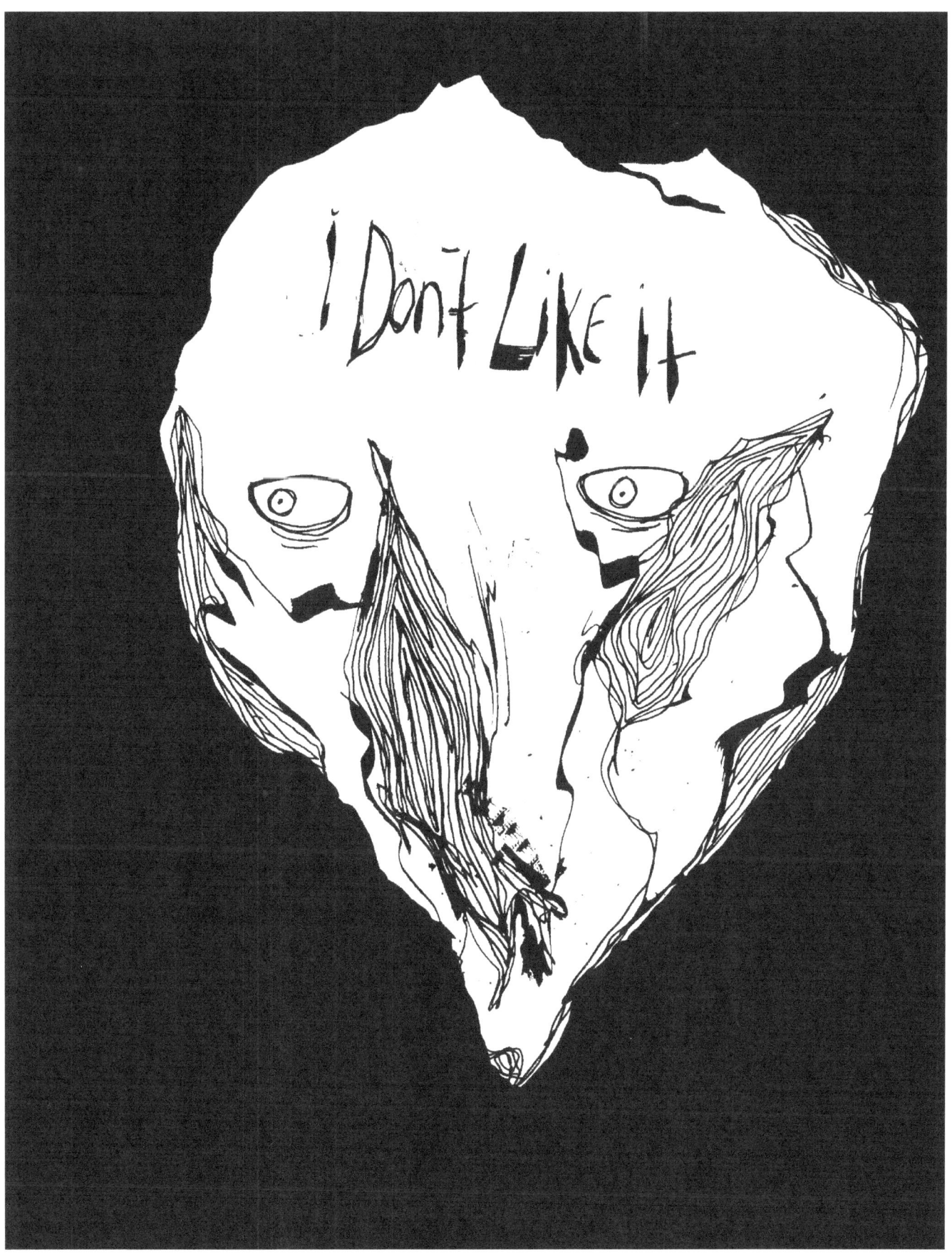

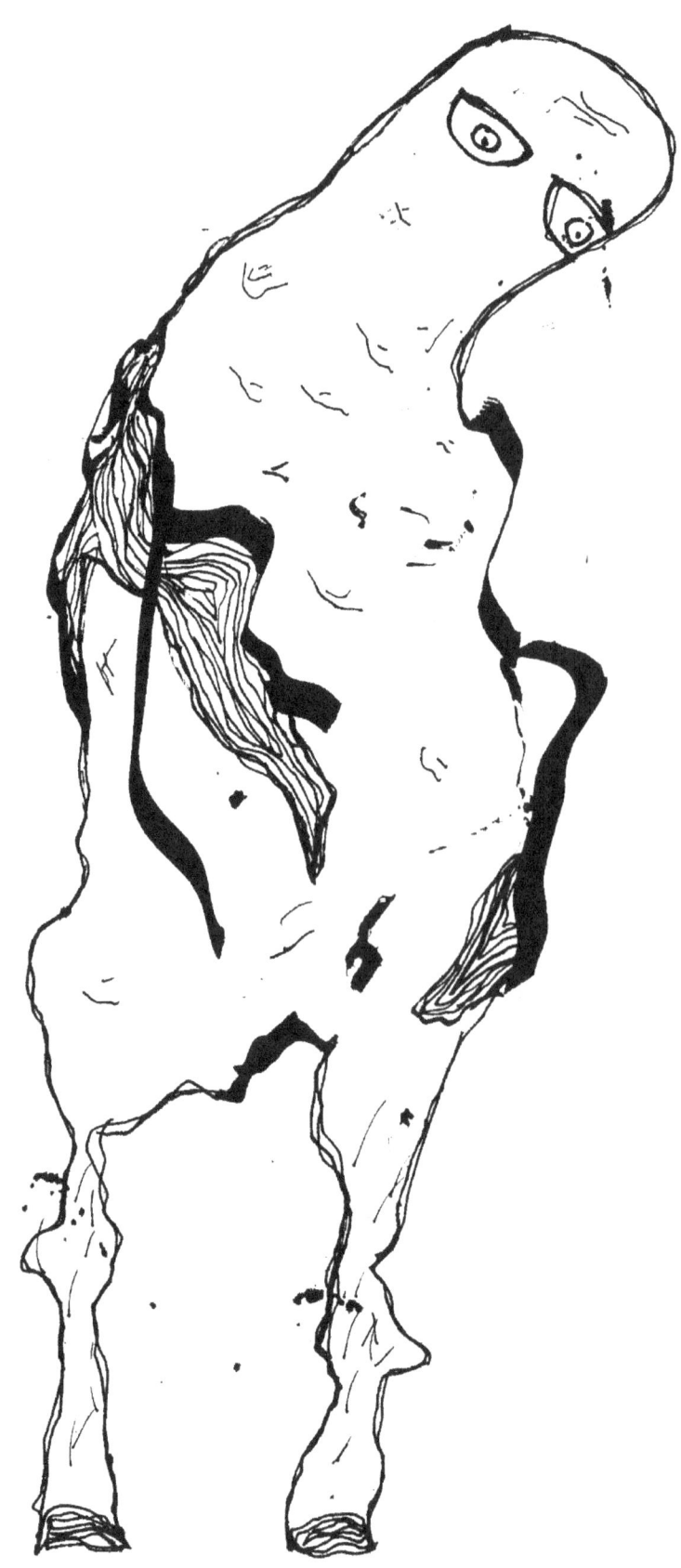

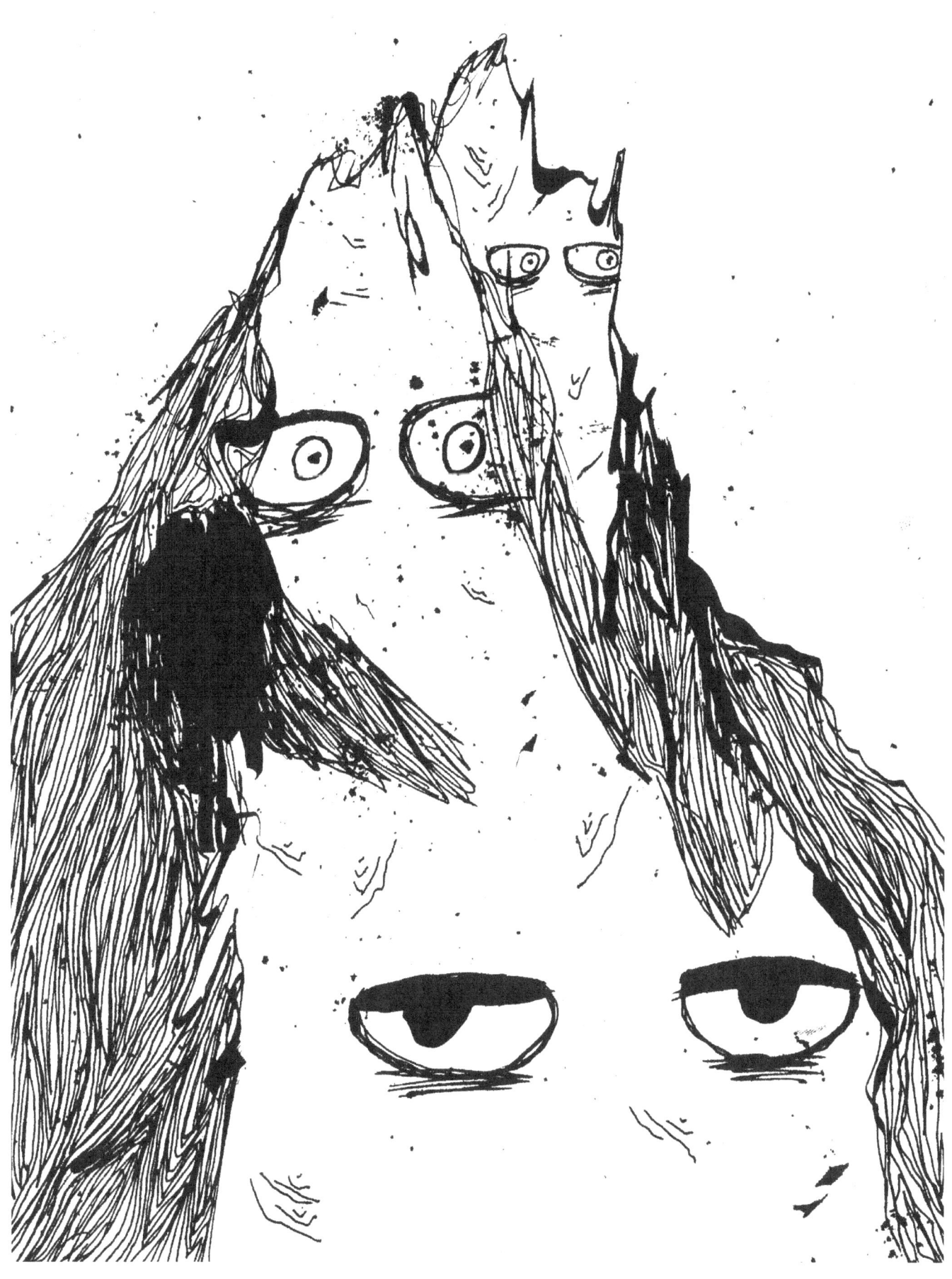

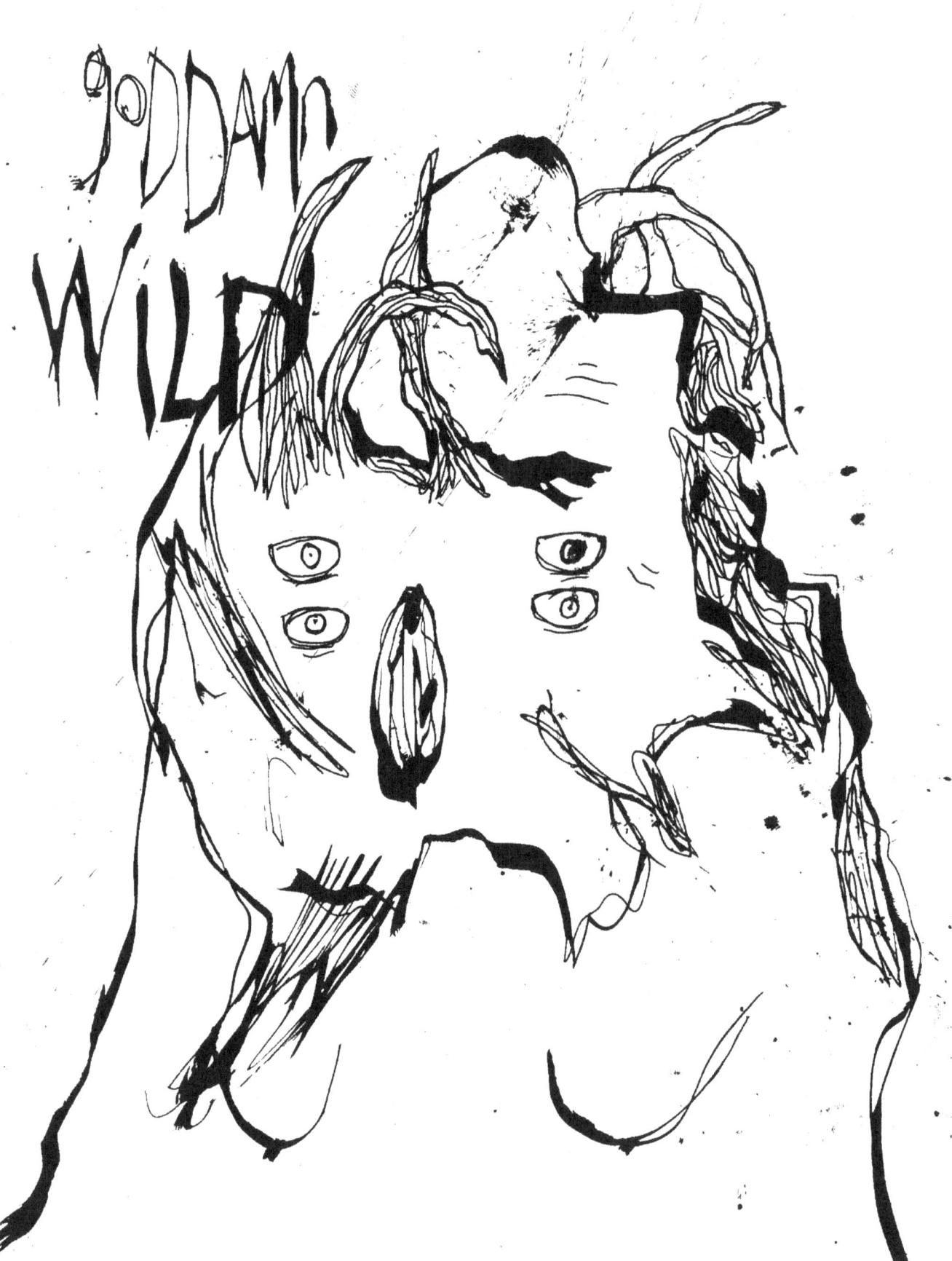

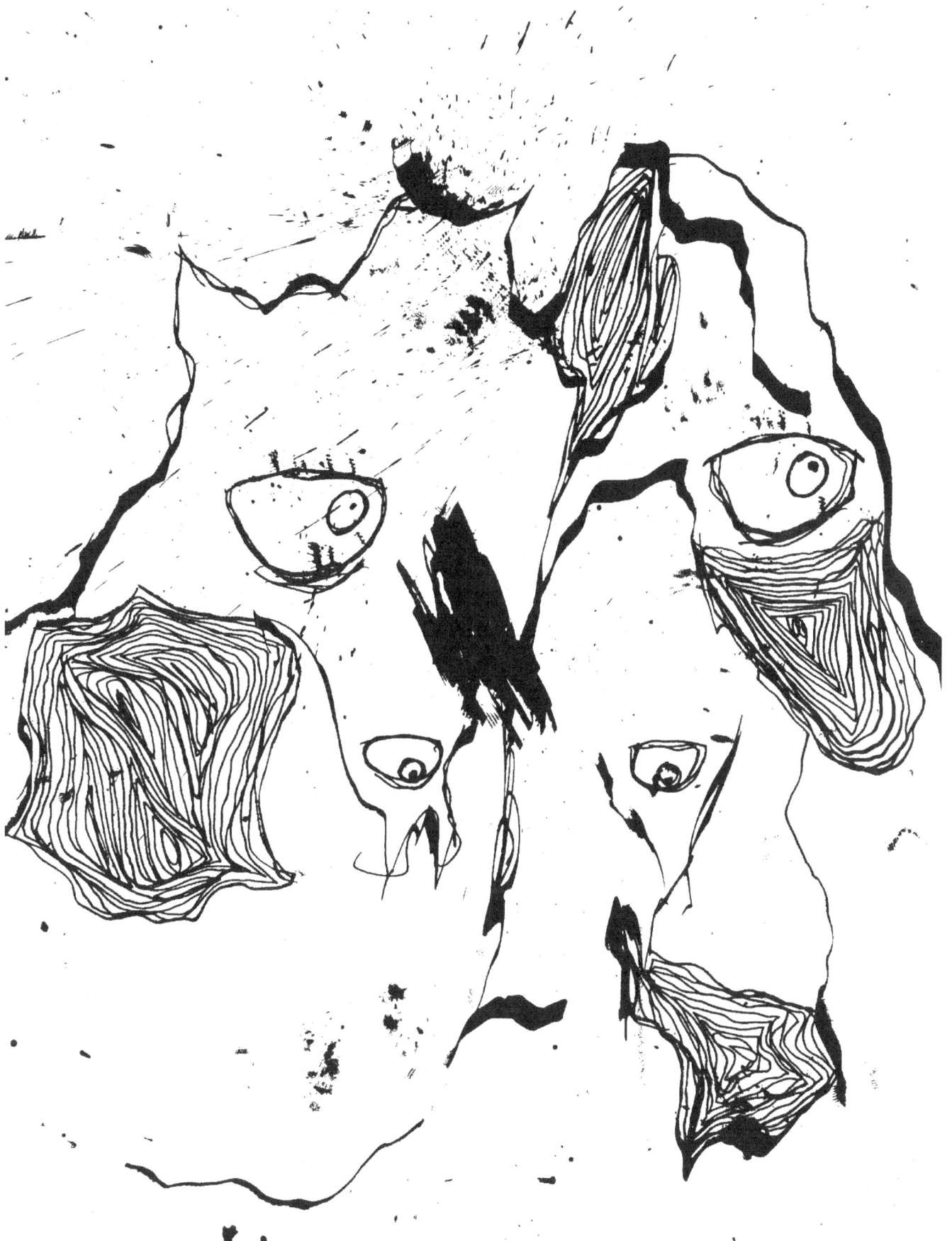

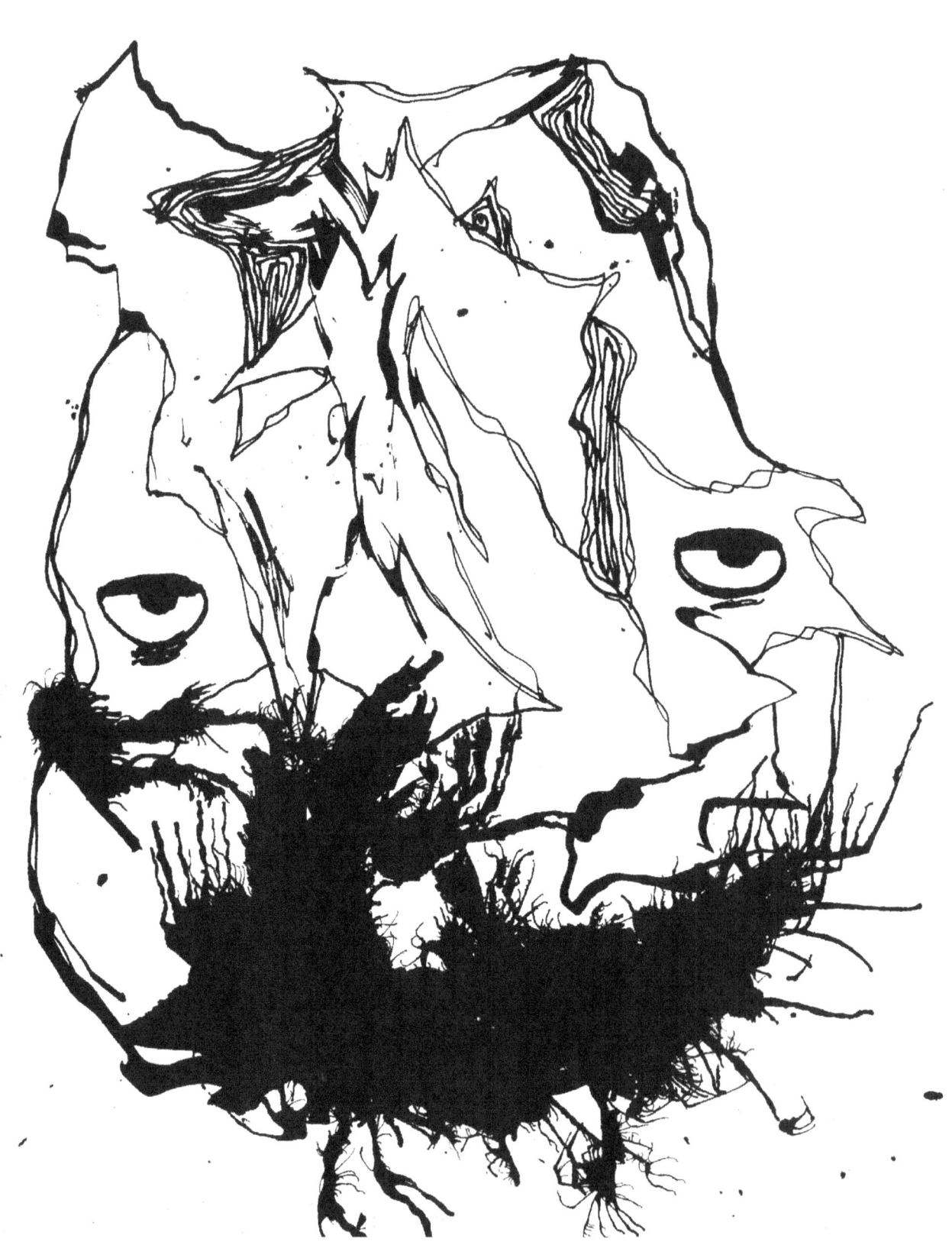

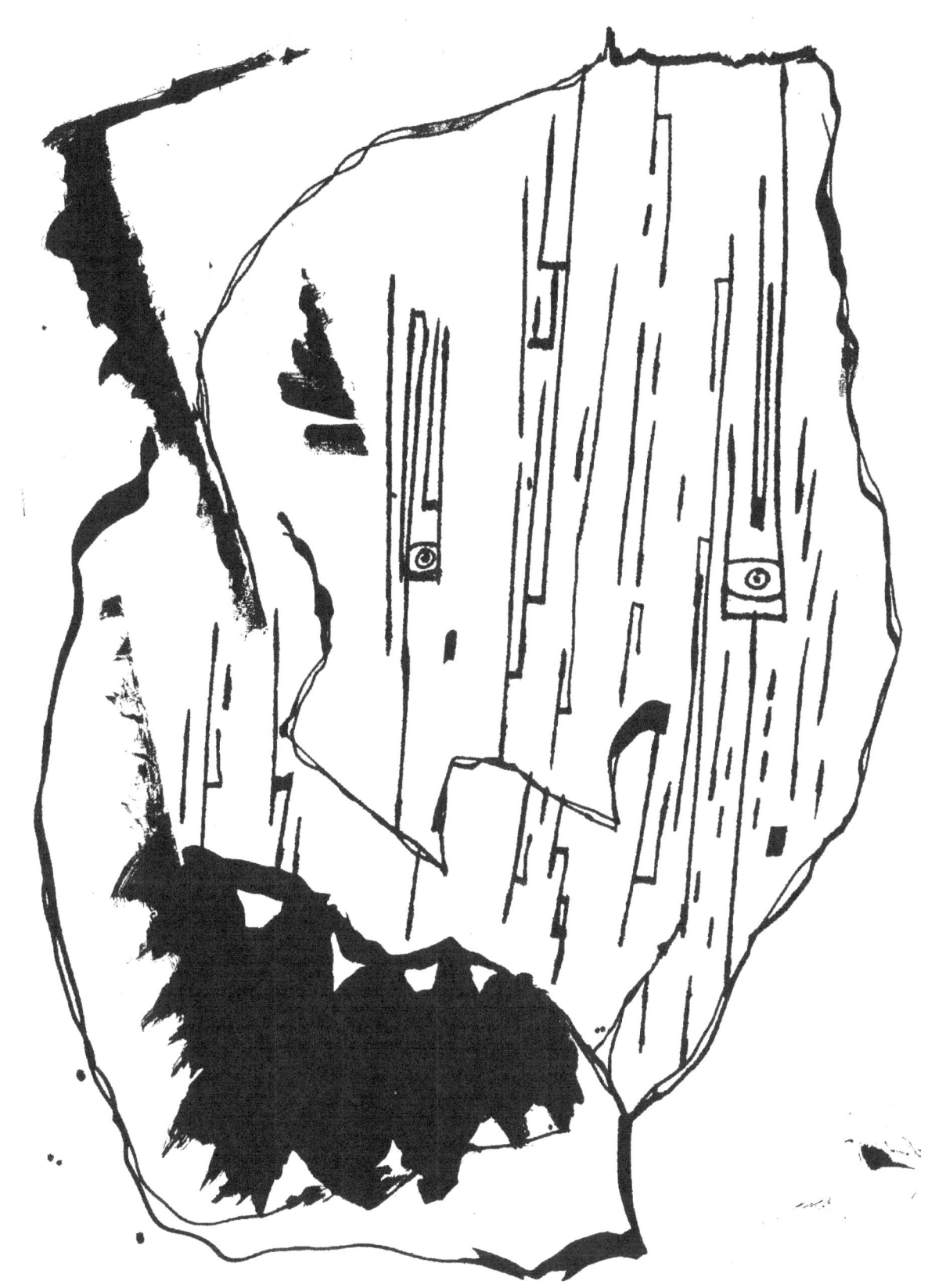

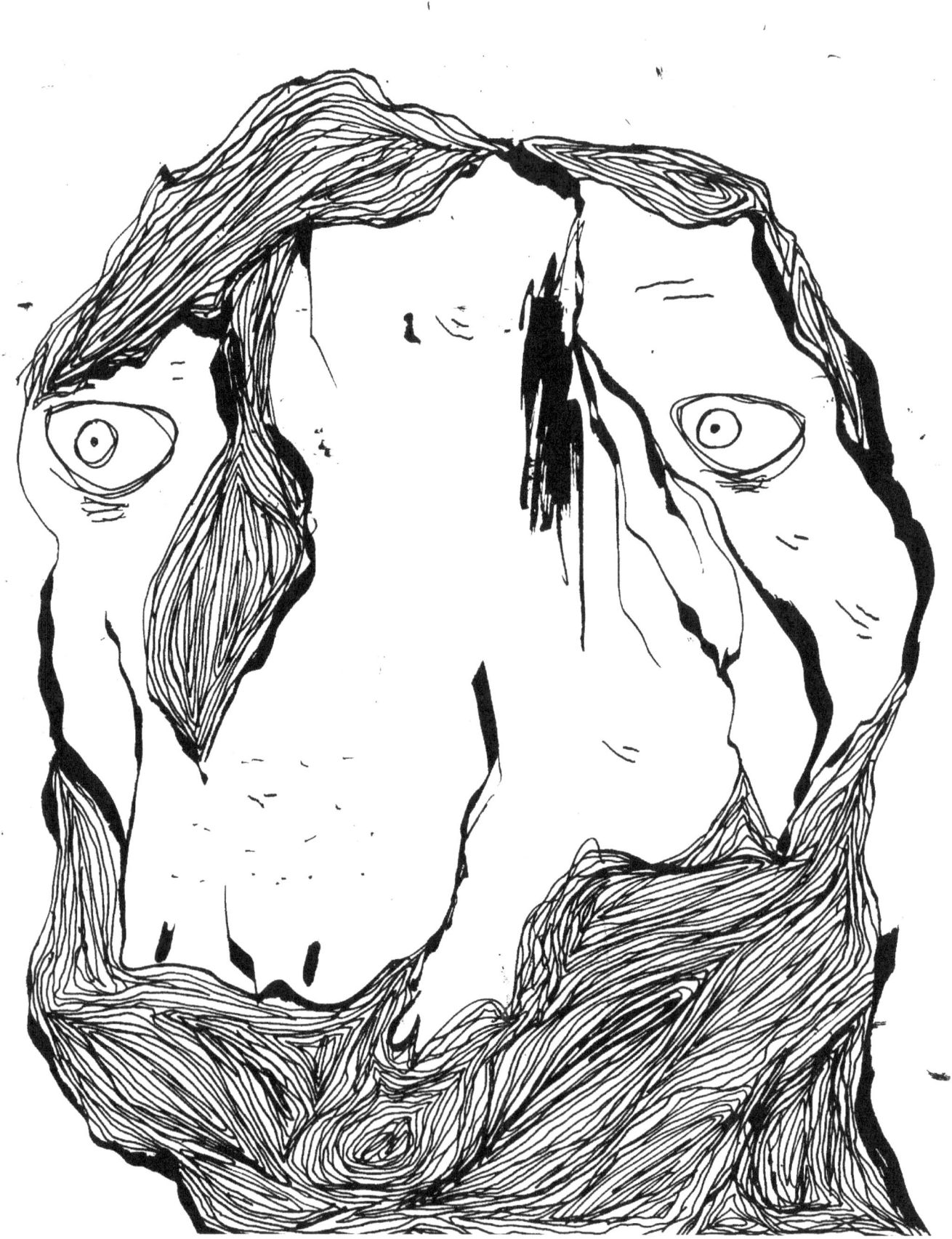

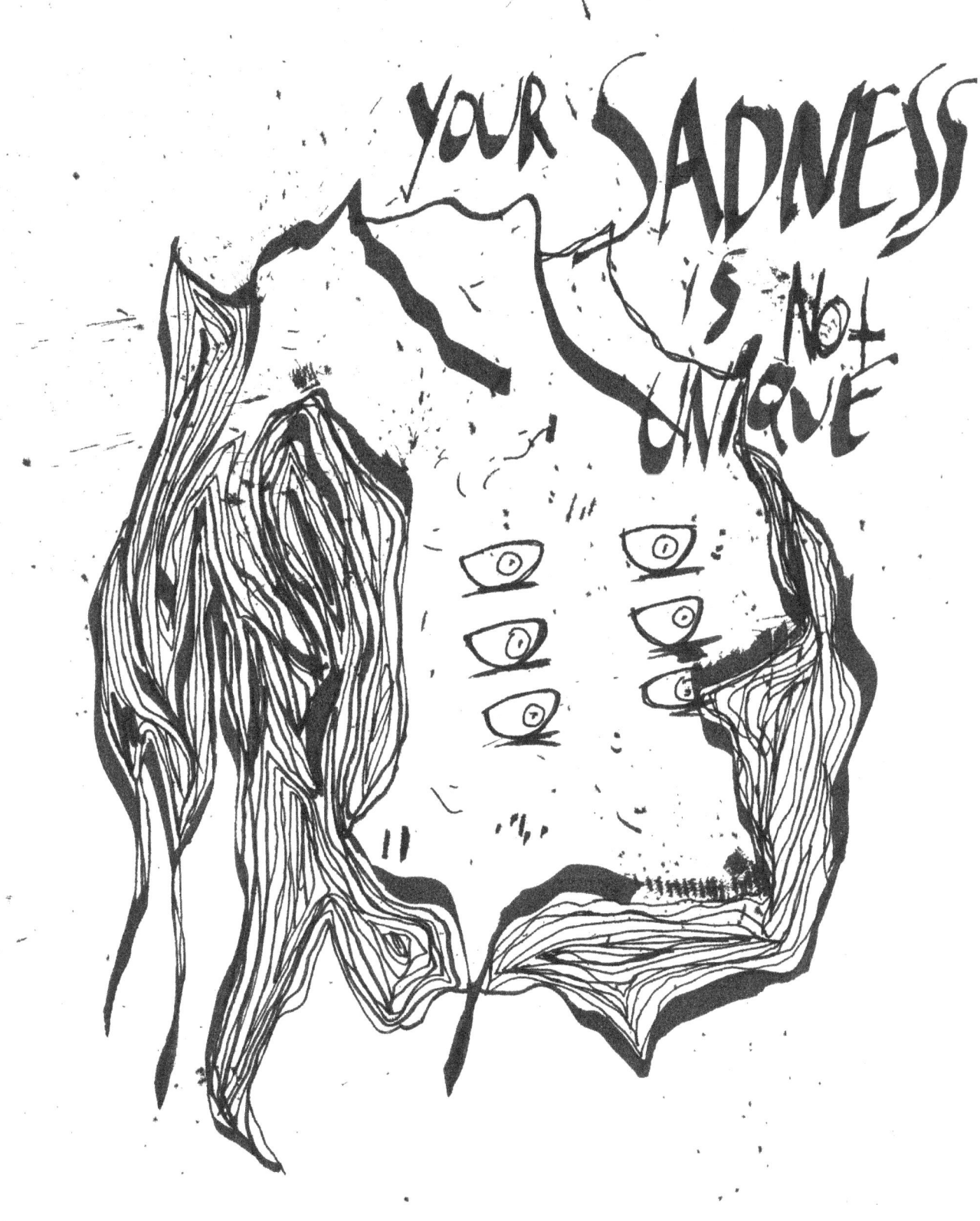

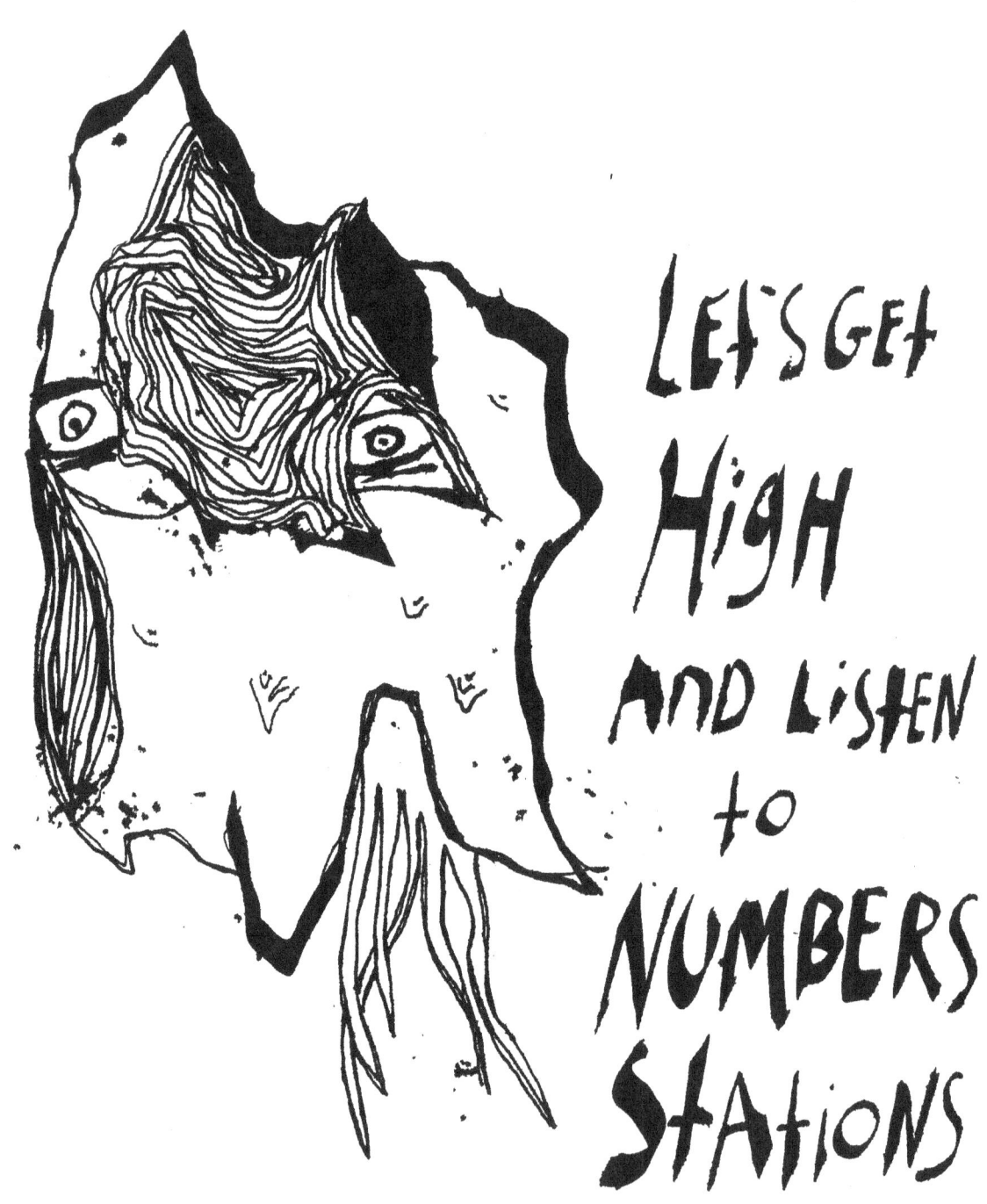

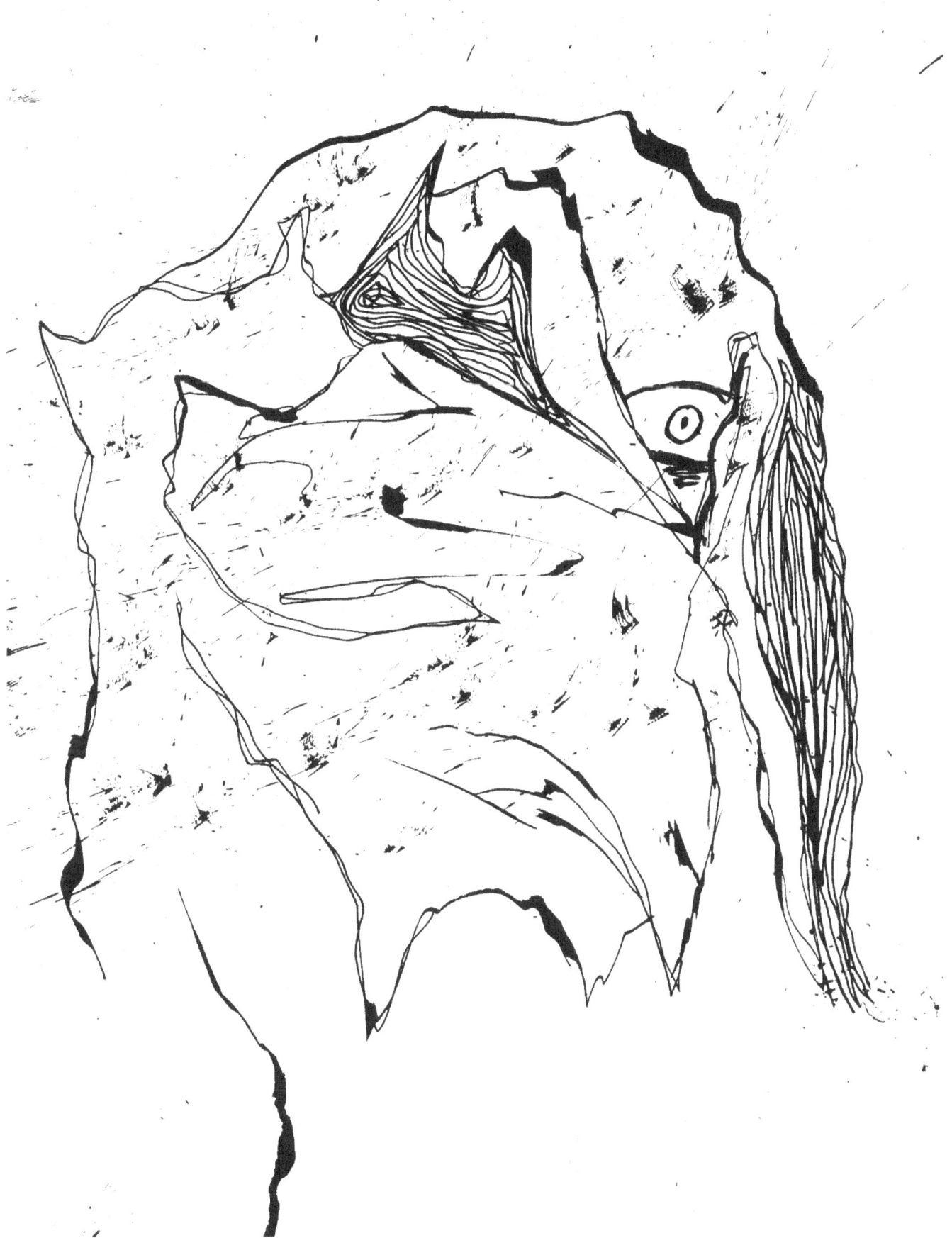

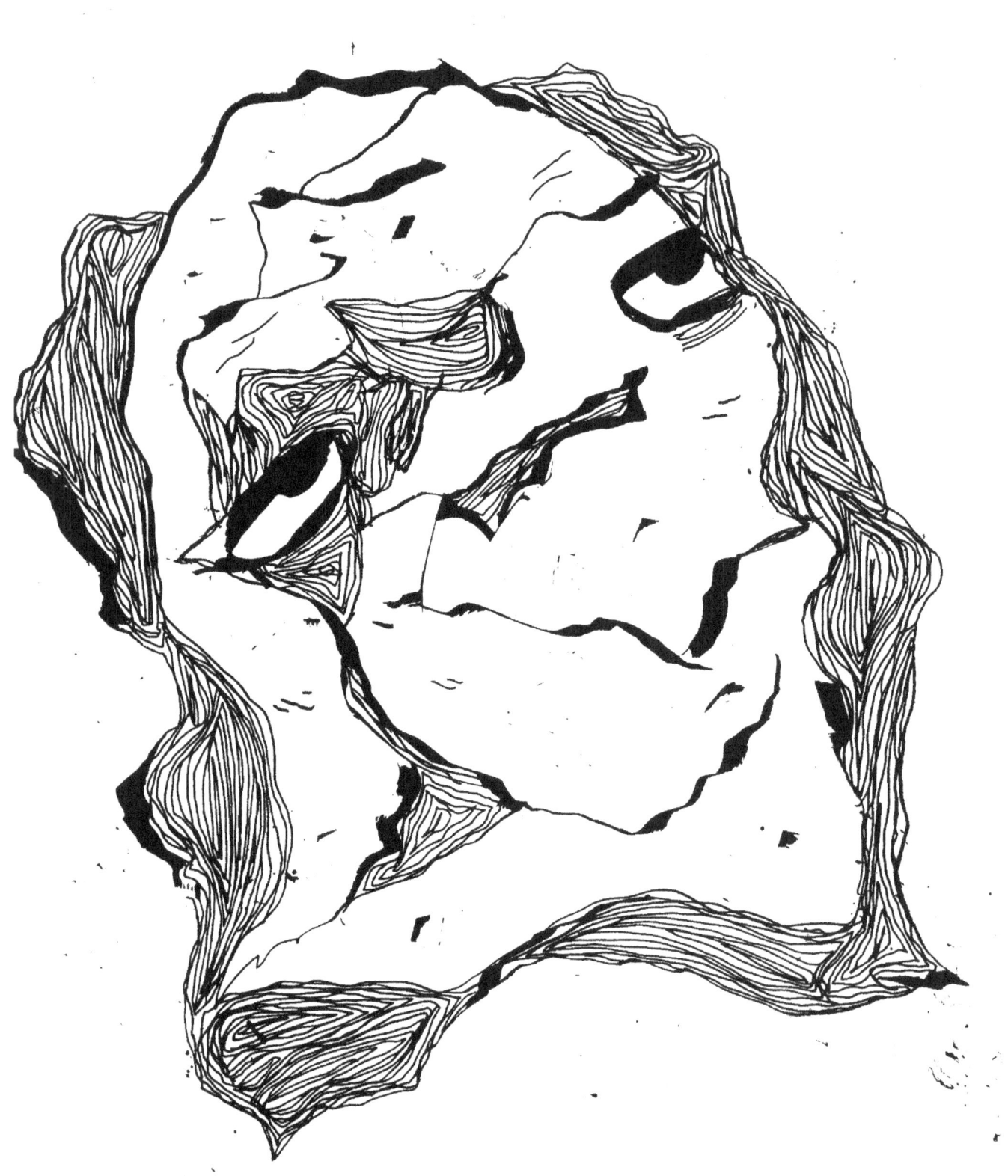

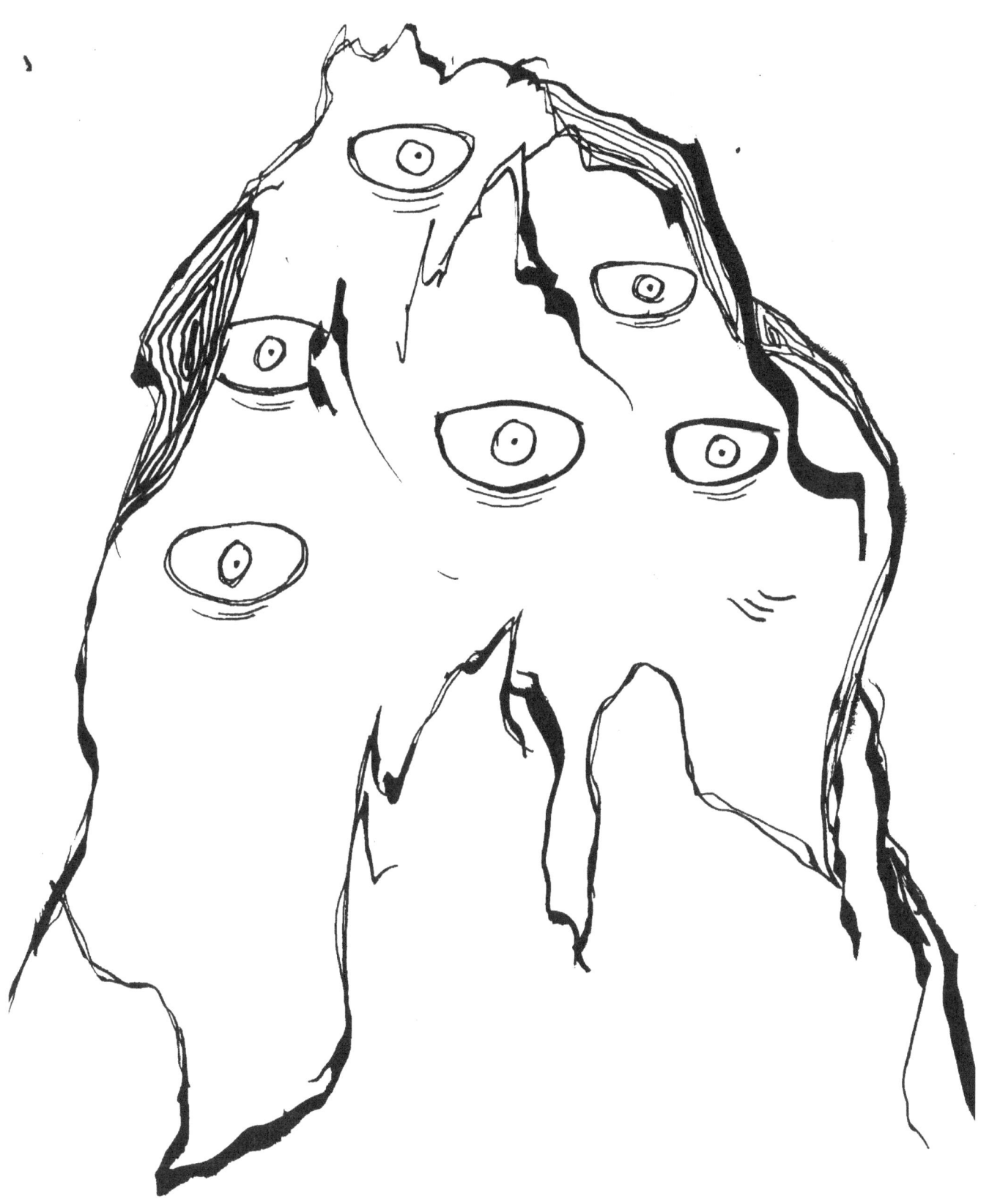

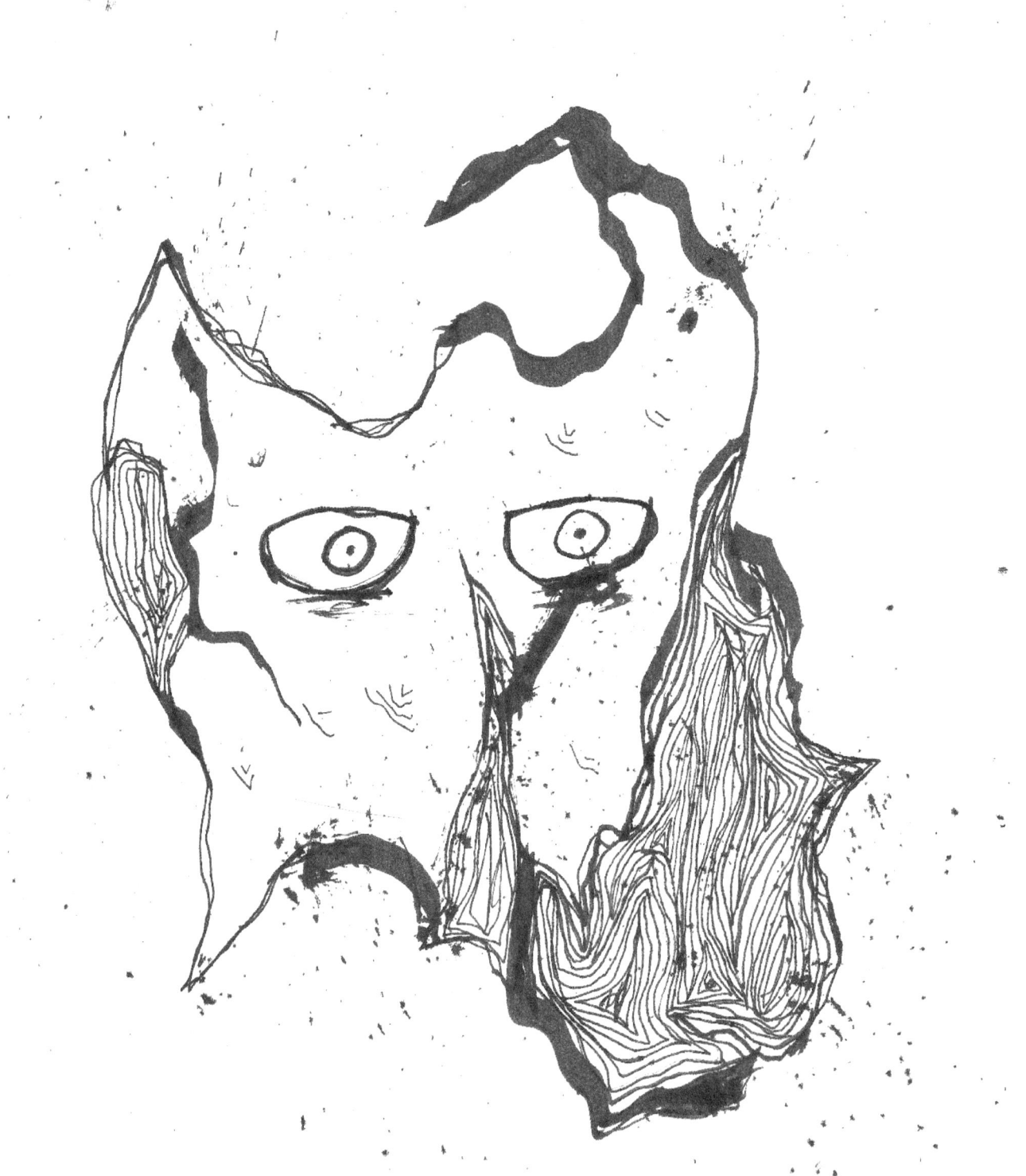

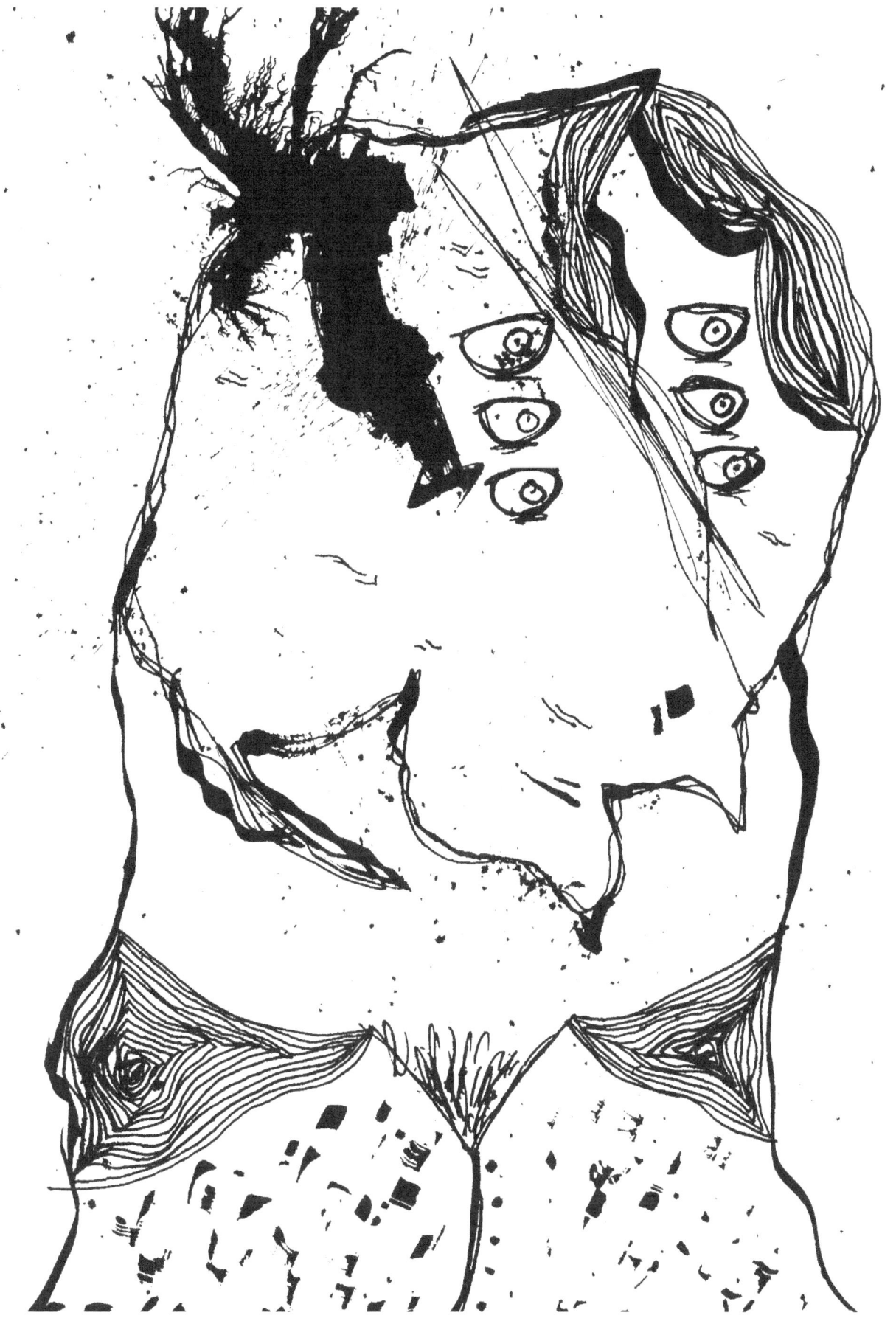

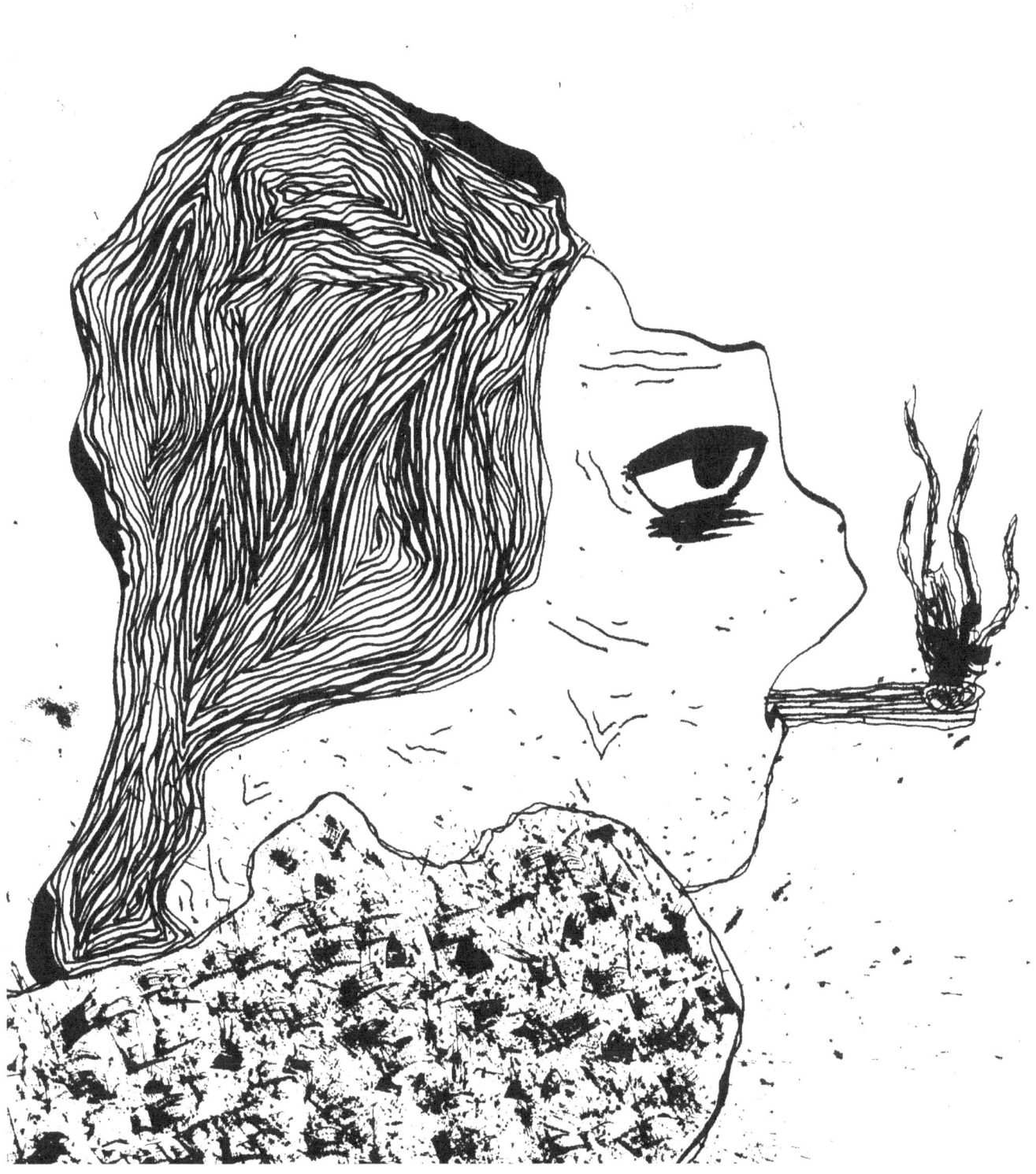

THE LAST MARS BIRTH

A terasecond later, I am born on mars
There's so little of me left.
I am held together with ice and sand
I drift in the wind
It's always dark
There is nobody to talk to, or to shoot me
no insects, no chants or songs
the only screams are my own

THE LAST DEATH

NO STARS. NO LIGHT. BARELY ME.
COLD. LONELY.
TIRED. BORED.
DEATH.
REST.
END.

Mick Malone is an artist, author and musician from Pittsburgh, Pennsylvania.

[this is all fleeting]
mpmmick [at] gmail.com
mickmalone.tumblr.com
instagram.com/gravebug

also available:

Doom Riddles (2015)
DOPE GRAVE (2017)
Cave Body (2018)

www.ingramcontent.com/pod-product-compliance
Lightning Source LLC
Chambersburg PA
CBHW082249220526
45469CB00009B/2935